Fine WoodWorking

on Boxes, Carcases, and Drawers

W9-BRD-909

Fine WoodWorking on Boxes, Carcases, and Drawers

41 articles selected by the editors of *Fine Woodworking* magazine

The Taunton Press

© 1985 by The Taunton Press, Inc.
All rights reserved

First printing: January 1985
International Standard Book Number: 0-918804-26-4
Library of Congress Catalog Card Number: 84-052097
Printed in the United States of America

A FINE WOODWORKING Book

FINE WOODWORKING® is a trademark of The Taunton Press, Inc.,
registered in the U.S. Patent and Trademark Office.

The Taunton Press, Inc.
Box 355
Newtown, Connecticut 06470

Contents

Introduction

Jewelry boxes, bureaus, cabinets, and closets: when we build storage furniture, we're wrapping wood around space. We need places in which to put our things away. We want to find the things again, so we divide and organize the boxed space. We want to retrieve our things quickly and easily, so we devise drawers, doors and lids.

Storage furniture won't work without good, strong ways to make flat pieces of wood turn corners: this is the art of carcase joinery. In 41 articles reprinted from the first nine years of *Fine Woodworking* magazine, authors who are also craftsmen tell you exactly how to choose, make and use carcase joints, with particular emphasis on the classic dovetail. Sometimes there's satisfaction or efficiency in making strong joints with hand tools. Sometimes, especially when there's lots to do, machine methods are best. Excellent results can be had either way, and this book explains both.

When we join four sticks together to make a rectangular frame, whether for a paneled door or a table or a stool, we're more likely to need the mortise and tenon joint in one of its innumerable forms. Frame joinery is another large subject, and there's a companion book devoted to it in this series. Its title is, simply, *Joinery*.

John Kelsey, editor

Carcase Construction

Choosing and making the right joints

by Tage Frid

Furniture construction is broken down into two main categories: frame and carcase. In frame construction, relatively narrow boards are joined—usually with a mortise and tenon joint—as in a chair or table base, or in a frame and panel door. In carcase construction, boards are joined end to end using dovetails, tongue-and-groove joints and the like, as in a drawer or hutch. When designing a carcase, the beginner may find it difficult to know which joint to choose. Some joints are excellent in plywood but weak in solid wood, and vice versa. Many beginners are so concerned with the "craft" aspect that they design in the most complicated techniques. They use a complex joint where a joint easier to make would work just as well. As a rule of thumb, I always choose the strongest but easiest joint to construct. I cannot see spending time over-constructing a piece. And I expect my furniture to last long after I do.

Most carcase joints can be made by hand, but are usually more easily and precisely made on a circular saw. I would advise people who don't own a circular saw to buy a table saw and not a radial arm saw. The latter is limited in function and not as accurate or flexible. It was designed for cross-cutting rough lumber to lengths, and even then is limited to a certain width. Many of the joints described here would be dangerous and impractical to make on a radial arm saw. I prefer at least a ten-inch table saw, and it does not cost that much more than an eight-inch. Buy one with at least a 1-hp motor, as an underpowered machine is much more dangerous to work with.

Joints at corners

Mattia's article (pages 14 to 18) states that dovetailing is one of the strongest and most attractive methods of joining the ends of boards together. This is true if you make the joints by hand. But most carcase joints lend themselves to machine fabrications. The closest machine joint to a dovetail is a finger or box joint. Because of the greater number of pins and the resulting total glue surface, it is stronger than a dovetail, far easier to make, and just as attractive.

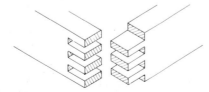

Tage Frid teaches furniture design and construction at the Rhode Island School of Design, and has been a professional woodworker for close to 50 years.

The lock miter is used for either solid wood or plywood. Its advantages are that it is hidden to the outside, and that it requires clamping in only one direction, because of the built-in locking action. The "double-tongued" lock miter is the best and fastest production joint for plywood but it requires a shaper with special knives. Only one shaper setting is required—the first piece is run through vertically, the second horizontally. The same clamping benefit holds true here. I use this joint only in plywood. In production work, the time saved pays for the relatively high cost of the cutter.

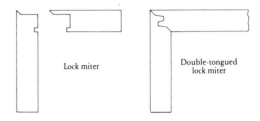

Lock miter | Double-tongued lock miter

The spline miter really lends itself to plywood, but can be used in solid wood on smaller pieces such as boxes. The grain direction of the spline must follow that of the pieces being joined. The spline should be placed 1/5 to 1/6 of the way in from the inside corner so as not to weaken the corner. Because of the 45-degree angle, all pieces must be glued up simultaneously, a real disadvantage in a piece with many parts. Also, a lot of clamps (in all directions) are required to ensure tight glue lines.

A lesser-used spline miter with a parallel spline has several advantages but can be used only in plywood. This spline is just as strong as the diagonal one. The spline slots are minutely offset (about 1/32 in.). Clamps are needed only parallel to the spline, and the offset pulls the pieces tightly together. The ease of clamping this joint is a real advantage. You can glue the inside members and sides first, and when they dry, glue on the top and bottom.

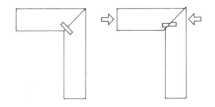

A corner tongue and groove, rounded or square, is good for either type of wood. In plywood the grain of the corner piece must run lengthwise along the edging. However, in solid woods, the grain must run in the same direction as the grain

Making a Lock Miter

Set the table saw fence to just inside the board thickness. Set a single blade to a height 1/5 to 1/6 of the thickness. Make the first cut using a miter gauge (1). Set the dado blades to the desired width (about 2/3 the thickness). Mark off the blade height from the other board and cut the dado. A tenoning jig is much safer here than using the fence (2). Scribe the other dado side to the first piece. Set a single blade to the height of the top edge of the dado. Saw to make the second tongue (3). Cut off the tongue on the dadoed piece to the right length (4). Tilt the blade to 45 degrees and miter the mating tongues (5 & 6). Keep checking back and forth between pieces as you make each cut to test for a good fit, or make a scrap set as you go along.

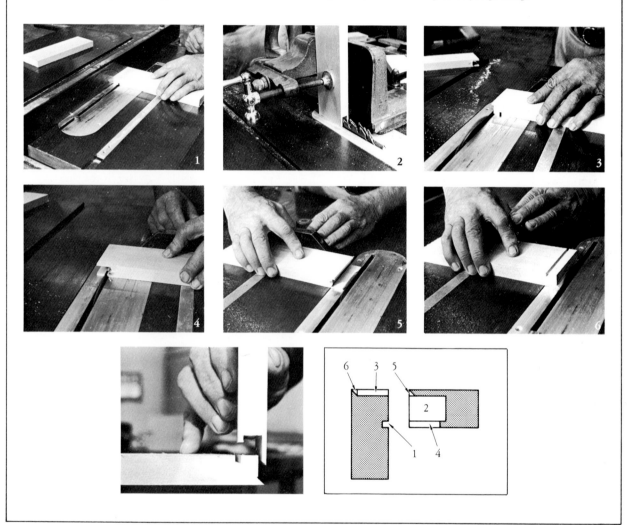

Making a Spline Miter

To make a spline miter set the blade at 45 degrees and cut the pieces using the miter gauge (1). Lower the blades, move the fence to the opposite side of the blade and cut the two spline slots (2). This method keeps the cuts parallel to the edge and prevents the pieces from skewing.

Making Multiple-Spline Joints

Mock Finger Joints

The mock finger joint is made using a simple jig on the table saw. The carcase pieces are first mitered and glued. A jig with a 45-degree vee cut out of it is made and a dado cut is sawed into the jig. A spline is fitted into the cut. The jig is screwed to the miter gauge. A cut is made at the desired arbitrary distance from the spline (1). The pieces are set in up against the spline and the first cut is made. The first cut slips onto the spline and the next slot is made (2). The process is continued down the length (3).

Mock Dovetails

For a mock dovetail the jig is exactly the same as in the mock finger joint. A fence is set up on the router table that is no higher than the bottom of the vee on the jig. A board is attached to the back of the jig to provide a greater surface running against the fence (1). The process is exactly the same as the mock finger joint (2,3). The length of spline is angled on both sides to fit into the dovetail slots (4).

Full-Blind Splines

The first piece is lined up with the left side of the jig and the second with the right so that the two align properly. Or a piece of plywood can be made to serve as a guide. If the joint is made with a dovetail jig the splines will have to be rounded on two edges. Or the splines can be made smaller and left square since there is plenty of glue surface. The joint can also be made on a mortiser, using a jig just as in the mock spline joints.

of the sides so that expansion is constant. The grain should run diagonally from tongue to tongue. Any shaped corner molding can be used. The inside is shaped first, the pieces are glued together, and then the outside is shaped.

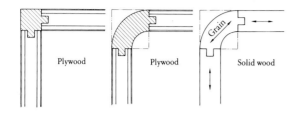

Plywood　　　　Plywood　　　　Solid wood

The doweled miter is used where structure is not crucial—in small boxes, knickknack cabinets, spice racks, etc. It is easy to make, and aligns itself correctly for gluing because of the dowels. A dowel center is useful for transferring the position of one hole to its corresponding hole. This joint works in solid wood or plywood.

I generally do not use a butt joint with dowels, but when I do, I find it advantageous to angle the dowels. This adds needed strength to the joint.

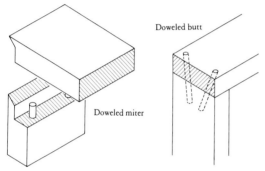

Doweled butt

Doweled miter

Several joints are made by cutting a miter, gluing the corners together, and then cutting slots to receive splines. Water-based animal glue in an electric glue pot is perfect for gluing the miters since the glue is strong and dries in just a few minutes so you can then finish cutting the joint. These joints have great strength and pleasing decorative qualities. With jigs, they can be made extremely fast. The first is a mock finger joint—it resembles a finger joint without the alternating fingers. For the same effect in a small piece, thin, handsaw kerfs are spaced down the joint. Pieces of veneer are hammered to make them thinner, and glue is squeezed into the saw cut. When the veneer splines go into the slots they swell from the moisture of the glue. (A loose through dovetail can be repaired in the same way, by evening out the gap with a saw cut and diagonally inserting a veneer strip.) A mock dovetail is made similarly, but using a router mounted in a table. If desired, a contrasting wood can be used for splines as a decorative detail.

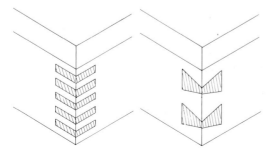

If the splines are to be hidden, the spline slots can be cut using a router with a machine dovetail jig. This joint is considerably stronger than a full-blind dovetail because of the greater glue surface.

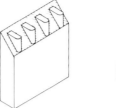

The tongue and rabbet is not the strongest joint but is good enough for the back of a drawer (although not as strong as a dovetail). It is very easy to make. The proportions must be strictly adhered to, as they are determined by factors of strength. The groove should be no deeper than 1/4 to 1/5 of the board's thickness.

The half-blind tongue and rabbet is made like a lock miter but without the miter. It is particularly good for drawer fronts, but in that case be sure to put the drawer stop somewhere other than in the front because of the limited joint strength. This joint can also be made with a router.

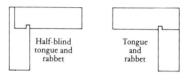

Half-blind tongue and rabbet　　　Tongue and rabbet

Machine-cut dovetails made with a router and dovetail jig are useful where great quantities must be cut, or where the extra strength of a hand-cut dovetail is not needed. I use them when I have stacks of drawers to do for kitchens. Otherwise, I prefer hand-cut dovetails for their strength and looks. Besides, when you've made them for many years you'll find them easier to do than setting up the router.

The through and half-blind hand dovetails are explained in the dovetail article by Mattia mentioned earlier (see pages 14 to 18). The full-blind dovetail (and similarly the machine-made, full-blind spline joint) is not used to be "crafty," but is used where strength is important, as in a freestanding cabinet without a back, or in a cabinet with glass doors.

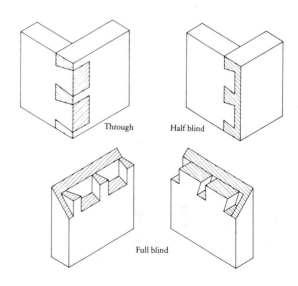

Through　　　Half blind

Full blind

Joints not at corners

A simple tongue and groove can be used for any type of wood except composition boards. At the ends of boards the tongue is set off center so that the outside shoulder isn't too weak. Fiberboard and particle board are made of waste materials and so there is no grain strength. Since a tongue would break, a spline must be used with these materials. The spline should go into the carcase side about 1/4 of the side's thickness, and twice that amount into the perpendicular piece. Setting the spline further into the side will weaken it, and keeping it shorter in the perpendicular piece will not add enough strength.

I would never use a fully-housed dado joint. There are no shoulders to lock the wood and help resist sideway stresses. Also, if the wood is sanded after the joint is cut, the piece becomes too loose. If there are imperfections in the wood, the piece will not fit tightly.

Another strong joint is a series of small mortise and tenons. For extra strength, the tenons should run through the sides and be wedged from the outside at assembly.

The sliding dovetail is an excellent joint for perpendiculars. The double-shoulder version is machine cut with a router and a dovetail bit. The single-shoulder joint is cut by hand with a dovetail plane and its corresponding saw, and with a router plane. The machine version is excellent for production. If

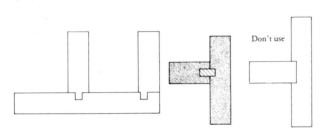

Don't use

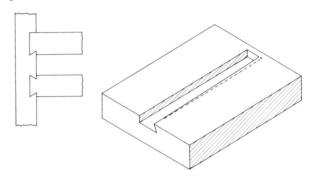

Making a Finger Joint

A simple jig on a miter gauge makes cutting this joint very simple. A correct fit is solely dependent on how accurate the jig is. Raise the blade a hair higher than the thickness of the boards: It is easier to sand a little off the ends of the joint than to plane the whole side. Make a cut in the board with the dado blades. Then make a spline that is exactly the same size as the slot and fits into it snugly (1). Line up the blade to a position precisely one spline thickness over from the first cut. Screw the jig to the miter gauge. With the spline in the slot, cut the first finger with the board edge up against the spline (2). Slip the finger slot onto the spline and continue down the board, moving over one each time (3). Start the second piece lined up to the open sawcut so the first cut makes a slot (4). Continue down the board (5) and the two should fit together perfectly (6). I recommend you do a small test to check the accuracy of your jig before cutting the final pieces.

Making a Full-Blind Dovetail

The pieces are marked and the excess above the pins and tails is removed. The remainder that will form the top miter must be a square. A 45-degree angle is cut at the edge (or at both edges). The pins are marked, cut and chiseled out. The tails are marked from the pins, sawed and chiseled out. With a little luck, they might fit. If for some reason the corner is slightly open, hit it lightly with a hammer when the piece is being glued. This will bend the fibers over and close the imperfection. For a round corner the dovetail is made exactly the same but without the upper miter.

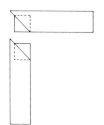 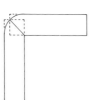 

Making Hand-Cut Sliding Dovetails

Hand-cut sliding dovetails require the special dovetail plane and saw (1). The position for the groove is marked with a framing square and scribed. The angle of the taper is drawn in. For lumber 3/4 in. or thicker I use about a 1/8-in. taper. If the groove is to be stopped in the front I mark off where the joint ends. All lines are scribed and scored deeper with a chisel. This is important since the cutting is across the grain. A slight vee is pared off of each line the whole way down (2). If the joint is to be hidden the end is chiseled out. This stops the groove and provides an opening to start the saw in. The straight side is sawed at 90 degrees and the tapered side is sawed at an angle using the saw shoulder as the guide (3). The router plane cuts out the mass of material and the groove is finished (4). The depth of the dovetail is marked onto the edge of the other board with the arrow-shaped blade in the dovetail plane which is available from Woodcraft Supply (5). I make the dovetail 1/32 in. shorter than the depth of the groove. The planing is continued until the piece appears to be the right size (6). It should slide in easily at first and become very tight in the last fifth of the groove. One or two more passes with the plane with testing in between should result in the desired fit. If the joint is hidden, the front of the dovetail is pared off.

only a few sliding dovetails are required, the hand method is preferred. It is extremely simple and much faster than one would expect. In the hand version the track is tapered so that the dovetail slides in easily at first and locks at the end as it is hammered into place. Consequently, as the dovetail is forced in tight, a small shoulder is pressed into the straight side and increases at the narrow end. In the machine version, the pieces should mate exactly and thus will require a lot of force to assemble. This is especially true if glue is used on a long dovetail, because the glue will swell the grain, making the piece increasingly difficult to slide in.

With both types of sliding dovetails, glue is not necessary, although a spot can be put at the front to fix it in position, or the whole length can be glued. If two different materials are used (e.g., plywood shelves into solid sides), only the front should be glued so that as movement occurs, the front will remain flush.

In a chest of drawers or similar carcase higher or wider than two feet, some sort of strengthening brace will be required. I use a sliding dovetail in the center brace, and if additional bracing is needed, a tongue and groove out to the sides. The sliding dovetail holds the center in tight.

If you wish to keep joints from showing through in front, you can stop the joints before the front or else cover them. In solid wood I sometimes cut a half-inch strip off the cabinet, run the joints through, and reglue the strip. In plywood I run the joints through and add a facing for the same result.

Backs for carcases

The back of a carcase is an important strength-determining factor. Various methods for inserting backs will require differing assembly sequences, which must correspond to that of the particular carcase joint used. This is an important relationship that must be decided at the design stage.

The easiest and most common way to insert a back is to make a rabbet around the four sides and screw on a piece of plywood after the carcase is glued. This method gives you a second chance to square a cabinet that has been glued slightly out of square. The plywood can be made square or slightly out-of-square the opposite way and this will counteract the mistake. This type of back is fine if the cabinet is designed to go against a wall. Most antique furniture was designed to be placed against a wall, and so the backs were usually crudely made and left rough. Today furniture is used much more flexibly, e.g., as room dividers, so it is advisable to design a piece with the back as nice as the rest of the cabinet. The cost and effort of sanding and finishing the back are minimal in light of the time spent designing and executing the piece. Of course, if the piece is designed to be fastened to the wall, the back must still be finished, but not to the same perfection.

A good method for a freestanding piece is to make a groove for a piece of plywood or solid wood which is inserted at the same time the cabinet is glued up. If solid wood is used, be sure the back is free-floating to allow for movement. You may pin or glue the back just at the center points, which will allow the wood to expand equally out to both sides. Leave a little space in the groove on each side to allow for expansion.

If the sides of the cabinet are frame and panels, a set-in flat back would look out of place. To keep your design consistent you can make a frame and panel back that is inserted using either of the assembly sequences described for a plywood back. □

Box-Joint Jig
Router template indexes cuts

by Patrick Warner

The box joint is being used less and less today and it's no wonder, considering the setup complications, the danger of holding workpieces vertically on table saws, the indexing hangups and the assembly problems. After studying most of the classical box-joint cutting methods and tools, I decided to design and build a template jig that could be used with a router. (For the table-saw method of making this joint, see "Making a Finger Joint," page 6.)

I've made dozens of boxes and drawers and have found that most don't measure more than 12 in. high and 36 in. on a side. Most stock used for small boxes is ⅜ in. to ¾ in. thick. I made my jig to accommodate these dimensions with no changes in setup.

In designing the jig, I aimed for simplicity of operation, safety, rapid setup and indexing, accuracy, precision, repeatability, and latitude in box sizes. I built it into a table that's split to allow the stock to be held vertically—the jig is on one side of the split, the press screws are on the other (see photo below). The table is both portable and stable, and has a utility drawer, my first box made with the jig.

The template, the heart of the jig, is made out of laminated phenolic—it's smooth, slippery and strong. The stock should be no more than ¼ in. thick, to use up as little of the vertical travel of the router as possible. I had mine milled at a local machine shop, although I first squared up the stock on a

Photo: Patrick Warner

jointer and carbide saw. The slots, 1⅛ in. deep, were milled with a ⁵⁄₁₆-in. end mill, leaving pins ³⁄₁₆ in. wide on ½-in. centers. A milling machine will easily hold ± .001, and I suspect ± .0025 is tolerable. Job shop time should not exceed 30 minutes, if the stock is presquared.

The template overhangs a pillow block, which is tenoned to an oak cross-member. Stops on either end of the template index the workpiece. When indexed on one end the yield is a pin; the other end yields a socket. The workpiece is clamped vertically against a piece of scab stock, and each side of the box is cut separately. The router with its ⁵⁄₁₆-in. outside-diameter template guide and ¼-in. bit traverses the tines of the template, as in dovetail-cutting jigs.

The scab stock backup board is especially important because without it the router bit will tear out the back side of the panel. One scab board will usually accommodate the four corners of one box because it can be used turned upside-down and backwards. The scab board is located to guarantee the entry of at least half of the diameter of the bit, and is held snug

Patrick Warner makes cabinets in Escondido, Calif.

against the template with standard spring plungers. (The plungers are available at the time of this writing, 1979, for about $2 each from Vliet Engineering Corp., 2333 Valley St., Burbank, Calif. 91505.)

If the template has been cut well but the first joint doesn't fit, the outside diameter of the template guide can be turned down. As a final measure, the router bit can be ground to correct the error in the fit. The router bit should be a ¼-in. carbide two-fluted straight-faced bit that needs sharpening, so if it doesn't fit you pay for sharpening only once.

To make the table frame for the jig, I used clear kiln-dried fir: 2x8s yield three pieces about 2¼ in. wide. I mortised and tenoned all frame members, which measure 1½ in. by 2¼ in. in cross section. I mounted the working parts of the jig on an oak member for stiffness and dimensional stability, then tenoned the member into the table rails. The four press screws that hold the work against the stock have custom-made handles so I could locate the nuts on 2½-in. centers without the handles interfering. They were made to my order by the Wetzler Clamp Co., 43-13 11th St., Long Island City, N.Y. 11101 for $7.50 each (1979). □

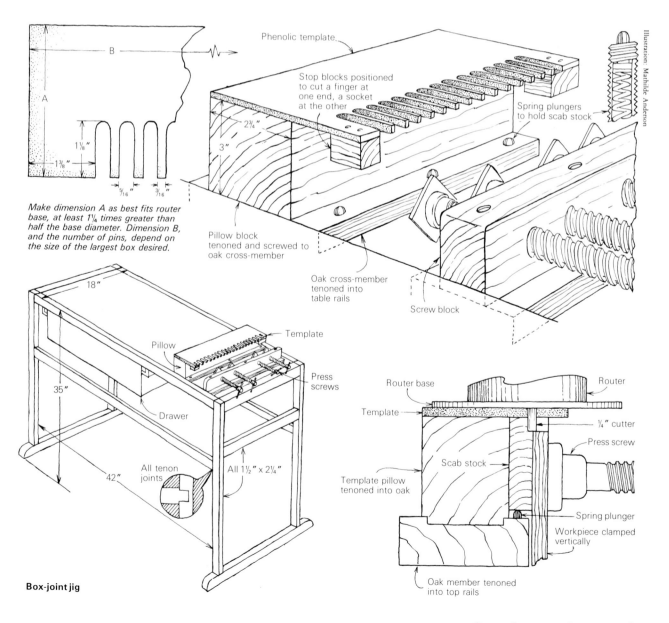

Make dimension A as best fits router base, at least 1¼ times greater than half the base diameter. Dimension B, and the number of pins, depend on the size of the largest box desired.

Box-joint jig

Cutting Box Joints on the Radial-Arm Saw

Sliding jig moves workpiece into blade for safe, precise cuts

by Ken Mitchell

Sooner or later, the owner of a radial-arm saw will want to use this machine for some operation that will tax both patience and ingenuity. My challenge arose when I wanted to make a substantial number of box (finger) joints for drawers, quickly. The obvious method—clamping the work on edge to the fence, running the blade parallel to the table, and lowering (or raising) the arm for successive cuts—soon proved impractical. If you have ever tried this method, which most owner's manuals recommend, you'll know that it is slow and deplorably imprecise.

Resolving to find a better way, I decided that the blade should remain fixed and that the stock should be raised in precise increments for each cut. The first requirement in working this out was finding a way to guide the work along the table for each pass into the dado head. Table saws have miter-gauge slots for guiding the stock into the cut, and I reasoned that such an arrangement could be worked out for a radial-arm-saw table. To make this guide slot, I first attached skirts to the sides of the table, and to these I screwed a guide rail parallel to the front of the table. As shown in figure 1

Ken Mitchell, an amateur woodworker, is an engineering supervisor for AT&T in San Francisco, Calif.

(facing page), the slot is created by a spacer glued along the bottom inside face of the guide rail. This spacer holds the rail a consistent ¾ in. away from the front edge of the table.

Next I designed a sliding jig for holding the stock on edge while it is being fed into the dado blade. The jig's travel across the table is guided by a bar that rides in the slot. To make the work go faster, I made the jig big enough to hold eight pieces of ¾-in. by 6-in. stock, which meant that I could cut the joints for four boxes at once. The jig (figure 1) consists of a plywood base, a guide bar that rides in the slot, a fixed fence, an adjustable fence and a stop block (for determining the depth of cut) that travels along a slotted rail and is secured at the appropriate setting with a wing nut.

To make the jig, first dimension the base to a size that is suited for your project and glue and screw the guide bar in place. Install the fixed fence on the base with glue and countersunk wood screws through the base. Make sure you brace the fence with blocks as shown, and be certain that the fence is precisely perpendicular to the base. The adjustable fence is made so it can slide toward and away from the fixed fence, sandwiching the stock in between. The distance between the two fences depends upon the thickness of the stock and the number of pieces being cut at one time. So it can

Here the stock is positioned for making a third pass into the blade. Successive fingers are cut by stacking precisely thicknessed shims under the stock, thus elevating it in precise increments.

With the stock aligned and clamped together between the two fences on the sliding jig, the work is passed through the blade. The jig is guided by a bar that rides in a slot at the front of the table. The adjustable stop block is secured in place along the slotted rail and determines the depth of cut. Photos: Ken Mitchell.

These crisp finger joints were cut quickly and accurately on a radial-arm saw, using the author's modified saw table and special jig for feeding the work into a stationary blade.

slide right and left, the adjustable fence has a base with a slotted hole at each end, through which ¼-in. hanger bolts protrude. The fence is fixed in position by tightening wing nuts down on the hanger bolts.

The slotted rail for the stop block is screwed to the fixed fence. Don't glue it, as you may want to add longer or shorter rails for different projects. The stop block should be almost the same height as the fences. Dado the block so it will slide along the rail and bore it for a ¼-in. hanger bolt.

Now that you have a means of holding the stock on edge and feeding it accurately into the blade, the next step is choosing the size of the fingers to be cut. The depth of cut will determine the length of the fingers, which should be just slightly longer than the stock is thick. With all pieces cut to final length, clamp opposite sides of the drawer or box together with ends flush. With the depth of cut scribed on one board, move the stock horizontally in the jig between the fences until the tip of the blade is aligned with the mark, as shown in figure 2. Now tighten the adjustable fence snug against the stock and bring the stop block into contact with the ends of the boards and secure it in place.

You must decide on the thickness of the fingers and proceed to cut a number of shims, which will be placed under the stock to elevate it for each successive cut. For ¼-in. thick fingers, the shims must be exactly ½ in. thick. For ⅜-in. thick fingers, the shims must be ¾ in. thick. The width of the shims is slightly less than the distance between the fences, and their length is the same as that of the fences. Shims that are too short and too narrow could allow the stock to wobble in the jig. In addition to the shims that are twice the thickness of the fingers you want to cut, you'll need one or two that are the exact thickness of the fingers. Take care to thickness the shims to the exact width of the cut made by the dado blades

mounted on your arbor. Don't assume because the chippers are supposed to be ⅛ in. thick that your blades cut in precise ⅛-in. increments. Make a sample cut with your blades and thickness your shims according to the width of this cut. If you don't have a thickness planer, you can rip the shims oversize and finish them with a hand plane, or you can rip them to final thickness if your saw is capable of fine adjustments.

Begin by cutting the sides that have fingers on their top edges (figure 3). With the saw carriage secured on the arm, the blade parallel to the table and the depth of cut established by the stop block, lower the column until the blade lightly touches the top edge of the stock. Return the jig; then slide a ¾-in. shim under the stock, switch on the saw and pass the stock through the blade. This produces a ⅜-in. pin (finger) on the top edge of the box sides. For the second cut, insert another ¾-in. shim on top of the first shim, replace the stock and pass it through the blade. For each cut, repeat this procedure, adding as many shims as the width of the stock requires. If tear-out is a problem, back the stock with a piece of scrap.

The other two sides must be notched on their top edges to receive the pins just cut. I insert a ⅜-in. shim under the stock for this first cut (figure 4) and then make all the subsequent cuts by adding ¾-in. shims, as I did previously.

I've used this system frequently and have found that it produces close-fitting joints. And it's fast, especially once you've established a rhythm in performing the discrete little parts of the process. Another virtue is that the slot at the front of the table can be used for other purposes. I've made a number of cut-off and mitering jigs that ride in this slot, and they give more accurate results than rotating the arm on the column and pulling the saw into the work. The point is that a radial-arm saw will perform more accurately if the blade is stationary than it will if you move the carriage along the arm. □

Fig. 1: Modified saw table and box-joint jig

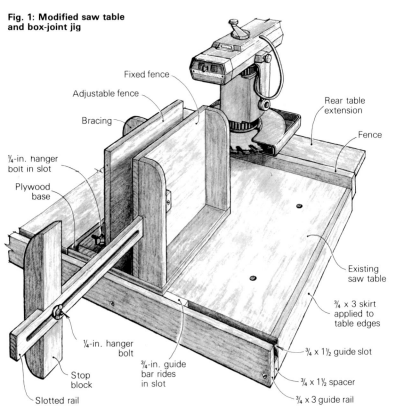

Fixed fence

Adjustable fence

Bracing

Rear table extension

Fence

¼-in. hanger bolt in slot

Plywood base

Existing saw table

¾ x 3 skirt applied to table edges

¼-in. hanger bolt

¾-in. guide bar rides in slot

Stop block

Slotted rail

¾ x 1½ guide slot

¾ x 1½ spacer

¾ x 3 guide rail

Fig. 2: Setting up the blade and jig

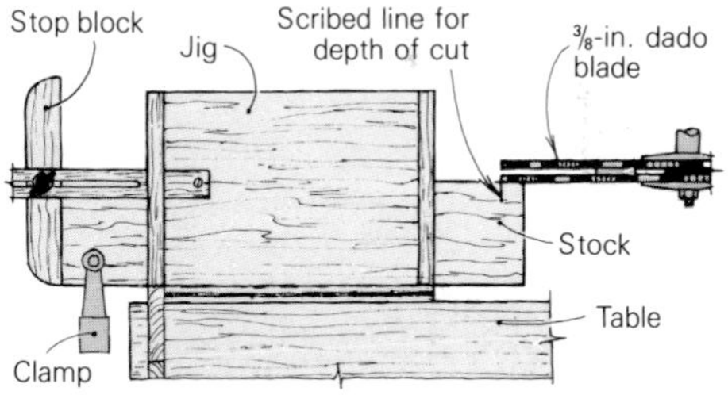

Stop block   Scribed line for depth of cut   ⅜-in. dado blade

Jig

Stock

Table

Clamp

Lower column until blade touches the top edges of the stock, then align tip of blade with scribed line for proper depth of cut.

Fig. 3: Cutting the pins first

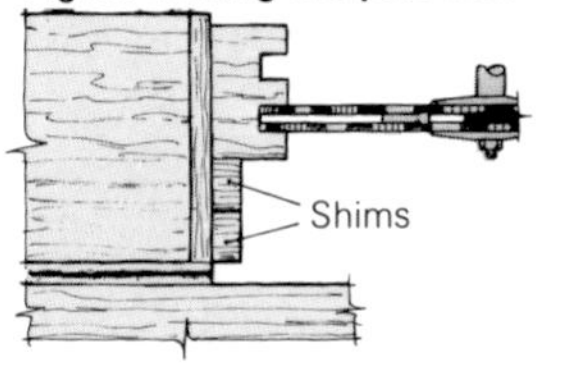

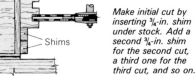

Shims

Make initial cut by inserting ¾-in. shim under stock. Add a second ¾-in. shim for the second cut, a third one for the third cut, and so on.

Fig. 4: Cutting the notch first

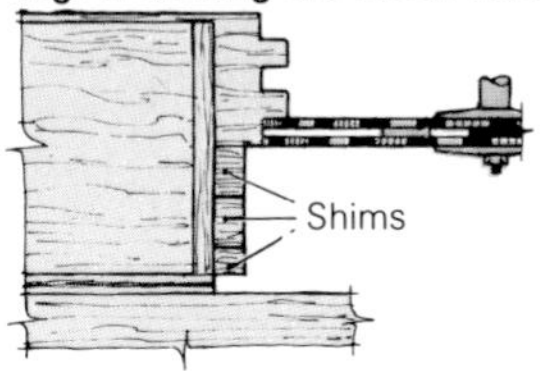

Shims

Cut notch at top edge of stock by inserting ⅜-in. shim beneath stock. For all following cuts, add ¾-in. shims under stock.

Making a Blind Finger Joint
Miter hides the router-cut fingers

by James A. Rome

The finger, or box, joint is one of the strongest choices for drawer, box or carcase construction. It's easy to make and easy to clamp, and there's a lot of long-grain to long-grain contact—the ideal gluing situation. In some applications, the finger joint is also quite handsome, but in others, the exposed end grain of through fingers clashes with the overall design. For that reason, I developed a method of making a joint that looks like a simple miter but retains the finger joint's strength.

Most of the steps in making my blind finger joint can be done on a router table and tablesaw, but some have to be performed by hand.

The completed joint is shown in figure 1E. The slots and fingers are cut on a router table using the jig shown in figure 2. Both halves of the joint are identical, each beginning with a finger and ending with a slot, so when one board is flipped over, the two parts mesh together.

After struggling with a small, metal router table, I built a big wooden one with a ¾-in. birch plywood top. I routed two grooves in the tabletop from front to back for the finger-joint jig to slide in. My router table has an adjustable fence which, for this job, acts as a stop behind the jig. A board clamped to the table would also work as a fence.

A note about routers: My first experiments using a Sears Craftsman 1½-HP router were unsatisfactory. No matter what I did, my slots were 0.011 in. oversize. I wrote to Sears about the problem, and received an answer from Singer, manufacturer of the router. Their specs permit runout of up to 0.007 in. at a distance of 1 in. from the collet. Since my bit was cutting farther from the collet, I got even more runout. Thus, the Sears router proved unsuitable for the job. I now use a Hitachi TR-12 plunge router, which cuts a slot accurate to within 0.001 in. With the router mounted on the table, however, it requires herculean strength to push upward against the router springs to adjust the depth of cut.

The jig must be rigid and accurately made to guarantee precision in the finished joint. I waxed the two hardwood runners on the bottom so that they would slide easily in the table grooves. Two screws countersunk into the side of one runner can be backed out to rub the side of the groove for a tight fit.

Router-bit diameter determines finger and slot width. I used a ½-in. straight-flute bit to make fingers and slots ½ in. deep, ½ in. wide and ¾ in. long, but you can change these dimensions for different size fingers. To index

Fig. 1: Steps in making the blind finger joint

Cut slots with ½-in. router bit.

A. First pass hogs waste.

Chisel cleans out corners.

B. Second pass squares up slot.

C. Define miter with tablesaw blade set to slot depth.

D. Cut miter with tablesaw blade set to 45°.

Chamfer corner.

E. Finish miter with dovetail saw and chisel.

45°

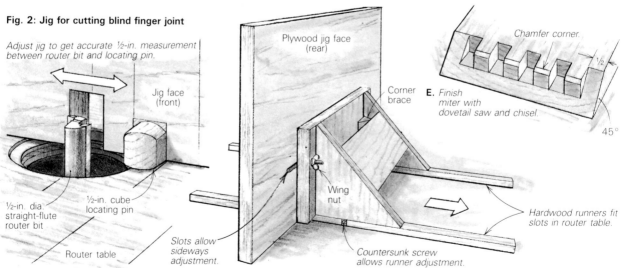

Fig. 2: Jig for cutting blind finger joint

Adjust jig to get accurate ½-in. measurement between router bit and locating pin.

Jig face (front)

Plywood jig face (rear)

Corner brace

Wing nut

½-in. dia. straight-flute router bit

½-in. cube locating pin

Router table

Slots allow sideways adjustment.

Countersunk screw allows runner adjustment.

Hardwood runners fit slots in router table.

Drawing: Ken Daniel

To cut first slot, clamp board vertically against jig face (left), right-hand edge against locating pin. First slot, placed over pin, locates next cut. Pencil lines on jig and router table make it easy to square up board. Bolts in jig face allow sideways adjustment of jig. After cutting slots, Rome readjusts router bit and makes a second pass with board horizontal (right), a light cleanup cut that flattens bottom of slots. Jig slides back until it stops against router-table fence shown at far right, behind jig.

the fingers, I installed a ½-in. cube-shaped locating pin in the front of the jig, as shown in figure 2. If you want larger or smaller fingers, make a pin with faces equal to your router-bit diameter. For ⅜-in. fingers, for example, use a ⅜-in. router bit and a ⅜-in. locating pin. Board width must be an even multiple of finger width. Finger length before mitering, as shown in figure 1A, must equal stock thickness. To make the joint shown, I used a board ¾ in. thick and 5 in. wide.

With the preliminaries out of the way, here's how to make the joint. The trick is to rout the slots between the fingers two times—once vertically, to remove the bulk of the waste, and once horizontally, to square off the round corners left after the first pass. With the jig set in the router table, adjust the router so that the bit extends ¾ in. above the table, to set the length of the fingers. Now adjust the fence behind the jig so that, pushed back against the fence, it stops when the front of the router bit extends ½ in. in front of the jig's face. Adjust the jig sideways to get exactly ½ in. between the locating pin and the router bit, as shown in figure 2. Clamp the board vertically against the face of the jig, with one edge against the locating pin as shown in the photo at left above. Use a square to ensure that the board is exactly vertical. (It's a good idea to test the setup using scrapwood before risking good stock.)

Cut one slot by pushing the jig toward the fence until it stops. Check the measurements and make any necessary

adjustment. To cut successive slots, position the slot over the locating pin and repeat the process, going from right to left. Do not cut a slot on the left edge, however. This edge must be mitered by hand later. The board at this point should look like the one in figure 1A. Cut the mating board in the same manner.

Next, lower the router bit so that it extends ½ in. above the table, and adjust the fence so that when the jig is pushed back against it, the bit extends ¾ in. in front of the jig's face. For this step, hold the board horizontal, with the slots and fingers down (photo, above right). Place the second slot from the left over the pin. Make a cut, move the board to your left one slot, and recut the remaining slots in the same way.

The first slot on the right of the board (shown at arrow in figure 1B) can't be recut with the jig. After cutting all the other slots on both halves of the joint, remove the jig from the table, put this slot over the router bit (with the router turned off), and clamp a guide board on the table against the right-hand edge of the board. Adjust the fence so that it stops the cut at the ¾-in. point and recut the last slot without the jig. After the second pass with the router, only the corners need to be cleaned up with a chisel.

On the tablesaw, adjust the rip fence so that it's ¼ in. away from the far side of the blade and adjust the blade height to ½ in. With the slots downward, and the end against the fence, cut a slot through the end of each half of the joint (figure 1C).

To recut far right-hand slot, a guide board clamped to router table substitutes for jig.

Cut the miter on the tablesaw with the blade at a 45° angle. I screw a wooden fence to the crosscut/miter gauge, make a cut through the fence, and use that kerf as a reference to see where the blade will cut. For accuracy, I clamp the board to the fence. The joint should now look like the one shown in figure 1D.

Now the outer finger and uncut slot in each board must be cut by hand to a 45° miter (figure 1E). I'm partial to a Japanese dovetail saw (*dozuki*) for this operation. Use the existing miter to guide the saw, or make a 45° guide block.

The final step is to chamfer the outer edge of each finger. When the joint is assembled, the fancy cabinetwork is invisible, but the joint is incredibly strong. □

James A. Rome is a full-time plasma physicist and part-time woodworker in Oak Ridge, Tenn. Photos by the author.

Hand Dovetails

They're really not that hard to do

by Alphonse Mattia

Dovetailing is one of the strongest and most attractive methods of joining the ends of boards together. Traditionally, handcut dovetails consist of a series of alternating pins and tails beginning and ending with a half-pin, with the tails usually about twice as large as the pins.

Nowadays, dovetails can be cut much faster by machine, but there are certain disadvantages to doing them this way. The pins and tails are the same size because they are cut together in one step. This makes the joint look very confusing and without character, as it is hard to tell the difference between the pins and tails. Machine dovetails also have a size limitation because there are only two sizes of dovetail router bits generally available. And, when machine cutting half-blind dovetails, there is no guarantee that the series will end with a pin. Taken together, these may not seem like serious points to consider when time is critical, but they do affect the quality of a fine piece of furniture.

With hand-cut dovetails the craftsman has no limitations. He can tailor the shape, size and pattern of his dovetails to suit the piece he is building. There are many types: through, half-blind (only visible from one side), hidden, and mitered dovetails. Simple and compound-angled are also possible.

In this article, I will go through the steps for cutting the through and half-blind dovetails. The most important thing about cutting dovetails is patience. You must be as precise as possible with each step, especially sawing. It takes practice, but in time you will find that they are not at all difficult.

The pieces to be joined should be dressed to the same width and thickness and the ends cut square. The surfaces that will be inside should be sanded and so marked.

It helps if you have a marking gauge. Sharpen it with a file

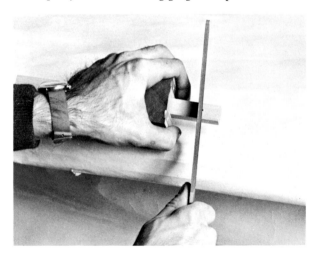

not quite parallel to the movable block. If angled in the right direction, this slight bevel will tend to draw the gauge tightly against the board being worked. (If the angle is reversed, it will tend to push the gauge away from the board.)

With the marking gauge set to the thickness of your boards, scribe a line all the way around the ends of your

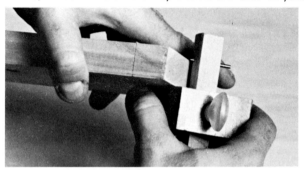

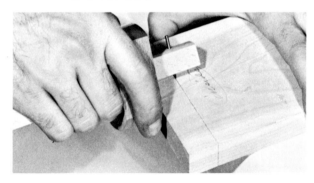

boards (front, back and edges). It helps if you set your marking gauge at a little more than the thickness of the wood (maximum 1/32). This will cause the pins and tails to extend above the surface of your boards when finished, so that after gluing, a little sanding will give a perfect corner.

(It is possible to join boards of two different thicknesses. If you do, you will have to use two marking gauge settings at this point, one for each thickness of board you are joining.)

Now the pins should be laid out on the end grain of one of the boards to be joined. In making through dovetails, I find it better to start with the pins, because later it will be easier to scribe the tails from the pins. But it is possible to cut the tails first and then the pins. When deciding which piece to lay out the pins on, remember that the dovetailed corner can be pulled apart from one side and not the other because of the wedging effect. For example, on a drawer, the tails would be on the sides and the pins on the front, so you are not depending on glue alone when pulling on the front. A hanging wall cabinet would have tails cut on the sides and pins on the top and bottom.

In any event, determine the size of the pins you will use. With handcut dovetails, the pins are usually about half the size of the tails. This ratio is optional, but if the tails are made too large, the strength of the joint is weakened as the holding power of the glue joint is in the long-grain areas between the pins and tails, not in the end-grain areas behind them. The

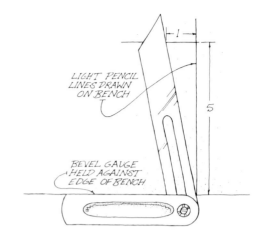

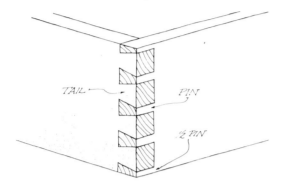

fewer the tails, the less the glue area. But if the tails are made too small, their strength is considerably reduced because there isn't enough wood across their narrowest point. With pins, however, strength is not significantly affected if they are made smaller (in some antique pieces the pins actually come to a point) because there is always enough cross-sectional area for what they have to do.

The first and last pins are called half-pins because they are angled on only one side, not because they are necessarily half the size of the whole pins. This is important when you are using very narrow pins because if you did make the outside pins half the size of the whole pin there would be danger of chipping or sanding through them. But in any case, begin and end a dovetail series with a half-pin rather than a half-tail, because a tail gets its strength only from being glued to a pin, not to the end grain it butts against.

Divide the width of the board that will have the pins into equal divisions, depending on the number of tails you have

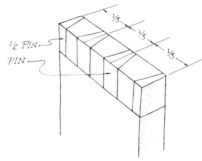

strength of the joint because of a flatter wedge.

At this point you should have the pins drawn out on the end grain of your board. The wider end of the pins should be toward the inside surface of the board. With a square you can carry your lines from the edges down to the marking gauge lines on both sides of the board. To avoid confusion, shade in the areas between pins. A common mistake is to saw on the

room for, e.g. divide in thirds for three tails, fourths for four tails. These division marks are the center points of your pins. If your pins are going to be 1/2-inch in width at their narrowest, measure in 1/4-inch from each end and 1/4-inch on either side of your division marks. This will give you the placement of your pins.

Check your divisions for accuracy. Then with a bevel gauge set to a 1-to-5 ratio, scribe in the lines with a sharp tool such as an awl or a scriber. Don't use a pencil (except for rough layout) because a pencil line is too thick.

The 1-to-5 ratio can be varied, but anything less will cause fragile corners on tails, and anything above 1 to 6 reduces the

wrong side of the line, or worse yet, to chisel out the wrong areas.

Now, with the piece held securely in a vise, you must make saw cuts down to the marking gauge line. You should use a fine dovetail saw. The thinner the blade, the easier it will be. Remember to split the line on the waste side. You'll find this easier if you imagine the line as having thickness to it, as a pencil line does. It is difficult to saw precisely at first, but you will get better with a little practice.

The piece should now be clamped over a rigid area of the workbench to support it while chiseling. Do not clamp over a vise or allow the piece to extend over the edge of the bench.

Before starting to chisel, it helps to deepen the marking gauge line between the pins with a chisel and then to remove a fine chip out to about 1/8-inch in front of the marking

gauge line. This will establish a positive edge to line the chisel against. It will also lessen the chance of the chisel drifting back beyond the marking gauge line during chiseling. Now you are ready to take a heavier cut.

With the chisel held vertically at the marking gauge line, a blow with a mallet will cut across the grain. Then a light cut in from the end grain will remove the chip. A few alternating cuts will get you about halfway through. Now turn the board over and repeat the process from the other side until you have chiseled out the material between the pins.

When you are making the vertical cuts across the grain at the marking gauge line, it helps to tip the chisel forward a few degrees. This is called undercutting and if done when chiseling from both sides it will result in a shallow, concave surface in the end grain between the pins. Remember that

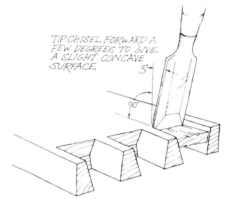

TIP CHISEL FORWARD A FEW DEGREES TO GIVE A SLIGHT CONCAVE SURFACE

this undercut is not visible and does not affect the strength of the joint, but it does result in a tighter looking joint.

Even with undercutting you will still have a little cleanup to do in the corners between the pins. If any of your saw cuts

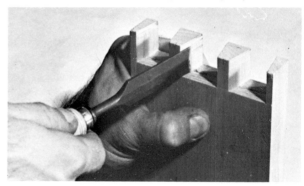

are out of square, you can clean them up a little also, but always use a sharp chisel, never sandpaper or a file, when cleaning up the pins.

You should now be ready to scribe the tails. Position the pins directly over the side to be joined. Make sure that the ends are flush, that the pins are positioned precisely at the previously drawn marking gauge line, that the inside surfaces are facing in, and that the widest end of the pins is toward the inside of the joint. Now scribe around the pins with a scriber or awl. It is important not to move the piece until all the scribing is completed. Clamp the piece in position if possible.

It is easier to scribe from inside the joint rather than out-side. The grain will work to your advantage in keeping the

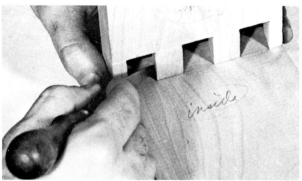

scriber tight against the sides of the pins. From the outside the tool tends to follow the grain away from the side of the pin.

After the pins have been scribed, use a square to scribe the lines across the end grain. Shade in the areas to be removed

and proceed as you did when cutting out the pins. Be as precise as possible with your saw cuts, remembering to split the line on the waste side. Deepen the marking gauge line with a chisel and remove a 1/8-inch chip. Undercut when chiseling.

It is probably neater and easier to saw rather than to chisel the ends out. Clean up the corners between tails with a chisel before trying the joint.

Do not force the joint together. If it is your first set, you will probably have more cleaning up to do. With practice you should be able to tap the two pieces together without any cleanup or splits or gaps.

The dovetails should be tight enough to require some tapping when putting them together; however, be careful of splitting. If your dovetails are very tight and require a lot of effort to drive them together, they are probably too tight and may split when the glue is applied (glue swells the joint slightly). Always dry clamp before gluing and use glue blocks —small pieces of a softer wood that are notched so they direct the clamp pressure over the tails. A little sanding to bring the ends down flush with the sides and your through dovetails are complete.

Half-blind Dovetails

Half-blind dovetails are those that show from only one side. They are most commonly used for drawer fronts but they can be used elsewhere quite effectively. The procedure for making them is basically the same as for through dovetails. I will list only the steps that differ.

Half-blind dovetails can be used for joining pieces of the same thickness, but because they are most commonly used for drawers, I will describe cutting them with pieces of different thicknesses—a thicker piece for the drawer front, a thinner piece for the side.

Dress the pieces to be joined to the desired thicknesses and sand and mark the inside surfaces. You will need two marking-gauge settings for half-blind dovetails. First the marking gauge is set to the thickness of the drawer side. With this setting scribe a line along the end of the drawer front on the inside surface only. Now reset the marking gauge to about 2/3 the thickness of the drawer front and scribe a line into the endgrain of the drawer front. The scribed line should be in 1/3 of the way from the outside (or 2/3 from the inside) surface of the drawer front. At this same setting scribe a line around both sides and edges of the drawer side.

The 2/3 proportion can be varied. It determines how long the tails will be. They can be longer, providing they don't interfere with any shaping or face carving on the drawer front. But as tails are shortened, the strength of the joint is reduced.

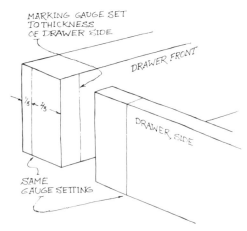

MARKING GAUGE SET TO THICKNESS OF DRAWER SIDE

DRAWER FRONT

DRAWER SIDE

⅓ ⅔

SAME GAUGE SETTING

When cutting half-blind dovetails I find it easier to cut the tails first because it is difficult to scribe inside the pins. But others say the pins should be cut first.

On the drawer side lay out the tails. This is done in the

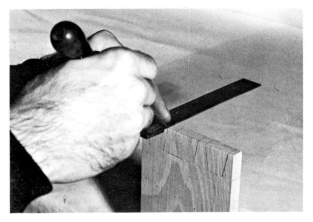

same way as when laying out pins for through dovetails except you will be working on the outside of the drawer side rather than on the end grain of the drawer front.

Saw and chisel out the areas between the tails you have just laid out using the same techniques as in through dovetails. Once the tails are cut out and cleaned up, you must scribe the pins onto the end grain of the drawer front. Clamp the drawer front in a vise flush to the workbench top and lay the

side over it. Be sure inside surfaces are towards the inside of the corner. Line the edges of the boards up, and position the ends of the tails exactly at the marking gauge line. This positioning is critical. If it is not done accurately, it will result in gaps. Clamp or hold the piece securely and scribe the pins from the sides of the tails. The lines should then be extended

with a square down the inside of the drawer front to the other marking gauge line. Novices usually expect the sawing and chiseling out of the pins to be difficult, but you will find that it is not much different than with through dovetails. Start sawing at the inside edge of the drawer front. Remember to split the line on the waste side, but do not saw past either of the two marking gauge lines.

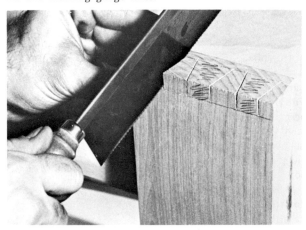

The chiseling is done with the same alternating cuts as for through dovetails. Remember to undercut slightly. The only difference here is that the inside corners will splinter as each chip is removed because the saw cuts do not extend back all the way. It helps to clean out these splintered internal corners after removing each chip. When you reach the marking gauge line do whatever cleanup is necessary and try the joint.

For purposes of clarity I have described procedures for cutting each of the types of dovetails on two pieces of wood. This is the best way to practice these joints. However, when actually making a box or a drawer, it is much more efficient and easier to be accurate if you work on all four corners at once. In other words, lay out and saw the pins on both ends of the front and back at once. Scribe the tails on both ends of the sides at the same time. Make all the saw cuts in one operation and then chisel out all the tails at once. But remember to letter each corner so you know which set of tails was scribed from which set of pins.

There are nearly as many methods for cutting dovetails as there are craftsmen. The methods I have described work best for me, and I hope with a little practice they will produce satisfactory results for the reader. ☐

Plate Joinery
We test two machines that make fast, tight joints

by Paul Bertorelli

Doweling is a quick and strong way to make carcase and frame joints, but the problem with dowels is accuracy. Even the best jigs maddeningly tend to misalign the holes in a way that isn't evident until after the joint is glued and driven home, with no hope of adjustment.

Faced with that trouble with dowels, a Swiss cabinetmaker named Herman Steiner during the 1950s tried substituting spline-like, eye-shaped plates of compressed wood. Instead of a drill and jig, he used a small circular saw to scoop out a short kerf, into which he could insert the thin plates. The joint proved quick to cut and to assemble. More important, the parts could be slid along the slot into alignment after assembly. The compressed beech plates then absorbed moisture from the glue and swelled, making the joint tight and strong.

Steiner's invention developed into biscuit or plate joinery, a technique widely used in Europe but just becoming known in North America. Plates can connect carcases or frames in solid wood or in plywood, and especially in particleboard. Plate-joining machines are as portable as routers and require very little set-up. When making large carcases whose components may be difficult to pass through machines, plate joiners can be brought right to the job.

Steiner Lamello Ltd., the firm that sprang from Steiner's tinkering, has marketed its system in the United States for over a decade. The German tool firm Elu now offers a similar system. The Lamello machine (called a Minilo) costs about $580, the Elu about $300 (1982 prices). Both companies say their machines are best suited for small shops where hand methods can't keep pace but where heavier equipment isn't justified. In my experience they've pegged the market. I used the Minilo in a small production shop for nearly two years and found that it worked well as a substitute for doweling, tongue-and-groove or even mortise-and-tenon. I recently borrowed an Elu machine from that firm's U.S. outlet for testing and found that, with some qualifications, it too makes an attractively quick and simple joint.

The plate does it—Steiner tried various sizes and shapes of wooden inserts, and even dabbled with plastic ones. He final-

Plate joints are made by inserting a beech biscuit into slots milled with a specialized portable plunge cutter. The cross-hatch pattern on the biscuit holds glue and speeds the biscuit's swelling, thus tightening the joint.

ly settled on three plates of the same thickness and shape (their edges are arcs of the same circle) but of different lengths and widths. Elu calls them biscuits, but the beech plates sold by both firms are virtually identical. Both make the same three sizes: No. 0 (about ⅝ in. wide and 1¾ in. long), No. 10 (¾ in. wide, 2⅛ in. long) and No. 20 (1 in. wide, 2½ in. long). The plates are die-cut from beech blanks with the grain running diagonally to the plate's length. Thus they are nearly impossible to snap across their width. The plates are compressed and embossed with a cross-hatch pattern that holds the glue, which you squirt into the slot before assembly. At first the plate fits its slot loosely. But as the compressed beech absorbs moisture from the glue, it swells in its slot. This swelling action is what makes the joint so tight and reliable. If there's enough glue in the slot, the joint tightens to maximum strength every time. Any water-based glue seems to work, sometimes even a little too quickly. I once misassembled a plywood carcase and tried to pull the yellow-glued Lamello joints apart after just ten minutes. I ended up with a lot of broken plywood.

Both machines consist of a high-speed motor powering a 4-in. carbide-toothed sawblade through a right-angle drive, attached to an adjustable base. Both machines have a spring-loaded mechanism that keeps the blade inside its base until you plunge it into the work to make the cut. Then the spring slips the blade back out of the wood and into its guard, while you move on to the next slot. The Minilo motor and blade move in a straight line, while the Elu swivels on a pivot; otherwise they both mill slots the same way.

Apart from speed, the big advantage of plate joints is being able to slide assembled parts into alignment. The machines cut a slot slightly longer and deeper than the actual dimensions of the joining plate. This tolerance allows the entire joint to slide along its length by as much as ⅛ in. The slot width is critical and is fixed at ⁵⁄₃₂ in. Spacing of the biscuits depends on the joinery situation, although the closer together they are, the stronger the joint. For maximum strength, the plates can be end-to-end (on about 2½-in. centers) and side-by-side (in stock thicker than about ⅝ in.). In most applica-

To cut slots with the Elu, above left, the cutter index is aligned with each pencil mark and the motor-cutter assembly is pivoted, plunging the blade into the stock. The edge of the mating board acts as a fence and must not be moved during the plunge, or an oversize slot will result. Slots in the mating part are cut by repositioning the machine, left. Above, glue has been squirted into the slots, and the beech plates inserted. The metering nozzle and glue bottle sold by Lamello are on the bench. Now the joint is assembled and pulled up tight with clamps, screws or nails. Clamps can be removed in as little as 10 minutes, because the plates swell, locking the joint.

tions, you cut the mating parts as if for nailing or butt-joining. You bring the parts together and strike pencil marks about 5 in. apart across the line of the joint. Then cut the slots in both parts by setting these marks to a centerline on the base of the machine. Add glue and the plates themselves, and assemble. The joints can be pulled up tight with clamps, screws or nails and need be held tight only until the plates swell. As with any joint, the final position of the parts must be marked accurately. And you have to hold the machine and its positioning guide rock-steady while cutting, or the slot will splay out and will be too wide for the biscuit.

Despite its versatility, the plate isn't always the best joint. When joining boards edge-to-edge, for example, a spline or an accurately placed dowel will draw warped or bowed surfaces into plane. Until the glue swells it, the plate is too loose in its slot to align two surfaces. I've tried to use plate joints to edge-join slightly bowed plywood panels and found that the method won't get the faces within a veneer thickness.

The plate joint can substitute for a mortise and tenon in a frame, but within limits. The rails have to be at least 1⅞ in. wide, the length of the No. 0 biscuit slot, or else the

edges of the slot will show. A protruding plate can be trimmed flush, but the result is never as neat as a well-made mortise and tenon. In frame stock thicker than ⅝ in., two plates should be used side-by-side.

Controlling the amount of glue in the slots is important. Too little and the plate won't swell. Too much and you get a river of squeeze-out. Lamello sells a split-nozzle bottle for metering glue, although at $20 (1982) it seems overpriced.

I've seen no data comparing the strength of plate joints with traditional joinery. So I assembled a few test joints in poplar with dowels, stub tenons and plates. I was surprised to find that only the plate-joined piece couldn't be wrenched apart by hand, although it did succumb to a swift kick that broke the wood, not the glue line.

Comparing the machines—Both the Elu machine and the Minilo are well-crafted. But after I used each in the shop for a few hours, I found the Elu system to be generally less refined. The Swiss-made Minilo has a slick, detent-type depth adjustment, a real help when you want to switch plate sizes. I had to struggle with the Elu's stiff, threaded stop for depth set-

These frame joints were cut by placing the parts together and marking them, as with doweling. Using two plates in stock thickness makes for a stronger joint.

The Minilo's front fence can be set at 45°, making it the better machine for slotting lengthwise miters. Spring-loaded pins in the machine's front guard lock the Minilo against sliding during the plunge, a feature lacking in the Elu.

The Elu and Minilo are similar in size and weight. The plates, center, are sold in the same three sizes by both manufacturers.

ting. To locate the plate in the wood's thickness, Lamello uses a flip-down fence that rides atop the stock. A simple plastic snap-on template accommodates thinner stock, and also does double duty as a guide for plate spacing, typical of this machine's thoughtful design evolution. Elu's base rides on the bench top, which means there must be no debris under the stock, and it uses a tedious screw to adjust the cutter to the stock's thickness.

Both machines are at their best when making carcase joints. For cutting frame joints, the Minilo is handier than the Elu. Its front fence flips down and locks parallel to the cutter, and gives you plenty to hang on to while making the plunge. The Elu has no front fence, making it tough to hold both stock and machine at once, unless you clamp the stock down.

The Elu does have one feature the Minilo lacks. With a clamped guide or side fence (sold with the machine), it can cut a continuous groove faster and cleaner than a router does. Set to its full depth, the Elu could even be used as a panel saw for stock up to ⅝ in. thick.

The real difference between these machines is price. When I bought my Minilo, it was the only game around, so I winced

and paid the $580. It turned out to be worth it. The machine paid for itself every day by speeding carcase and frame joinery, and I soon wondered how I had ever gotten along without it. Yet, after trying the Elu, I'm sure it is more than half the machine for half the money. And despite its design shortcomings, I'd put up with its relative crudeness—particularly if I weren't going to use it in production every day.

The decision whether to buy a plate joiner ought to be guided by clear purpose. If you enjoy creating complicated, fussy joinery with little regard for time, one of these machines would only take some of the joy out of your woodworking. But if you find joinery a chore anyway, the plate joiner will make you wonder why you ever bothered with many traditional joints. A plate joiner is fast—a specialized power tool for doing lots of work quickly. □

Paul Bertorelli is on the editorial staff of Fine Woodworking *magazine. The Lamello system is available through local tool outlets. It is imported by Colonial Saw, Inc., 100 Pembroke St., Kingston, Mass. 02364. The Elu is sold by Elu Machinery, 9040 Dutton Dr., Twinsburg, Ohio 44087.*

Cutting Gauge
The right tool for cross-grain layout

by John Lively

Nothing quite beats the cutting gauge for scoring across the grain. For striking dovetail baselines and shoulder lines for tenons, dadoes and rabbets, it's an especially accurate and handy tool. It can also be used to eliminate splintering when crosscutting by scoring the wood prior to sawing, though this requires an initial crosscut to within an inch or so of the final length to give the gauge an edge to ride against.

Unlike the ordinary marking gauge whose steel scribing pin is designed to mark along the grain, the cutting gauge is equipped with a cutting spur, which when properly ground and honed, severs cross-grain fibers cleanly. Used across the grain, the marking gauge can tear the wood and produce a ragged line, but the cutting gauge incises a neat, clearly visible cut, just the right thing to accept the edge of a sharp chisel when paring away the last bit of end-grain tissue.

The only commercially available cutting gauge on the American market, made by Marples (England), is sold by most mail-order tool suppliers for about $14 (1982). Usually made from beech, the fence has two brass wear strips let into its face, and is bored and tapped to receive a plastic thumbscrew which tightens against the stock and locks the fence in place at any distance from the spur. The Marples cutting spur is ground to a spear point and beveled on both skewed faces and is flat on the back. The spur is held firmly in the stock by a brass wedge. If you buy one of these or already have one, you'll get it to work better by regrinding the spur to a round-nose profile as described below.

Instead of buying a cutting gauge you might want to make one. Start by selecting and dimensioning the material for the fence and stock. A stable, relatively dense hardwood like maple or cherry will do. Though the pieces themselves are small, it's best to cut the blanks large enough to machine them. The fence blank should be planed to a finished thickness of 1 1/16 in., ripped to a final width of 2 3/16 in., but leave the block about 14 in. long for now. Thickness the blank for the stock (bar) to 3/4 in. square, cut it to its finished length of 7 1/2 in. or 8 in. and put it aside.

Now pencil the outline of the fence in the middle of the blank. The fence is about 2 3/4 in. long (its length really depends on what size most comfortably fits your hand), and it is radiused top and bottom. Orient the layout so the grain runs vertically, from one rounded end to the other. To mortise the fence to receive the stock, locate the center of the fence and construct a 3/4-in. square about it, knifing-in the lines on both faces so that you have two squares directly opposite one another. Next bore a 5/8-in. hole through the block, centering the bit in the square. Enlarge and square up the hole, finally paring from knife line to knife line on all four sides of the mortise. The stock should slide freely through the mortise, but with no wobble side to side or up and down.

Fence and stock are locked together by a wedge, which requires tapering the top of the mortise at about 10°. Find the angle with a sliding bevel, and knife a line on the inside of the fence the proper distance above the top of the mortise. The tapered slot for the wedge is 5/8 in. wide; this will leave a 1/16-in. wide untapered shoulder on either side of the mortise. These keep the stock from flopping up and down when the wedge is removed. Pare down the end grain with a 5/8-in. chisel to form the slot, taking care to stop the taper just short of breaking through at the other end. Cut the wedge to fit the angle of the slot, but make it about 1/16 in. narrower than the slot is wide. The lateral play here, along with the prominent hump on the rear of the wedge, lets you wiggle the wedge side to side when you want to remove it.

Cut a 1/2-in. wide by 1/8-in. deep rabbet down both sides of the block on the face side (opposite the wedge side). These receive wear strips which you can make from a dense tropical wood like lignum vitae, ebony or rosewood. Finally, bandsaw the fence from the blank and epoxy the wear strips in place. When the glue has cured, sand the strips flush with the face, and smooth the rounded top and bottom edges.

Grind the cutting spur from a length of old hacksaw blade. It is 5/16 in. wide and 1 1/2 in. long. You ought not break it off until you've ground and honed the edge. The business end is first rounded and then beveled to a sharpening angle of about 20°. The rounded edge keeps the tool from digging in and dragging. Back off the unbeveled side on a stone, hone the bevel, then back it off again. Soften the upper edge with a file after snapping it off.

Cut the mortise for the spur and its retaining wedge about ½ in. from the end of the stock. Proceed as you did when mortising the fence, only taper the outside wall the full width of the mortise; lastly, fashion the wedge from the same tropical wood you used for the wear strips.

Traditionally used, the cutting gauge (and the marking gauge for that matter) is pushed into the work rather than pulled. This requires adopting a special grip to get consistent, accurate results. As shown in the photo at right, the index finger wraps around the top of the fence, while the thumb, positioned against the stock directly above the cutter, powers the tool. If you try to push the tool by its fence, it's liable to get slightly askew and bind against the wood. Trying to cut the full depth in the first pass can also cause the cutter to bind, drag and even wander; so first make a light pass. Having easily cut a shallow groove straight and true, you can make a second pass to final depth without risk of binding or wandering, because the scoring spur cannot deviate from the groove it cut first, and half the work is already done.

The orientation of the cutter is important, and can be different, depending on whether you are left or right-handed. If the toe of the spur is inclined toward the fence even slightly, you'll have a hard time getting a straight cut because the spur will want to push the fence away from the edge as you move the tool along. If the heel of the spur is angled toward the fence, it will wedge the fence against the edge during the cut, tight enough to cause binding if the angle is too great. Ideally the cutter should heel-in toward the fence one degree or less; this combines ease of operation with a slight wedging action, which means that you don't have to jam the fence against the edge of the board with barbaric force. Shave small amounts of end-grain tissue off the rear wall of the mortise in the stock until you get the right degree of skew.

For most woodworking operations, the bevel of the spur

Used across the grain, a cutting gauge will score wood cleanly. A marking gauge has torn the wood fibers and left a ragged mark.

should face the fence, a condition that means that the beveled side of the scored groove is in the waste and that the groove wall on the other side is perfectly vertical to the face of the board. The vertical wall will be plainly visible (since the end-grain has been burnished by the spur), and this will make the task of end-grain paring considerably easier. You'll already have a ledge about $\frac{1}{32}$ in. wide on either side of the board to position the edge of your chisel for the final, leveling shave.

The cutting gauge is more than a marking tool. Its spur actually cuts the visible shoulder line of the joint it's laying out. The careful chiseling you do between the scored lines, the nice end-grain surface you leave behind, gets covered up when the joint goes together. But the clean, straight line you scored with the cutting gauge is what you see and feel once the shoulder is pulled up tight. In laying out a joint with a cutting gauge, you make the final cut first. □

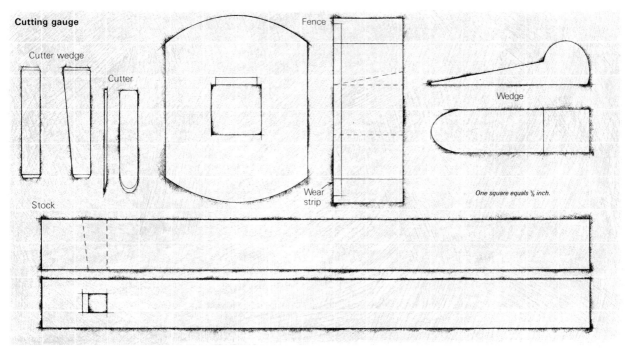

Cutting gauge

Cutter wedge

Cutter

Fence

Wedge

Stock

Wear strip

One square equals ½ inch.

Illustrations: E. Marino III

On Dovetailing Carcases
Which to cut first, pins or tails?

by Ian J. Kirby

The through dovetail has become synonymous with quality woodworking, a hallmark of distinction. This is understandable because the joint must be handmade—we don't have a machine that can produce variations in the dimensions and angles of its tails and pins. I do wonder, however, why so many woodworkers see the joint as a standard of craftsmanship. In terms of skill it is considerably easier to make than the mortise and tenon or the secret mitered dovetail. Cutting the through dovetail is little more than sawing to a line. I make this point not to demean the work, but to encourage anyone who might feel inhibited about attempting dovetail joints. The through dovetail is not difficult, and it should not be thought of as the ultimate in woodworking skill.

The through joint was routinely used by 17th- and 18th-century cabinetmakers to put a carcase together very quickly. It doesn't take much experience before you can lay out and cut the joint with the minimum of marking out. If you make the end of the board square and knife the depth-line around, you will find it easy to gauge the spacing of pins and tails by eye. Lines may be penciled square across the end grain as an assist, but with practice even this is not necessary. It doesn't matter if the angle on the tails varies, since the pins will be marked and sawn from the tails; the interface will still be tight. It was usual 200 years ago to cover the through joint with an applied molding. The outlook and attitude of the times was to conceal structure behind some embellishment. Note the direct contrast with 20th-century attitudes—our urge is to expose structure as part of the dynamic of the object, and to read structural detail as the mark of quality. Figure 1 illustrates some layout possibilities.

The details of laying out and cutting the joint have been written about by other authors (see pages 14 to 18 and 30 to 31). I will concentrate instead on the associated and attendant techniques. There is, however, one point about making the joint itself: whether you should cut the tails first and mark the pins from them, or whether you should start with the pins and mark the tails from them. Woodworkers disagree, and either way will achieve the result. If you understand both, then the answer to which is correct has to be, whichever method you are most comfortable with, and whichever gives the better result. The decision is often determined by which board in a carcase—the vertical or the horizontal—is to have the tails, and which board is the longer. For example, take the proportions of a carcase as shown in figure 2 and assume we want the tails on the longer piece. They will therefore show from the top. If the tails are made first it is simple to put the pins board upright in the vise, position the tails board on it, and mark the pins through the tails. If the pins were made first, then to mark the tails you would have to balance the pins board vertically on the tails board. This is usually done by clamping the pieces in place on the edge of the bench. If the pins board is in any way cupped or twisted,

the problem is compounded by having to clamp straightening battens across it. When the tails are made first, a cupped or warped piece can be straightened by blocks or by clamps put across the bench. Having come this far, I should say that for through or lapped dovetails I make the tails first. It seems to give better control over the marking out and cutting, and better control of the boards themselves. On the other hand, when cutting a secret mitered dovetail, you must make the pins first and mark the tails from them—it can't be done the other way around.

The sawing of the joint also takes on different flavors depending on whether you cut the tails or the pins first. If you make the tails first, then the first thing is to get the sawblade at right angles to the face of the board, and the kerf is made just $\frac{1}{32}$ in. or so deep right across the end grain, as shown in figure 3. Make this initial kerf by keeping the saw vertical and don't yet be concerned about the tail angle. The small amount of vertical cut will not affect the extreme tip of the tail. Right-angularity having been achieved, set the saw at the angle to which you wish to cut the tail.

Once started, the angle must not be adjusted or the result will be a bent line. This bent line cannot be "mirrored" on the pin—and anyway, if the angle varies a little from one tail to another, does it matter? The important thing is to have all the sawcuts at right angles to the face of the board. If you make the pins first, cutting them follows this same procedure. But once the tails have been marked from the pins, there is no room for any variation in sawing the angle. The kerf is made across the wood to about $\frac{1}{32}$ in. deep, and the

Fig. 1: Dovetail layout

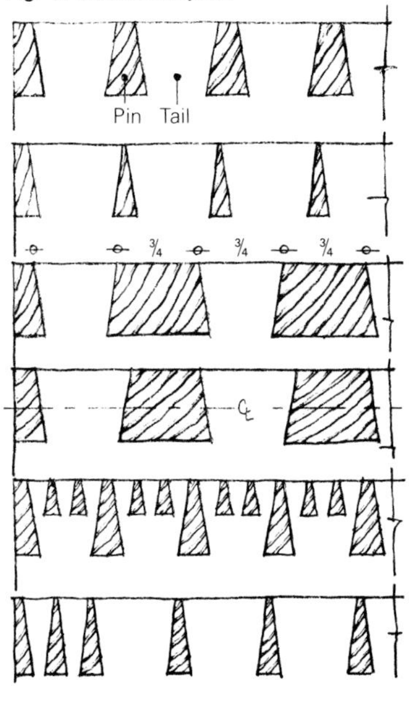

Common proportional layout—tails are two or three times as wide as pins.

Very fine pins were used by 18th-century drawer-makers. A fine chisel is used to clean out between the tails.

Equal spacing on the end grain does not produce equal pins and tails.

To make equal pins and tails, measure along a centerline and strike angles from there.

There are many decorative variations. This one adds glue area at ends and edges.

Small tails and extra pins increase gluing area at the carcase edges.

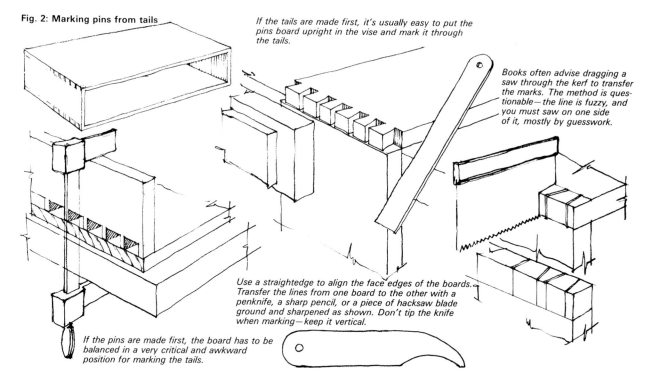

Fig. 2: Marking pins from tails

If the tails are made first, it's usually easy to put the pins board upright in the vise and mark it through the tails.

Books often advise dragging a saw through the kerf to transfer the marks. The method is questionable—the line is fuzzy, and you must saw on one side of it, mostly by guesswork.

Use a straightedge to align the face edges of the boards. Transfer the lines from one board to the other with a penknife, a sharp pencil, or a piece of hacksaw blade ground and sharpened as shown. Don't tip the knife when marking—keep it vertical.

If the pins are made first, the board has to be balanced in a very critical and awkward position for marking the tails.

saw is sighted and set exactly at the angle which must be achieved to give a good interface.

Whatever the method, getting the saw into the correct angle is probably best achieved by beginning the cut on the far side of the wood—not, as one might expect, from the near side. Use light strokes to start, almost lifting the weight of the saw off the wood. Once the shallow cut is made and the saw will remain in the kerf, then saw across the line toward the near side—don't cut any further down the back side of the workpiece. You must concentrate on achieving the angle, not on reaching depth of cut, at this stage. Starting from the far side seems to give better vision into the workpiece—the saw does not hide the line, and the dust is easily blown away. All you have to accomplish is the shallowest kerf across the end grain, to give the saw teeth a register in which to work. If you lift the saw out, the kerf should be well defined across the board but too shallow to have direction downward. Now you can set the saw to the required direction—at an angle for a tail, or vertical for a pin. All of this assumes that you have placed the board vertically in the vise for sawing. If you want to become skilled with the saw, there is no virtue in tilting the wood in the vise. Keep the workpiece square to the bench and learn to saw at the required angle.

To gain skill, the amateur craftsman should look for and take every opportunity to practice. This often leads to experiments in softwood, for utility work around the home and shop, but it can be a disappointment. Generally, softwood tissue is alternately hard and soft, and the soft part readily crumbles if forced into too tight a joint. When cleaning out the bottoms of either pins or tails, that is, when paring across the grain, the wood will crumble badly unless the chisel is absolutely sharp. It helps to ease the under-edges of the tails when working in softwood (figure 3) or when you have made one or more pins a little too tight. With the sharpening bevel of a wide chisel toward the wood, remove a sliver of material from the corner of the tail which is going to come first into

contact with the edge of the pin. Don't cut away any tissue that will be visible, and remove an absolute minimum only. It may seem wasteful to practice with good wood such as a mild-working mahogany, but the feedback of information through your tools and hands, plus success achieved at a critical learning time, makes it worth the expense.

From the outset you should work toward making a through dovetail straight from the saw. The cross-grain surfaces must be chiseled flat, of course, but if the beginner thinks that long-grained surfaces should be sawn fat and chiseled back to the line, adequate results will be a long time coming. You can get the result you want directly from the saw, and to a very high standard, after only a few practice tries.

Having become skilled at making the joint, you may wish to try a mild variation: a very slight off-square cut when making the tails (figure 3). Mark out the joint as usual, with the face side of the board toward the inside of the finished piece. But instead of sawing the line of the tail square to the face, very slightly angle the saw so that the normally parallel gap on the end grain of the tails is wider toward the face side of the board. The gradient of the tail isn't altered, but the tails have a larger pin gap on the face side of the board than on the outside of the carcase. When the pin is subsequently marked from the larger profile, it will tighten as it is driven home and the top interface will be mildly crushed. Be cautious: Overdoing this can ruin an otherwise good joint. The angling of the saw is more an opinion than a visible amount off-square. At worst the outside edges of the pins will be crushed at the top and won't present a parallel line—you went too far.

Use a steel hammer to drive the tails into the pins. A mallet can't be directed at a single tail, if it hits the workpiece on the twist it very easily marks the wood, and its tone upon impact gives no clue as to the tightness of the joint. The hammer should be slightly domed on its face—most hammers are anyway—so that each tail can be struck individually. The hammer will do little damage to the tissue if each blow is

Fig. 3: Sawing dovetails

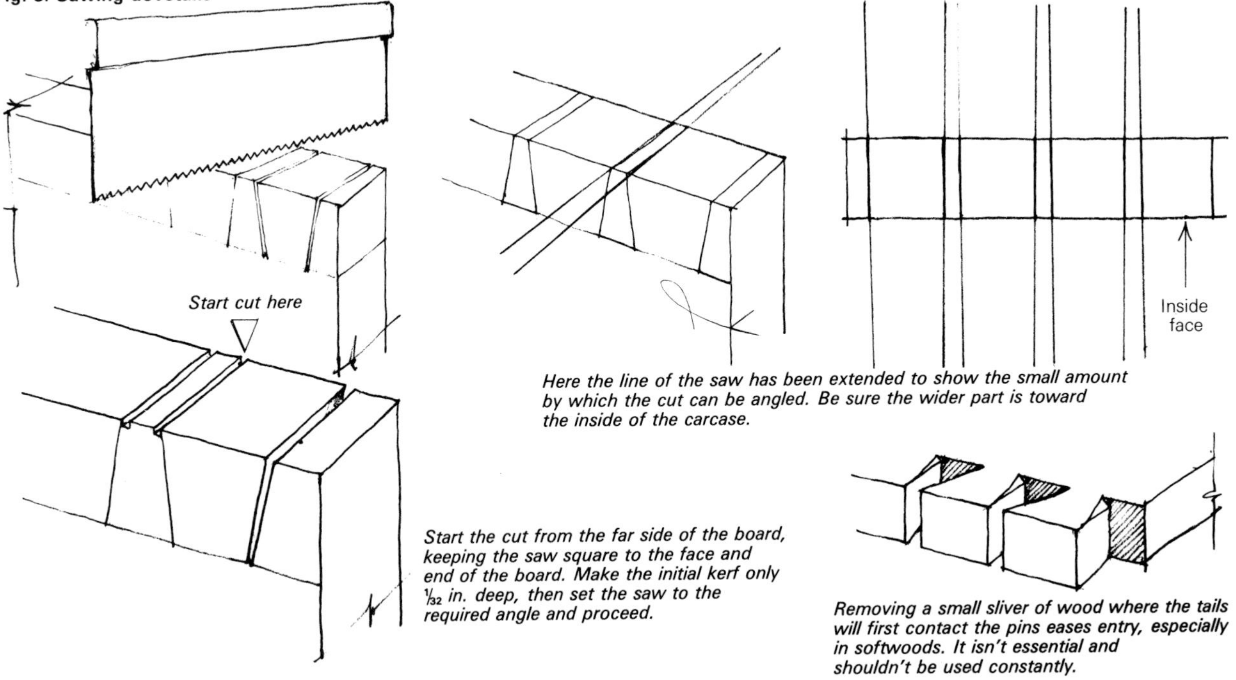

Plan view

Inside face

Start cut here

Here the line of the saw has been extended to show the small amount by which the cut can be angled. Be sure the wider part is toward the inside of the carcase.

Start the cut from the far side of the board, keeping the saw square to the face and end of the board. Make the initial kerf only 1/32 in. deep, then set the saw to the required angle and proceed.

Removing a small sliver of wood where the tails will first contact the pins eases entry, especially in softwoods. It isn't essential and shouldn't be used constantly.

delivered squarely. Each tail can be driven independently, and you will hear a distinct change in tone if a tail is binding and getting too tight. As well as the change in tone, the hammer will now bounce, as though hitting solid end grain. If this makes you queasy, protect the work with a small block of wood. The alternative to a hammer is a bar clamp. It has its greatest effect at the very end of assembling the joint, when the tail should be sitting down tight on the end grain at the base of the pins. When driven with a hammer the tail will travel the last few thousandths of an inch and may then bounce back or simply absorb the shock. Either way you can be fooled into thinking the tail won't sit down tight. Try a clamp and it goes the final fraction without problem, giving a clean, gap-free interface.

One sometimes sees a woodworker making up a set of castellated clamping blocks for each dovetailed carcase—the idea being to put pressure only on the pins or tails on each side of each corner. To me, this practice reflects fundamental misunderstanding of sound cabinetmaking technique.

In a through dovetail, when determining the length of the tail and the pin, we have three options (assuming that the pieces of wood to be joined are all of the same thickness). We can make the tails and pins longer than, equal to or shorter than the thickness of the wood. The method that seems to be most common is to make the tails and pins longer than the thickness of the wood. When the joint is put together the ends of the tails and pins protrude, later to be planed or sanded flush with the carcase sides. Unless you plan to feature this protrusion by carving in some way, there is no virtue here. This approach means you must saw to a greater depth than necessary, only to plane away the effort when cleaning up. In the process, you destroy a vital registered edge. Furthermore, clamping turns into a juggling act with all those little blocks, which tend to crush the tissue mercilessly, or you waste time making a set of special blocks.

Instead, I make the tails and pins fractionally shorter than

the thickness of the stock. Considering this point takes us back to the initial selection of which faces are to go on the inside or the outside of the carcase. Assuming that the more handsome side is to face out, then the less handsome side or inside should be prepared as the face side, having all the normal properties of a face side—it should be flat in length, flat in width, and out of winding or twist. It is likely that the boards will have been passed through a thickness planer after receiving their face side and face edge, but this is not necessary to the manufacture of the carcase. For the sake of argument, the outside of the boards could be left rough from the mill. But the ends of the boards must be cut to length and squared. The end grain should be clean and free of any tearout. Do this by knifing round the ends fairly deeply (figure 4), then plane down to the knife line with one of the bench planes—the wider the boards, the larger the plane, and the 22-in. jointer is not too large. A shooting board can be a big help here, since it allows you to lay a heavy plane on its side, gives good vision into the work, and with practice the plane can be made to cut almost like a bacon slicer.

Probably the most useful assist I have found when teaching this and other aspects of woodworking is a magnifying glass about 4 in. in diameter and of 4× or 10× magnification. The enlarged view of the work and the tools brings understanding not only of how and where one is cutting, but also of the quality and sharpness of what one is cutting with.

I am always surprised by how often I meet a woodworker who believes a block plane is the correct tool for end grain. This plane is a small thing, not easy to grasp firmly and push through end grain, where you need the heft and two-hand grip of a larger tool. The fact that the block-plane iron is set at a low angle is of little consequence. Since it is also mounted on the frog with its bevel uppermost, the cutting angle is the same as on a larger plane.

Having got the ends square they need to be knifed round. It is at this point that one has to settle the length of the tails and pins. Set a cutting gauge a bare $\frac{1}{32}$ in. less than the thinnest part on the boards. Knife a line round the ends of the boards, using the accurate end of the board as the face from which to gauge. The gauge knife should be sharpened to the profile shown in figure 4, flat side away from the gauge fence. This puts the beveled surface of the knife into the wood on the waste side of the line. Because the pins and tails are marginally short of the outside face of the carcase, during assembly there is no need for special clamping blocks. The clamp heads can be place directly on the tails to press them home, or a straight, simple clamping batten is all it takes. When cleaning up the carcase on the outside, one simply has to plane off the whole surface and come down just to the end grain on the tails and pins—the original end grain prepared by saw or plane. When we reach it and take the finest feather off, then the outside of the carcase is accurate to thickness and parallel to the inside, or face side. This method is not used for the sole purpose of achieving accuracy of carcase thickness—this is only a consequence. Another consequence is that the gauge line from marking out will be removed when cleaning up. Most importantly, carcase squareness was achieved long before the joints were made.

This procedure also permits a delightful refinement in fitting drawers (figure 5). Assume we are making a drawer or set of drawers as shown, and that the carcase is 18 in. deep (front to back). The ends of the top and bottom pieces are made deliberately not square. They are made with $\frac{1}{64}$ in. extra on the back edge at each end. Thus the top and bottom pieces are $\frac{1}{32}$ in. longer on their back edges than on their front edges. The end-grain edges are prepared as previously explained; the difference being that when one gauges from these edges the assembled carcase will be longer at the back than at the front. When the drawer is made, the boards for its front and back are cut and planed to fit exactly the carcase opening. Then the sides are joined to them with lap dovetails at the front and through dovetails at the back. The drawer sides are also made proud of the end grain of the front and back pieces, then planed down just to the end grain, front and back. Such a drawer will fit exactly into its opening, and will enter the carcase with a mild friction-fit left and right. Because the carcase gets fractionally wider toward the back, this friction does not increase significantly as the drawer goes farther into it. When the drawer is pulled out, the resistance increases as it approaches maximum opening—the action is very sweet. Making a traditional drawer in a traditional carcase relies on this technique of leaving long grain proud on the carcase sides and on the drawer sides. It cannot be done by having end-grain surfaces of tails and pins protrude.

In conclusion, there are two small points to consider when making a carcase with through dovetails. At the outer edges it is generally good to have two or three quite small dovetails, to increase the number of gluing surfaces. This helps if someone should be tempted to lift the piece by grasping the outer edges of the board, and it also increases resistance to cupping. The second consideration is to miter the outside joints, giving a more vital flow to the front edge of the carcase. Making this miter is not difficult—the common mistake is to saw down the line of the first pin, and you don't need to. Figure 6 should make this clear. ☐

Ian Kirby directs Kirby Studios, a school of woodworking and furniture design, in Cumming, Ga.

Fig. 4: Planing end grain

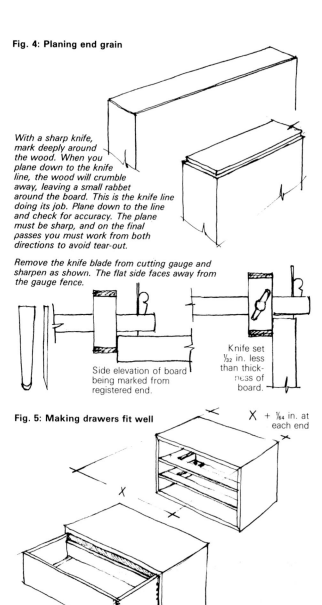

With a sharp knife, mark deeply around the wood. When you plane down to the knife line, the wood will crumble away, leaving a small rabbet around the board. This is the knife line doing its job. Plane down to the line and check for accuracy. The plane must be sharp, and on the final passes you must work from both directions to avoid tear-out.

Remove the knife blade from cutting gauge and sharpen as shown. The flat side faces away from the gauge fence.

Side elevation of board being marked from registered end.

Knife set $\frac{1}{32}$ in. less than thickness of board.

Fig. 5: Making drawers fit well

X + $\frac{1}{64}$ in. at each end

When drawer is made it won't fit into the opening—it has to be planed down to end grain of pins, front and back, which were made to the opening's exact size.

X + $\frac{1}{32}$ in.

X

Drawer front

Fig. 6: Mitering end pins

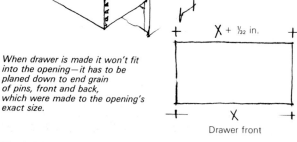

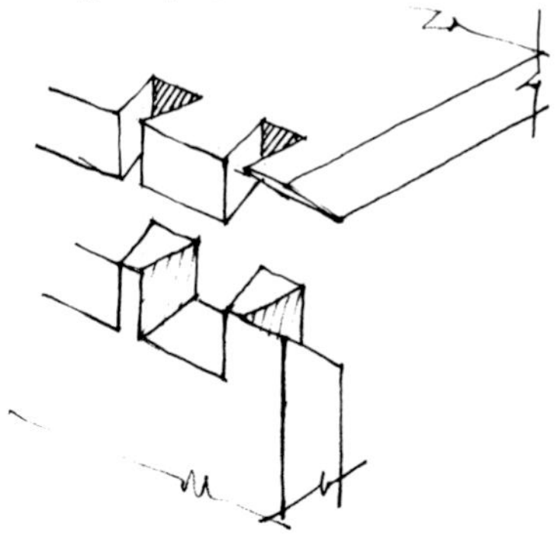

Cutting Dovetails With the Tablesaw
A versatile way to join a stack of drawers

by Mark Duginske

For joining such basic casework as small boxes, chests and drawers, I've always felt that there was a missing link between the tedium of hand-cutting dozens of dovetails and the faster method of producing monotonous-looking joints with a router jig. With that in mind, I developed this table-saw dovetail method which combines hand-tool flexibility with power-tool speed and accuracy.

With this technique, you can vary both the width and the spacing of the pins and tails for practically any aesthetic effect. The blocks that set the spacing are self-centering and will produce perfect-fitting, interchangeable joints, eliminating the need to mark boards so that individual joints will fit, as with hand-dovetailing. Besides a good combination sawblade and dado head for your tablesaw, you'll need a marking gauge, a bevel gauge and a couple of sharp bench chisels. Before proceeding, screw a wooden fence to the saw's miter gauge. A 3-in. by 20-in. fence will safely support most work.

Begin by squaring the ends of the boards to be joined. Take your time with this step—inaccurately prepared stock virtually guarantees sloppy results. I spaced the pins equally for the 4¼-in. wide drawer parts I'm joining in the photos. You can mark the pin centers directly on the pin boards, or, as I did here, you can just cut the spacer blocks to create whatever spacing you want the pins to have. In any case, the width of the blocks should equal the distance between pin centers. You'll need one block for each full pin, plus one.

The pin size is also controlled by the blocks. When they're lined up edge-to-edge, the total width of all the blocks should be less than the width of the stock by an amount equal to the width of the narrow part of each pin, that is, on the outside face of the pin board. I chose ¼-in. pins for the drawer sides shown in figure 1; if you want finer pins, decrease this dimension. The blocks must be of consistent width, so I crosscut them from the same ripping, then sandpaper off any fuzzy corners so that they'll line up with no gaps. To mark the depth of the pin and tail cuts, set your marking gauge to the stock thickness, and scribe a line on the faces of the pin board and on the face and edges of the tail board.

Cut the tails first with the saw arbor (or table) tilted to 80°, an angle that I've found produces the best combination of appearance and strength. A bevel gauge set at 80° can be used to set both the sawblade for the tails and, later, the miter gauge for the pins. As shown in figure 2, position and clamp a stop block to the miter-gauge fence so that when all the blocks are in place, a half-pin space of the correct size will be cut. At its narrowest width, the half-pin space should equal the narrow width of a pin. Raise the sawblade until it cuts right to the gauge line, then, with all the blocks in place, begin cutting the tails, flipping the board edge-for-edge and end-for-end (photo, right). Continue this process, removing a spacer block each time, until all the tails are cut.

A good-quality carbide-tipped blade will saw crisp pins

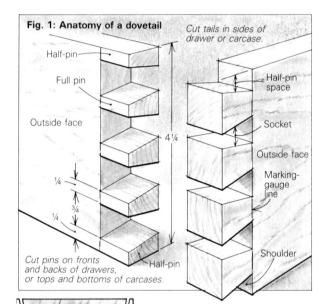

Fig. 1: Anatomy of a dovetail

Cut tails in sides of drawer or carcase.

Half-pin

Full pin

Outside face

4¼

Half-pin space

Socket

Outside face

Marking-gauge line

Shoulder

¼

¾

¼

Half-pin

Cut pins on fronts and backs of drawers, or tops and bottoms of carcases.

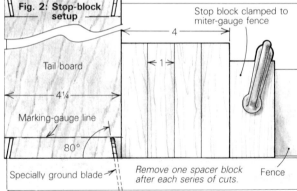

Fig. 2: Stop-block setup

Stop block clamped to miter-gauge fence

4

1

Tail board

4¼

Marking-gauge line

80°

Specially ground blade

Remove one spacer block after each series of cuts.

Fence

In Duginske's tablesaw dovetail method, the tails are made first in a series of cuts with the table or arbor set at 80°. After each series, a spacer block is removed and the cuts are repeated for the next tail. The last tail is made with one block in place.

Photos: Bill Stankus; drawings: David Dann

Machine-cut dovetails don't have to have the stiff, predictable look dictated by many router jigs. Using your imagination and the author's tablesaw technique, you can vary the width and spacing of pins and tails for infinite visual variety.

and tails, but set at an angle it leaves a small triangle of waste at the bottom of the cut that must be chiseled out later. To minimize handwork, I had the tops of the teeth on a carbide blade ground to 80°. The grinding cost $12 (1983) and the blade can still be used for other work. If you have a blade ground, make sure that all the teeth point in the same direction, and when you tilt your saw, match the tooth angle.

To cut the pins, clamp the boards together and scribe either of the outermost tails onto the pin board with a knife, as in the photo at right. Mark the wood to be wasted with an X. Only one pin need be marked; the spacer blocks will automatically take care of the others. The pins will be formed in the series of three cuts illustrated in figure 3.

First, return the arbor or table to 90° and install a ¼-in. dado blade raised to cut right to the gauge line. Adjust the miter gauge to 80°, and with all the spacer blocks in place, reset the stop block so that, with the outside face of the board positioned away from you, the first dado cut will be made just to the inside of the knife line. Make sure that the board is positioned correctly, or else you'll end up cutting the pin angle in the wrong direction. Make the first cut, flip the board end-for-end and cut only the opposite corner. Then remove the first block and repeat until one side of each pin is cut.

For the second series of cuts, set the miter gauge to 90° and waste the material between the pins. You'll have to remove a lot of wood in several passes to form widely spaced pins, in which case it's handier to judge the cuts by eye rather than relying on the spacer blocks. Don't waste too much material, else you'll nip off the opposite side of the pins. While the miter gauge is at 90°, use the dado blade to waste the wedge of wood remaining in the sockets of the tail board. If the sockets are narrower than ¼ in., nibble out the wedges on the bandsaw or with a coping saw and a chisel. Use a backsaw or the tablesaw to trim the shoulders where the half-pins fit.

Next set the miter gauge to 80° in the opposite direction, and reset the stop block so that the dado blade cuts just inside the other knife line. Make the third series of cuts like the first, but before proceeding, slip three or four strips of paper between the last spacer block and the stop block. Complete the cuts and try the joint. It should slip together by hand or with light mallet taps. If the joint is too tight, remove one or more paper shims, repeat the cuts and try again. Smooth the space between the pins and the tails, pare any tight spots with a chisel, and you're ready to glue up. □

Mark Duginske is a cabinetmaker in Wausau, Wis.

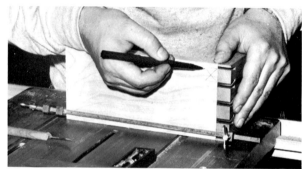

The tail location is scribed directly onto the outside face of the pin board with a knife. A bold X marks the material that will be wasted to form the pins.

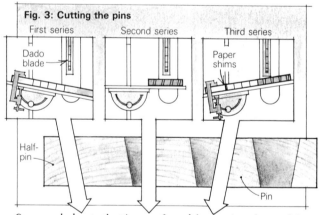

Fig. 3: Cutting the pins

First series   Second series   Third series

Dado blade

Paper shims

Half-pin

Pin

Once marked out, the pins are formed by wasting the wood between with dado-blade cuts. In the photo below, Duginske completes the second series of pin cuts.

Triangle Marking

A simple and reliable system

by Adrian C. van Draanen

Suppose you are making half a dozen drawers. You have cut all the pieces for them, and they are neatly stacked up. Your next steps are dovetails and grooves for the bottom. As you pick up a piece, you can probably tell whether you are holding a front, side or back. But can you tell which way is up, or which is the outside? Can you tell the left sides from the right? If the drawers are of different sizes, can you find matching pieces without remeasuring?

If you can answer "yes" to all these questions, you must have an adequate system for marking your work. If not, I'd like to suggest the triangle method.

Textbooks ignore marking. One is often advised to "mark the face," or "mark the top." But a particular method is never mentioned, and it is left to the worker to adopt or develop a system. Hence the use of lines, letters, numbers and other devices.

European carpenters and cabinet-makers use a system that employs a triangle, and nothing else. This system is widely used, and it is taught in trade schools. But it doesn't seem to be known outside Europe.

The rules of the system are:
—the triangle is an isosceles triangle and it must point up, or away, from you;
—each piece of wood must have two lines of the triangle on it.

Here is a glued-up panel, marked according to these rules:

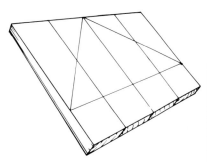

It is possible to take away each piece and put it back in the same place later. And each piece can immediately be identified. If, for instance, you were holding this piece,

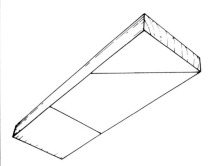

you would know right away that it is an inside piece, located to the left of the center of the panel.

If you had picked up this piece, you

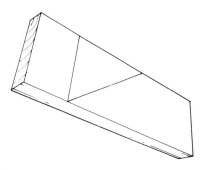

would know that you were holding it upside down. You would also know that it is the rightmost piece of the panel.

A glued-up tabletop is similar to a panel that has been rotated 90°.

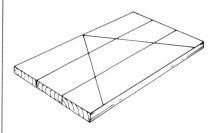

You may draw the base of the triangle on the tabletop, but it is not required and in practice it is never done. Look at each board and you'll find two lines, the two sides of a triangle that points away from you.

Now we have marked a panel and a tabletop. You can mix all the pieces any way you like and you can always put them back together. Each piece can be identified as either part of a panel (a vertical construction, because the base of the triangle is drawn at right angles to the sides of the individual pieces), or a tabletop (a horizontal construction, because the base of the triangle is parallel to the sides of the individual pieces). Just two lines give you all this information.

You may say at this stage that your own method is just as simple and fool-proof, and you are probably right. Very few constructions are as simple as a panel or a tabletop, though. When the work becomes complicated, as with drawers, the triangle method remains as simple as for the tabletop. Let's consider something that has both vertical and horizontal components, such as a door.

Here are the stiles,

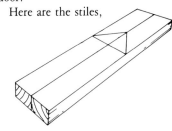

and here are the rails.

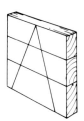

The completed door looks like this:

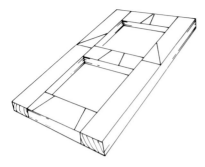

For simplicity the panels have been omitted, but you already know how to mark them. If this door had two panels of equal height, and both were marked the same way, it would be possible to get the pieces mixed up. To avoid this confusion, a double line on the second panel distinguishes it from the first.

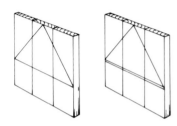

The base line on the second panel is the one to double, because it is the only line that is common to all the pieces.

Two identical tabletops would be marked thus:

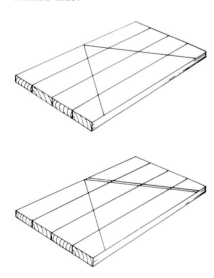

Again, a mix-up is impossible, because of the double line.

So far we have worked only with flat, two-dimensional assemblies. A set of four legs introduces a third dimension. There are front and back legs, left and right, and mortises are worked in the two inside surfaces of each leg.

A triangle drawn across the face of the front legs is clearly not enough.

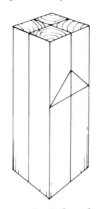

We must mark all four faces of the bundle. Going around clockwise, we draw the second triangle (A), doubling

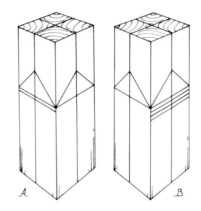

the base line, as this line is common to the two legs, then the third (three lines) and the fourth triangle (B).

It makes no difference whether the piece has four legs, or more than four

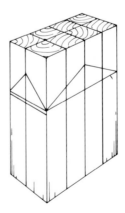

legs; they are all marked in the same manner.

Until now we have marked the sides of the stock, because that was the way the pieces had to be assembled. But in a box or a drawer, the edges, not the sides, are in the same plane; therefore marks are put on the edges.

Here is a drawer:

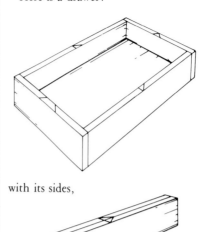

with its sides,

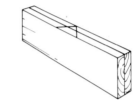

and its front and back.

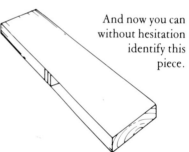

And now you can without hesitation identify this piece.

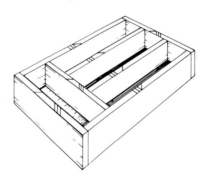

It belongs to a drawer. It is the right-hand side of it. You also know which side is the inside, which way is up, and that it belongs to the third drawer. □

Adrian C. van Draanen has worked as a cabinetmaker in his native Holland and in Ottawa, Canada, where he is now a government computer expert.

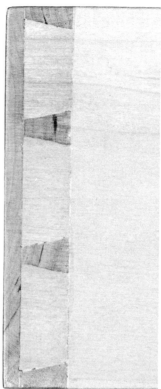

The small, conventional drawer and five shallow trays in Frid's compact, knockdown drawing table provide plenty of storage, and illustrate the basic drawermaking techniques that you can apply to any kind of furniture.

How to Make Drawers
Design for drawing table illustrates the principles

by Tage Frid

About twenty years ago, when I first started teaching at the Rhode Island School of Design, I was commissioned to make drawing tables for the school dormitories. The tables were to be plain and inexpensive, yet sturdy and able to withstand abuse. Because dormitory rooms are small, each table had to be space-efficient. This last requirement made the tables a good exercise in an important cabinetmaking skill—designing and building drawers.

When I design a piece with drawers, I first consider what will be put in them. This helps determine how I will build both the carcase (the body of the cabinet into which the drawers go) and the drawers, and of what materials. The overall size of the drawing table described in this article (see plans, p. 38), which is an improved version of the one I made twenty years ago, is based on standard sizes of drafting paper and parallel rulers. For storing big sheets of paper and finished drawings, I wanted an open compartment below the

adjustable drawing surface. For odds and ends, I added a drawer to the right of the space where your knees go. For instruments, pencils and pens, I also included some shallow trays that slide in grooves milled inside the carcase.

Once I had decided on the drawer and trays, I worked out the construction details for the carcase. There are three basic ways to make a carcase that will contain drawers: with glued-up solid wood, or with a frame-and-panel system, or with cabinet-grade plywood. I used plywood for my drawing table because it's good for knockdown joinery, and because it's simple and fast to work with. Lately, though, I've been using more and more solid wood for my furniture because I can do more with it, such as shaping, carving and bending. Of course, solid wood shrinks and swells with the seasons, so you must account for this in your drawer-hanging. A frame-and-panel carcase, with a solid or plywood panel, isolates most of the wood movement, but it limits your shaping choices, and

Photos: Roger Birn; drawings: Lee Hov

complicates the joinery and drawer-hanging.

There are several ways to hang a drawer. When I was an apprentice in Denmark, I learned the method shown in figure 1, which is the one I used for the top drawer of my drawing table and in all of my best furniture. The drawer slides in and out of the carcase on two horizontal members called runners, which fit into grooves milled in the sides of the carcase. At the front of the carcase, the drawer rests on a stretcher or a rail, which also ties together the front edges of the carcase and provides a surface to which drawer stops can be glued. For a drawer to work correctly, it must have some sort of guide to keep it from tilting down when it is pulled out. This guide, which bears against the top edges of the drawer sides, is usually called a kicker. In a chest of drawers, the bottom edge of the runner above acts as a kicker. The top drawer usually kicks against the inside of the carcase top, but in some cases (my drawing table is one) you have to install a separate kicker because the carcase doesn't have a top, or because the top is too far above the drawer to act as a kicker.

This method, called bottom-hanging (figure 1A), is good for almost any kind of furniture, whether plywood or solid. The runners are very strong and will carry the weight of a drawer filled with heavy objects. If lubricated with paraffin and made of a hardwood, such as oak or maple, the runners (and drawer sides) will last a long time. The big disadvantage is that to work right, a bottom-hung drawer must fit snugly, making it liable to stick in humid weather.

A drawer can also slide on runners that ride in grooves in the drawer sides, as in figure 1B. You don't need stretchers and kickers for each drawer, but you do need to tie a big carcase together with at least one front rail in the middle to keep the sides from bowing outward. Side-hanging is best for small, light drawers, such as in writing desks and jewelry boxes. I wouldn't use it in a chest of drawers or a kitchen cabinet, though, because the sliding surfaces are small and they would wear out pretty fast.

Some people think that metal runners (figure 1C) are used only in cheap factory furniture, but for heavy drawers, such as a desk file drawer or a kitchen-cabinet flour bin, I prefer them. Good-quality metal ball-bearing runners will support a heavier drawer than wood will, and some kinds allow the drawer to be fully extended so you can get what's in the back without removing the drawer. These runners last forever, and they never stick, no matter what the weather. Always buy your runners—or any hardware, for that matter—before you make the piece. Some types of runners require a drawer that is 1 in. narrower than the carcase opening; others need 1½-in. clearance. Nothing is more frustrating than to build a piece, only to find that the hardware you want to use won't work.

Getting started—If you want drawers that fit well, you have to take your time and make an accurate carcase. My drawing table consists of a permanently joined plywood carcase which holds the drawer and trays. To this, I attached (with knock-down fasteners) the panels that form the sides, the back, the storage compartment, and the shelf under the drawing surface. A really fine carcase should be made about $\frac{1}{32}$ in. wider at the back than at the front so that the drawer action won't stiffen up from increasing friction as the drawer is pushed in. There are a couple of ways to do this. If your carcase is solid wood, you can join it up square and hand-plane a few shavings off the thickness of the back inside third of each carcase

Fig. 1: Drawer-hanging methods

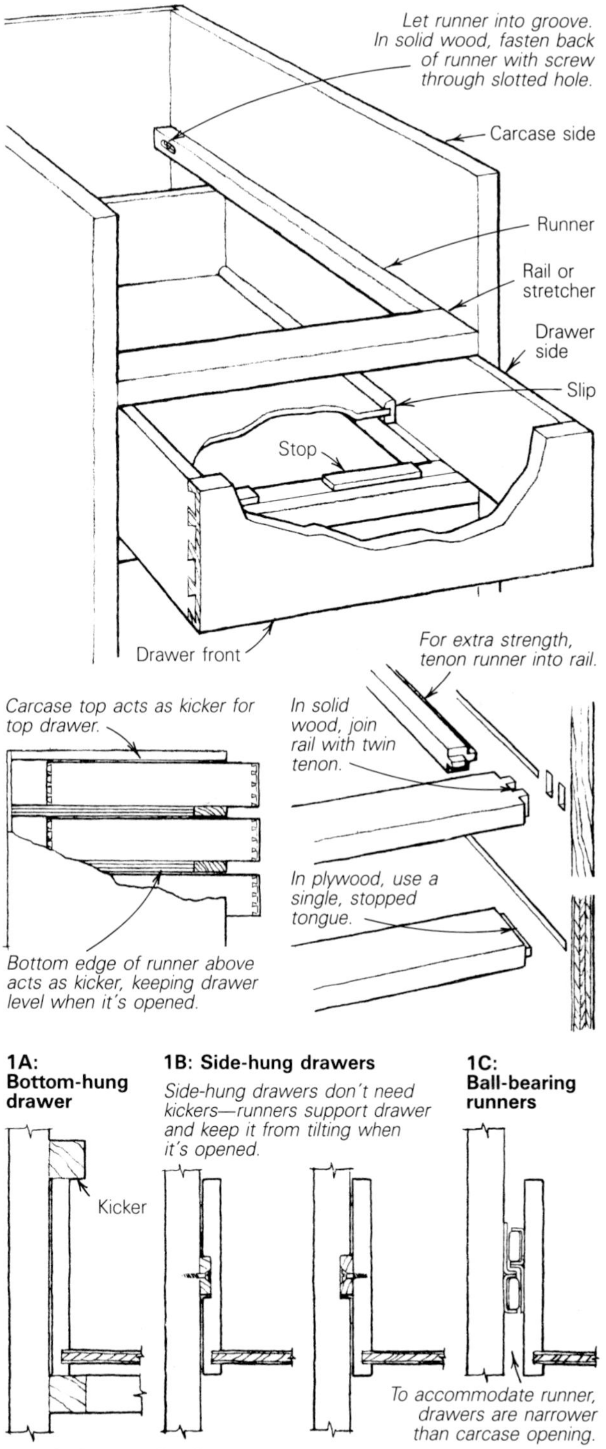

Let runner into groove. In solid wood, fasten back of runner with screw through slotted hole.

Carcase side

Runner

Rail or stretcher

Drawer side

Slip

Stop

Drawer front

For extra strength, tenon runner into rail.

Carcase top acts as kicker for top drawer.

In solid wood, join rail with twin tenon.

In plywood, use a single, stopped tongue.

Bottom edge of runner above acts as kicker, keeping drawer level when it's opened.

1A: Bottom-hung drawer

Kicker

1B: Side-hung drawers

Side-hung drawers don't need kickers—runners support drawer and keep it from tilting when it's opened.

1C: Ball-bearing runners

To accommodate runner, drawers are narrower than carcase opening.

Fig. 2: Drawer details

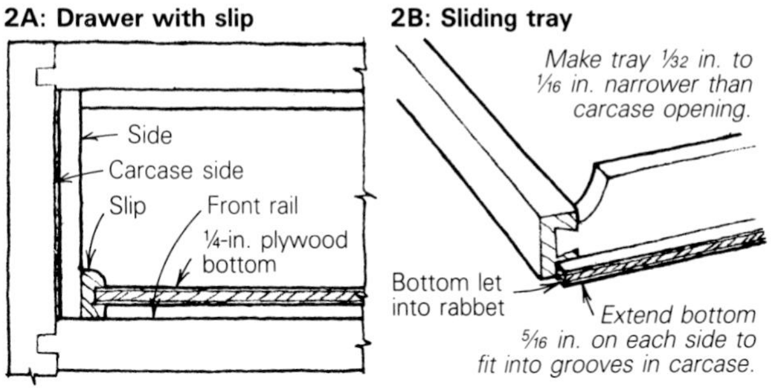

2A: Drawer with slip

Side

Carcase side

Slip

Front rail

¼-in. plywood bottom

2B: Sliding tray

Make tray $\frac{1}{32}$ in. to $\frac{1}{16}$ in. narrower than carcase opening.

Bottom let into rabbet

Extend bottom $\frac{5}{16}$ in. on each side to fit into grooves in carcase.

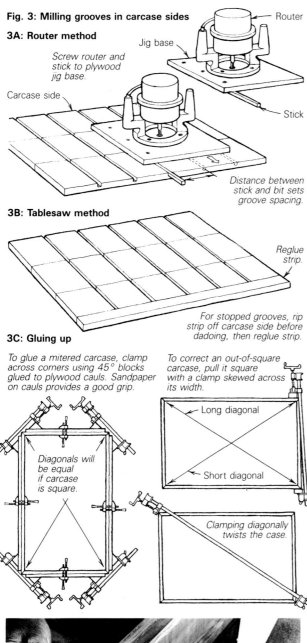

Fig. 3: Milling grooves in carcase sides

3A: Router method

Router

Jig base

Screw router and stick to plywood jig base.

Carcase side

Stick

Distance between stick and bit sets groove spacing.

3B: Tablesaw method

Reglue strip.

For stopped grooves, rip strip off carcase side before dadoing, then reglue strip.

3C: Gluing up

To glue a mitered carcase, clamp across corners using 45° blocks glued to plywood cauls. Sandpaper on cauls provides a good grip.

To correct an out-of-square carcase, pull it square with a clamp skewed across its width.

Diagonals will be equal if carcase is square.

Long diagonal

Short diagonal

Clamping diagonally twists the case.

For a perfect fit, Frid fits the drawer parts individually before he assembles them, first trimming the drawer front to a tight fit in the carcase opening. If the drawer front's length can't be scribed from inside the case, mark it directly from outside.

side before final assembly. Or, in solid wood or plywood, you can cut each end of the carcase top and bottom slightly out of square. The article by Ian Kirby on pages 24 to 27 tells more about this type of carcase construction.

The drawing table has only one drawer, so I didn't bother making my carcase wider at the back. I cut the parts I needed out of a sheet of ¾-in. veneer-core cherry plywood, squaring each panel carefully and joining the carcase with tongue-and-groove joints. Where the raw edges of the plywood would be exposed, I glued on a ¼-in. thick by ⅞-in. strip of solid cherry, planing it flush with the plywood and sanding it after the glue had dried.

Next I cut the grooves for the solid-oak drawer runners and the sliding trays. This step is a critical part of making the carcase—the runners (and so the grooves) must be square to the front edges of the carcase and spaced the same distance apart on both carcase sides. Some people mount the drawer runners in a sliding dovetail joint, which is stronger. But it's a lot of extra work, and since the load is all downward, you don't really need that much strength. You could avoid grooves altogether by screwing the runners directly to the carcase, though this method isn't as accurate. For the trays, I decided to make lots of grooves relatively close together so that there would be maximum flexibility in tray arrangement.

The grooves can be crosscut with a dado blade in the tablesaw, or with a router, using the jig shown in figure 3A. I usually use the router because it's easier for an old guy like me, and if I don't want the grooves to show at the front edge of the carcase, I can stop them short. If you use the tablesaw, be sure to mill each pair of mating grooves in both carcase sides before you change the fence setting. Figure 3B shows how to stop a tablesawn groove.

If I were making a chest of drawers, I'd cut the joints for the front rails at this point. In solid wood, I'd join the rails to the sides with a twin tenon, as shown in figure 1. I usually mill the twin mortises with a router. Then, with a marking gauge, I lay out the tenons on the rail and cut them (by hand or on the tablesaw) to a tight fit. A rail can be joined to plywood with a tongue that stops short of the front edge of the carcase, so it won't be seen. For extra strength, you can tenon the runner into the back edge of the rail.

Assembling the carcase comes next. A tongue-and-grooved plywood carcase, such as my drawing table, is easy to glue up with clamps and battens. When I'm joining solid wood, I usually use dovetails or splined miters. If they fit right, dovetails don't need to be clamped at all. You just put some glue on and tap them home. Miters should be clamped across the corners, or else the pressure of the clamps might distort the case. I use the clamping fixture shown in figure 3C, and I check the carcase for square by measuring diagonally from corner to corner. If both diagonals measure the same, it's okay. Don't try to correct an out-of-square carcase by clamping the corners diagonally, or else you'll twist it. Instead, clamp across the width of the carcase, with the clamp angled slightly to pull in the long corner.

When the carcase comes out of the clamps, you can install the drawer runners. Plane or sand them smooth first, otherwise the little ripples left by machine-planing will make your drawers noisy. Because the drawing-table carcase is plywood, which won't shrink and swell, you can glue the runners right in, all the way across. If the sides of your piece are solid wood, runners should be glued only at the very front.

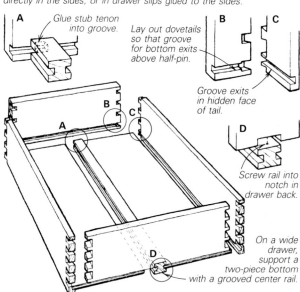

Fitting the drawer—Getting a wooden drawer to work like it's gliding on ball bearings is not all that difficult if you take the time to do it right. The trick is to fit the drawer *before* you make it. First, rough-mill all the drawer parts you will need. I like to use maple, oak, cherry and walnut for drawer parts. Pine and poplar are too soft. For drawer sides higher than 10 in., ½-in. Baltic birch plywood is good because it is less liable to warp. I make the sides and backs of small drawers ⅜ in. thick, and their fronts ⅝ in. thick. Larger drawers should have ½-in. sides and backs, with ¾-in. fronts.

The drawer front should be fitted first. Cut the wood to width so that it will just about go into the opening, then finish the fit with a hand plane. Now cut the front to length: Square one end (if it isn't already) and fit it into the opening, then mark the other end by scribing the back of the drawer front from inside the case. Cut it a hair long at first, then trim it to fit. If for some reason you can't reach inside, mark the length by holding the front outside the case, as shown in the photo on the facing page. The drawer front should fit so snugly that it can be just pushed in halfway. Mark and cut the drawer back exactly the same length as the front, but make the width less, to leave space for the drawer bottom to slide in and also to allow a little space to make fitting easier later on. I usually make the back about ¾ in. narrower than the front.

Fit the drawer sides the same way as you did the front, by planing the width until they will just slide in snugly. Crosscut the back ends square, then push the drawer sides back as far as you want them to go. Drawer sides should not go all the way to the back of a solid-wood carcase because when the carcase sides shrink, the drawer will pop out a little. Also, I don't like to stop a drawer against the back of the carcase unless I have to—it sounds clunky. I allow about ¼ in. between the back of the drawer and the carcase. One way to make sure the clearance is right is to place a scrap shim temporarily against the case back as you push the sides in.

When the drawer front, back and both sides have been fitted, the drawer is ready to be assembled. But before I do that, I mark the parts as shown in figure 4.

Assembling the drawer—The traditional joint for a drawer is a half-blind dovetail at the front and a through dovetail at the back. Other joints will do, but they aren't as strong. The box on p. 36 shows some examples. Some craftsmen use solid wood for drawer bottoms, but I think that ¼-in. hardwood plywood is better. It's more than strong enough and quite stable. Although it doesn't really matter, running the grain of the bottom in the same direction as that of the front looks nicest. In my best furniture, I mount the bottom in grooved strips, called drawer slips, which are glued inside each drawer after assembly, as shown in figure 5. This technique allows me to work with thin drawer sides, which are better-looking, and still leave a wide wearing surface for the drawer to slide on. To prevent the bottom from sagging in really wide drawers, use thicker plywood, or make the bottom in two pieces and support it with a rail down the middle of the drawer.

Normally, I put slips only on the sides, letting the bottom into a groove cut in the drawer front. But on my drawing table, the finger pull routed in the bottom edge of the drawer front would have exposed the groove, so I glued a slip on at the front as well. For quick drawers in kitchen cabinets, I just mill a groove directly in the drawer sides and fronts. Cut the grooves before you lay out your joints, so a groove

The drawer sides should be made equally snug, then trimmed to a length that will stop them from banging against the back of the carcase.

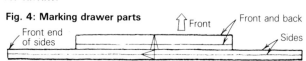

Fig. 4: Marking drawer parts

Points of triangle always face forward or upward. Put numbers on triangles to distinguish parts of multiple drawers.

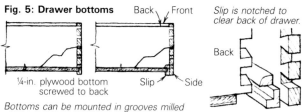

Fig. 5: Drawer bottoms

Bottoms can be mounted in grooves milled directly in the sides, or in drawer slips glued to the sides.

On a wide drawer, support a two-piece bottom with a grooved center rail.

A finger pull that Frid routed in the drawing-table drawer front would have exposed the groove into which the plywood bottom is normally let—a problem Frid solved by gluing a slip to the front, as well as to the sides. The carcase rail, visible at the bottom of the photo, is relieved to give access to the pull.

Instead of dovetails...

Whenever I can, I prefer to join a drawer with handcut dovetails, half-blind at the front and through at the back. This combination of joints is mechanically strong against all the pushing and pulling that happens to a drawer, and it's quite attractive, especially if you use different colored woods for the drawer sides and front.

Other easier-to-make joints are okay for drawers, too. But remember that when a drawer is pulled out, the front-to-side joint bears most of the load, so it must be designed to resist this stress and should be strong mechanically, without relying entirely on glue. You could, for example, use dovetails at the front and a tongue-and-rabbet or a half-blind tongue-and-rabbet at the back. For quick drawers in a set of kitchen cabinets, the half-blind tongue-and-rabbet would also be okay for the drawer fronts. But if you use it, stop the drawer at the back instead of at the front, otherwise the weak short-grain of the grooved piece might crack off. Both of these joints can be

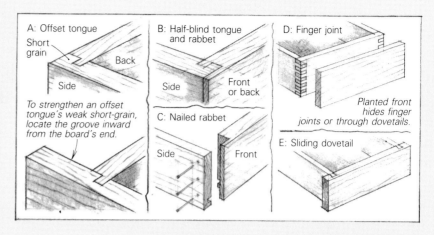

A: Offset tongue
Short grain
Back
Side
To strengthen an offset tongue's weak short-grain, locate the groove inward from the board's end.

B: Half-blind tongue and rabbet
Side
Front or back

C: Nailed rabbet
Side
Front

D: Finger joint
Planted front hides finger joints or through dovetails.

E: Sliding dovetail

made on the tablesaw. Remember to allow for them when you cut the drawer sides to exact length. A rabbet reinforced with Swedish dowels (nails) is fine for quick drawers, too.

A box or finger joint is another good drawer joint that can be cut on the tablesaw. I might use this joint for drawers in a tool chest, but I wouldn't want it in furniture because I think that the end grain of the exposed fingers is ugly. To hide the fingers, or the end grain of through dovetails used on a drawer front, you could glue on a planted front.

If a drawer is narrower than the inside of the carcase—as it would be if you were using ball-bearing runners—or if you wanted the drawer front to overhang and cover the front edges of the carcase, a sliding dovetail is a good choice for joining the drawer front to the sides. Sliding dovetails work well in both solid wood and plywood. If you set up to make this joint, you can also use it to join the back to the sides.   —T.F.

Drawer-stop ideas from three makers

Sometimes it's not practical to install a stop that works against a drawer's front, as Frid does. In this case, I stop a drawer at the back by gluing and screwing small wooden eccentrics inside the carcase, as shown in the drawing below. Before the glue dries, I rotate the eccentrics so that the drawer stops just where I want it to.
—David Hannah, Newtown, Conn.

Drawers in really well-made furniture should have outward stops, but I don't like to spend a lot of time making them. Usually, I use the method in the drawing below, which works for practically any style drawer. The stop is a small block screwed to the rail (or to the inside of the carcase top) above the drawer. As the drawer is opened, its back strikes the block and stops. So that the drawer can be inserted, the block pivots to align with a notch cut into the back. A felt pad glued to the block gives the stop a quieter action.
—Ben Mack, Mt. Tremper, N.Y.

I learned about the outward drawer stop shown below from Stephen Proctor, my teacher at the Wendell Castle workshops. It consists of a notched wooden leaf spring let into a mortise in the rail above the drawer. If you need a lot of stops, it's easy to mill the shape into a wide board, ripping the leaves off to the required width. For strength and springiness, ash is the best wood to use. Locate the stop where you want the drawer to stop, then scribe and cut the mortise. A countersunk wood screw holds the stop in place.
—Wendy Stayman, Scottsville, N.Y.

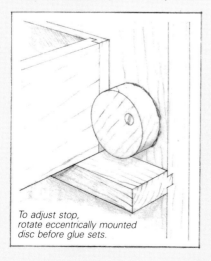

To adjust stop, rotate eccentrically mounted disc before glue sets.

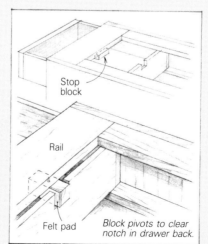

Stop block
Rail
Felt pad
Block pivots to clear notch in drawer back.

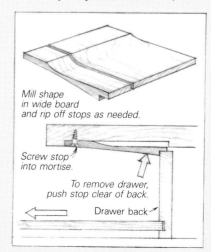

Mill shape in wide board and rip off stops as needed.
Screw stop into mortise.
To remove drawer, push stop clear of back.
Drawer back

won't come out in middle of a dovetail pin.

I had only one drawer to dovetail for my drawing table, so I did it by hand. If there are a lot of drawers to do, I use a dovetail fixture with my router, sanding or planing the inside of the drawer parts before the joints are cut. I don't dry-assemble drawer joints because if they are as tight as they should be, testing them will compress the wood fibers and the joint will be too loose later. Put just a little bit of glue on the top of the pins and front edge of the tails, and tap the joint together with a hammer. Check your drawer for square and put it on a flat bench to make sure it isn't twisted. When the glue is dry, cut the drawer slips to length and glue them in.

Next, I clean up the joints by sanding lightly with a belt sander, and planing or scraping the top and bottom edges of the sides and front. To hold the drawer for sanding, I prop it over a wide board clamped between two bench dogs, as shown in figure 6. After sanding, I try the drawer. Usually it will slide right in. I move it in and out a few times and remove it. Where the drawer binds against the runner, kicker or carcase side, there will be a shiny spot on the wood. I scrape or plane off these spots until the drawer fits perfectly.

If I'm making a drawer in January, I'll make the fit a little loose so that the drawer will still work when the wood swells up in August. Don't take too much off, or the drawer will end up too loose and will bind instead of sliding. To plane the top of a drawer, start at one end of the front and plane toward the back. When you get to the joint between the front and side, just turn the corner in one continuous motion. If you want to finish the inside of the drawer, you can do it at this point. I use two coats of 2-lb.-cut shellac. I wouldn't use oil—it smells too strong and will bleed out of the wood later.

When everything fits, slide the bottom in and fasten it with screws driven into the drawer back. To locate the drawer stops, set a marking gauge to the thickness of the drawer front and scribe a line on the top surface of the rail. Glue two 3-in. by 1-in. by ³⁄₁₆-in. blocks to the rail. Don't make the stops smaller, or someone slamming the drawer might knock them off. I don't use outward stops, but many wood-workers like them. The box on the facing page shows some good methods.

Rub paraffin on the runners, kickers, slips and inside of the carcase. Don't put any other kind of finish on the outside of a drawer or the inside of a carcase where drawers will go, unless you are using ball-bearing runners. The finish will just gum up the works and might cause the drawer to stick.

Making the trays—Making the trays is a lot easier than making the drawers. The tray parts can be kept small in dimension because the assembly is solidly glued and screwed to the plywood bottom. You don't have to fit the parts first, just cut them so that there will be ¹⁄₃₂ in. to ¹⁄₁₆ in. between the side of tray and the inside of the carcase (figure 2, p. 33). No grooves or slips are needed for the bottom, but you should let it into a rabbet milled in the tray front.

When you assemble a tray, make sure that it is square and that the bottom overhangs equally on each side. Complete the final fitting by testing the trays in the grooves and sanding the plywood lightly where necessary.

Correcting problems—Sometimes drawers won't work right, no matter how careful you are. Bowed sides are one reason. If you notice this before you assemble the drawer, position the

Fig. 6: Trimming a drawer

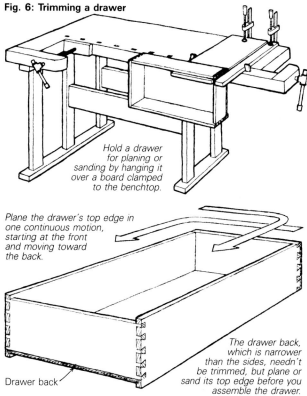

Hold a drawer for planing or sanding by hanging it over a board clamped to the benchtop.

Plane the drawer's top edge in one continuous motion, starting at the front and moving toward the back.

The drawer back, which is narrower than the sides, needn't be trimmed, but plane or sand its top edge before you assemble the drawer.

Drawer back

Fig. 7: Drawer fixes

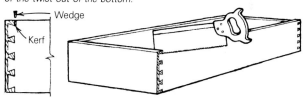

Correct a bowed side by pulling it in with a clamp and holding it true with a small glue block.

Bowed side

Bottom

Correct twist by first kerfing the high corners to the depth of the first tail. Then insert wedges to partially flatten the drawer, planing the rest of the twist out of the bottom.

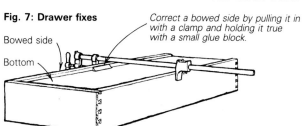

Wedge

Kerf

Excessively sloppy drawers can be corrected with a center guide, which fits into a track glued to the drawer bottom. Mount the guide between the front rail and a rail added to the back of the carcase.

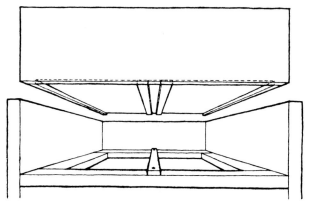

bulge of the bow to the inside of the drawer. That way, when you slide the bottom in, the side will be pushed straight. If a drawer side bows out after you put it together, pull the bow in with a clamp and hold it with a small glue block, as shown in figure 7, page 37.

A slightly out-of-square drawer will usually be forced into true when the bottom is put in. Just make sure the bottom is truly square and fits exactly to the bottom of the grooves, and put the bottom in before you do final-fitting. A twisted drawer, which won't sit flat but teeters on two corners, is more difficult to fix, but it isn't hopeless. Take some of the twist out by driving small wedges into kerfs sawn at opposite corners in the joints between the sides and the front and

back. The kerf should go down just to the first tail of the joint. Plane the remaining twist out of the bottom edges.

A drawer that really rattles around—either because you planed too much off or because the carcase is too wide—can be fixed with a center guide, or by gluing veneer shims inside the carcase. Shims work best when the looseness is mostly at the back of the drawer. I don't like to use the center-guide method unless I have no other choice. □

Besides teaching at Rhode Island School of Design one day a week, Tage Frid is building furniture as well as writing about it—his third book for The Taunton Press is to be published in the fall of 1985.

Fig. 8: Drawing table

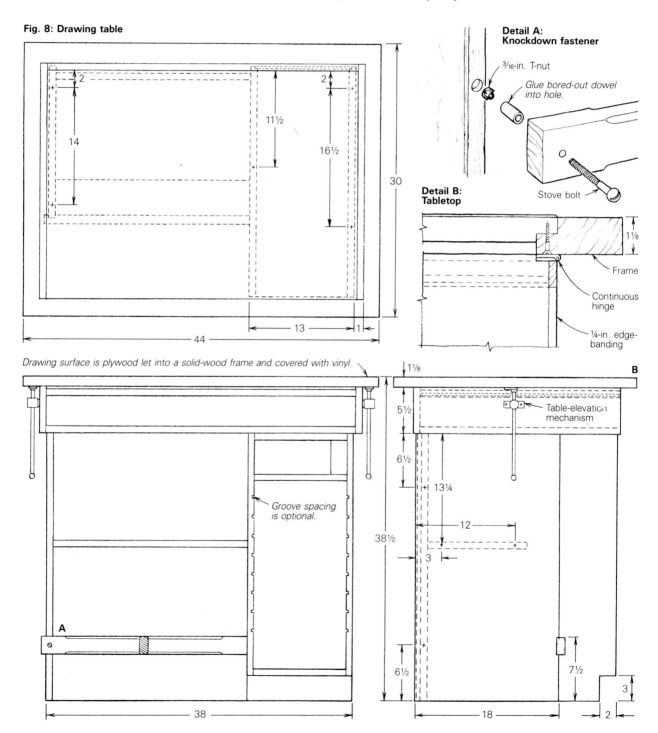

Drawing surface is plywood let into a solid-wood frame and covered with vinyl.

Drawer Bottoms

Six variations on a theme

by Alan Marks

Drawers have long been considered one of the most difficult elements in cabinetry, probably with justification. Done in traditional fashion, they are time-consuming and require exacting work if they are to operate properly. This accounts on the one hand for industry's preference for stapled particle board, hot-melt glues, and ball-bearing steel suspension glides; and on the other hand for the tendency of today's craftsmen to avoid traditional drawers in favor of compartments, shelves or pigeon holes. Dovetailed construction, however, remains the strongest way of making a drawer, and also the most attractive.

The many types of construction possible using dovetails allow for innovation and flexibility, as witnessed by these six examples from Malmstens Verkstadsskola in Stockholm. Although the Swedes agree that the dovetailed drawer is the sturdiest, they often consider the decorative aspect incidental. All of the front dovetail joints shown here are half-blind. The conservative Swedes generally eschew through dovetails in drawer fronts because they interfere with the design requirements and overall style of traditional pieces. Drawer fronts on such cabinets often are delicately inlaid with veneers or carved or profiled around their edges,

all unsuitable situations for through dovetails. Also, problems of uneven swelling and shrinkage can occur with through dovetails, when the wood of the solid drawer front shrinks while the end grain of the tails does not. Through dovetails are, however, used in the backs of drawers, where the unevenness ordinarily remains unnoticed.

French bottom

The traditional drawer bottom is made of solid wood, as opposed to Masonite or plywood. Thought to have originated in France, the so-called ''French'' drawer bottom floats with its grain running parallel to the drawer

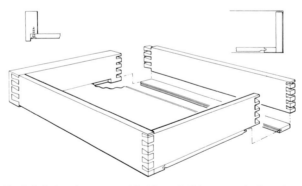

Exploded view from rear, with side and glide removed, shows how French-bottom drawer is put together. Section at left shows bottom screwed to front rabbet; right, section shows side, glide and bottom.

The little chest shown here is used to teach drawer construction at Malmstens Verkstadsskola (workshop and school) in Stockholm, Sweden. It was made in 1960 by master cabinetmaker Artur Joneröt, from drawings by guitarmaker Georg Bolin, then rector of the school. Of mahogany, it stands 65 cm (25 in.) high, 25 cm (10 in.) wide and 31 cm (12 in.) deep. From the top, the drawers are kitchen, NK, false French, French, NK with ply bottom, and side-hung. The work of Carl Malmsten, who died in 1972 at age 83, was an inspirational source for the commercial furniture style now known as Scandinavian or Danish modern. Many of his designs are still in production; his school, which he founded in 1930, is now state-owned. In preparing drawings for manufacturers, he usually offered alternative constructions and indicated the one he thought superior. The second would be accompanied by a comment such as, 'This construction probably won't even last a hundred years.'

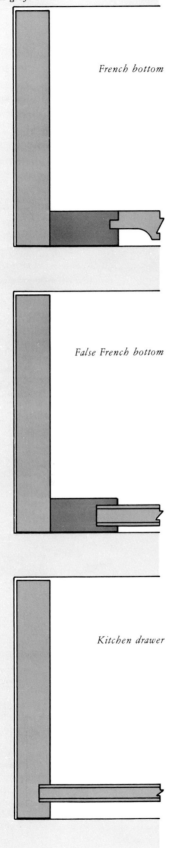

Full-size sections through drawer sides and bottoms (medium grey): Carcase sides and rails are light grey; glides are darkest grey.

French bottom

False French bottom

Kitchen drawer

front, grooved into a two-piece frame formed by the glides. The drawer front is rabbeted to receive the bottom, which is slid home after glides have been glued to the drawer sides. Then the bottom is secured at the front with screws or a few brads, thus allowing later removal for cleaning, refinishing or repair, or else it is simply glued at the front edge. Either way, the wood bottom is free to expand and contract in its grooves. On a drawer this small, the bottom need be only 8 mm (5/16 in.) thick; it is raised 1-1/2 or 2 mm (1/16 in.) above the bottom of the glides to get around problems of sagging and scraping. The tongues should be made about 2 mm (3/32 in.) thick and 3 mm (1/8 in.) long.

The back of this drawer—and all the drawers discussed here—is made 5 mm (5/16 in.) lower than the sides; this keeps the back from scraping as the drawer is pulled out.

The bottom edge of the drawer front protrudes about 4 mm (5/32 in.) below the drawer side to act as a stop. This overhang slides into a corresponding rabbet in the carcase rail; the drawer may be made to close flush or to recess by varying the depth of the rabbet.

False French bottom

Because the French bottom is somewhat complicated to make and not compatible with large series production, the obvious shortcut is to take advantage of such dimensionally stable materials as plywood and Masonite. The resulting false French bottom simplifies construction and saves time. It looks the same at the front, but from the back the scalloped profile of the genuine French bottom is missing and three plies, two of veneer and one of Masonite or plywood, show up. This procedure creates a problem: The bottom might warp upward or become uneven if it is not restrained in some way; a tongue cut in Masonite or plywood would be much too weak. The solution is a glide with a groove wide enough to accommodate the whole thickness of the bottom, glued to the sides and butted against the front, as before. This creates a ledge inside the drawer, like the edge of the frame in conventional panel construction, which can be rounded. The final fitting of the glides is left until sides, front and back have been assembled. Then the glides are held in place at the front, marked at

French bottom, back view.

the back, and rabbeted with a chisel the small amount needed to make the bottom of the glide flush with the bottom of the side, enabling the bottom to be slid home. The drawer bottom projects into a rabbet in the drawer front and is fastened there with brads or screws and a bit of glue.

Kitchen drawer

The kitchen drawer bottom carries the cheapening of quality construction to its extreme. It is nothing more than a veneered plywood or Masonite bottom held by grooves in the sides and front and glued in place. There are disadvantages: rubbing on sides, little torsional strength, a small gluing surface, sides weakened by the groove, and a tiny gliding surface that eventually wears grooves in the rails.

NK drawer

The traditional French bottom and its counterfeit version share a weakness with most drawers made ever since

NK glide; pins are pared flush with side.

chests of drawers replaced lidded chests: the sides present a large scraping surface. This is noisy and can make the drawer difficult to extract. A solution is found in the so-called NK (pronounced enco) drawer.

NK is the abbreviation for a large store with several branches, Nordiska Kompaniet. Founded in Stockholm in 1902, a time of revolution against cluttered overdecoration in Swedish interiors, NK set up its own furniture factory. It was able to design, build and market tasteful contemporary pieces more in keeping with the timeless advice of William Morris: "If you want a golden rule that will fit everybody, here it is: Have nothing in your homes that you do not know to be useful, or believe to be beautiful."

The glides, usually 10 to 12 mm (1/2 in.) thick, are glued to the bottom of the sides and protrude about 3 mm (1/8 in.) beyond them. This is done by cutting the pins on the drawer front about 3 mm deeper than the thickness of the sides. Thus the drawer is steered by the narrow side surfaces of the glides alone. After assembly, the protruding full pins are pared flush with the sides, while the half-pins at the top and bottom of the front are trimmed to horizontal. A solid bottom is screwed or glued into a groove in the drawer front.

This construction gives ultimate ease in sliding, especially when used for high drawers, and is quite strong because of the bracing the glides provide by being glued across the corner.

NK ply bottom

The one drawer that provides all possible strengths is the NK style with a veneered Masonite or plywood bottom, although it may offend those who insist upon solid wood. The version shown here has a half-open front, intended for use inside large cabinets with doors or within secretaries with drop leaves. Since it needs no pull, the cabinet door can close quite close to the drawer front, an optimal use of space. The bottom of the front entirely overlaps its supporting rail.

In construction, the veneered bottom is cut to width such that its edges on either side lap the drawer sides by half their thickness. It is then glued into a rabbet in the glides. The glides butt against the front, where the bottom enters a rabbet. This assembly, if squared properly, automatically ensures

NK glide with low front, recessed side.

that the drawer front closes parallel to the cabinet. Excellent fits are easily made possible if the bottom and glide assembly is first fitted to the drawer opening before it is glued to the front, sides and back.

Side-hung

The side-hung drawer slides on runners inset into the cabinet sides and screwed in place. These runners also butt the end of the groove in which they ride and act as stops for the drawer. Thus the drawer front need have no overhang. The grooves may be made with a router, shaper or dado head, and squared up with a chisel. The veneered Masonite or plywood bottom acts as a cross brace for the front, back and sides. The sides are rabbeted, leaving a lip of about 3 mm (1/8 in.), and the bottom is glued, or glued and screwed, to them. At the same time it is glued to the back and let into a rabbet in the drawer front. □

Side-hung drawer, back view.

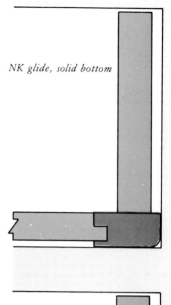

NK glide, solid bottom

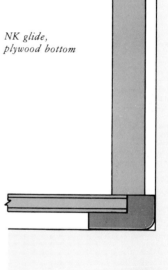

NK glide, plywood bottom

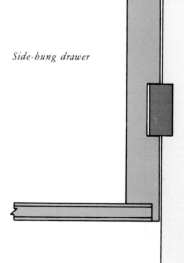

Side-hung drawer

Drawers
Logical assembly ensures proper fit

by Adrian C. van Draanen

With the exception of those who make only chairs, the makers of furniture are regularly called upon to produce pieces with one or more drawers. Often the design of the drawers must meet specific requirements. For example, a china cabinet usually has at least one felt-lined drawer, with dividers; one drawer in a desk should have provision for pens, pencils and other small supplies. Drawer exteriors may also demand special attention. A chest of drawers is a good example of a piece of furniture whose appearance depends on the proportions, shape and material of the drawer fronts.

In this article I will look at what goes into making and fitting a drawer. The methods and recommendations given here apply to traditional, first-class work, and they involve handwork. For the large production jobs a shaper or router with dovetail attachments significantly reduces the time.

A drawer has a front, two sides, a back and a bottom. The front must match or complement the piece of furniture of which it will become a part, and therefore the wood is chosen mainly for appearance. The thickness of a solid front should not be less than 2 cm (¾ in.) in order to have enough material for dovetails, and for a mortised lock if the customer wants one. As a rule the grain of the front runs horizontally. To do otherwise would result in a drawer which would have no strength without unusual measures to reinforce the joints. Moreover, the drawer front would undergo considerable dimensional changes caused by fluctuations in humidity.

These problems do not exist with plywood fronts, because the direction of the grain in the face veneers is of little consequence. Plywood fronts are often used in simple, modern furniture and in kitchen cabinets. To preserve the pattern of the face veneers, particularly when the grain is vertical, no rails show between the drawers. Because of this, and because plywood drawer fronts need a veneered top edge, their construction and fitting are quite different from solid-front drawers and fall outside the scope of this article.

The wood for the sides and back does not need to match the front. Ability to resist warping, to be hard-wearing and to finish nicely are the most important considerations. Depending on availablity, ash, beech, birch, maple, oak or sycamore can be used. Cedar, fir, pine, poplar and spruce are less satisfactory because they do not stand up to hard wear. Sides are 8 mm to 12 mm (⁵⁄₁₆ in. to ½ in.) thick, and the back has either the same thickness as the sides or a little bit more. The direction of the grain in a drawer side must permit you to plane it from front to back along the top edge and on the outside. If the grain runs the wrong way and the drawer sides cannot be planed from front to back, you risk damaging the drawer front when fitting the top edge or when the outsides

of the drawer are being cleaned up after assembly. The second thing is that when a drawer side has any tendency to bow, it must be placed with the hollow side out. When the bottom is put into the drawer, the side will straighten automatically. If the drawer side curves out, binding will be a constant problem. Naturally, if the side has anything more than just a slight bow, it should be rejected.

The bottom is usually made of plywood, 3 mm to 6 mm (⅛ in. to ¼ in.) thick. Heavier plywood may be used for extra-large drawers or when the weight of the contents is going to be excessive, although thinner plywood with a reinforcing center strip glued underneath it is preferred for better work. Birch and beech are good choices for plywood bottoms and they are readily available in several thicknesses. For first-class work, Douglas fir or poplar plywood should not be considered unless the bottom is lined. Convention dictates that the grain on the bottom run in the same direction as that of the drawer front. This means you have no choice but plywood when the drawer has a vertical front, since there is only one way a solid bottom can go in: with the grain running from side to side. The grooves for the bottom must be neither too tight nor too loose—in the first case, the bottom may force the sides apart or cause them to split; in the second, the drawer may rattle. It is also important that the width of the bottom be accurate, to ensure that the drawer remain square and that the sides stay straight. The bottom should be long enough to extend 2 mm to 3 mm (⅛ in.) beyond the back of the drawer, but not so long as to be even with the ends of the sides. If you should have to shorten the sides during the final fitting, you do not want to have to trim the bottom too.

Before plywood became available, and even after that but before it was accepted for high-grade furniture, drawer bottoms were always made solid. I see no advantages in using solid bottoms for contemporary work. But they are a must for certain reproductions if they are to appear authentic, and in the repair and restoration of old furniture when the original condition must be preserved or restored. A solid bottom requires a fair amount of work and it is not something that is highly visible or immediately apparent to an uninformed observer, and for that reason not appreciated.

Suitable timbers for solid bottoms are clear pine, spruce, fir and basswood. If woolens are to be stored in the drawer, aromatic cedar might be considered. Preference should be given to quartersawn boards, and the wood must be thoroughly dry. You should aim for a bottom with maximum stability and maximum freedom from warping and cupping. The boards are edge-glued to obtain a width equal to the depth of the cabinet. The grain of a solid bottom must run from side to side, so that the shrinkage and expansion of the bottom can then be allowed for at the back of the drawer, the bottom can be glued to the front, and the sides will be kept square with the front because there is no movement of the

Adrian C. van Draanen has worked as a cabinetmaker in his native Holland and in Ottawa, Canada, where he is now a government computer expert.

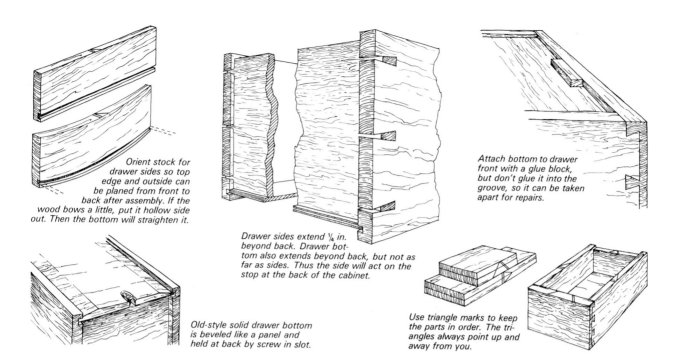

Orient stock for drawer sides so top edge and outside can be planed from front to back after assembly. If the wood bows a little, put it hollow side out. Then the bottom will straighten it.

Drawer sides extend ¼ in. beyond back. Drawer bottom also extends beyond back, but not as far as sides. Thus the side will act on the stop at the back of the cabinet.

Attach bottom to drawer front with a glue block, but don't glue it into the groove, so it can be taken apart for repairs.

Old-style solid drawer bottom is beveled like a panel and held at back by screw in slot.

Use triangle marks to keep the parts in order. The triangles always point up and away from you.

bottom in that direction. A thickness of 5 mm to 6 mm (¼ in.) is good for most drawers if they are not too wide, but in repair work or in reproductions the thickness may have to be much more. When the original was made, thicknessing was done by hand, and the sawmill did not provide boards much thinner than 1 in. The bottom was made like a panel, with the center part left the full thickness and a border about 1½ in. wide all around it planed down to ¼ in. or ⅜ in. The flat side of the panel was placed on the inside of the drawer. The width of a solid bottom must be a perfect fit in the drawer. The grain runs in this direction, and this dimension therefore doesn't change. The front to back length of the bottom (across the grain) must be such that at its driest the bottom is at least even with the backside of the drawer back, and that at the other extreme the bottom does not extend beyond the drawer sides. The bottom is screwed to the back with flat-head screws. The screw holes in the bottom are elongated across the grain of the bottom, so that the bottom can move and still be held. This eliminates the danger of splitting (winter) and buckling (summer). The bottom must be glued to the drawer front with good-sized glue blocks. Do not glue the bottom into the groove at the front, because this would make future repairs very difficult. It is imperative that the bottom and the front be securely kept together, else the bottom will pull out of the groove when the wood dries.

Assembly

Assuming that all material has been chosen and cut slightly oversize, and all the components have been paired and marked (see "Triangle Marking," pages 30 and 31), fitting and assembly can begin. Note the order: the drawer is made to fit before it is joined and assembled.

Take the drawer front and plane the bottom edge. It must be made true and parallel to the top edge, and the height of the drawer front must be a perfect fit in the drawer opening. Square one end of the drawer front and place it in the opening to scribe the other end. It does not matter whether this mark is made on the face or on the inside of the drawer front,

but cutting must be done on the face because cutting from the inside may leave the face rough. When the second end has been cut you have a front that fits the opening exactly. No force should be necessary to place the front in the opening, but there should be no clearance either at this stage.

The back is next. Its top and bottom edges must be parallel to each other. The distance between them, that is, the height of the back, is less than the height of the front. It is not possible to give exact measurements, but it is from 2 cm to 2.5 cm (¾ in. to 1 in.) less. The bottom of the back must clear the drawer bottom when the bottom is slid into place, and the top edge is lower than the sides by about .5 cm (¼ in.). This clearance at the top of the back allows air to escape when the drawer is being closed. Without it a well-fitting drawer acts like a piston. The length of the drawer back must be the same as that of the front.

The drawer sides must have a true bottom edge, and the ends of the sides must be square to this bottom edge. The height of the sides is of no consequence yet, provided that it is more than is ultimately required: The sides should be just a little too high to fit into the drawer opening. The length of the sides is equal to the full inside depth of the cabinet (from the face of the front rail to the inside of the back) minus the .5 cm (¼ in.) or so you leave in the drawer front for half-blind dovetails. In a cabinet without a back, or whose back is not sturdy enough to act as a drawer stop, measure to a rail or stop, securely fastened as close as possible to the back of the cabinet. Thus the drawer stops are always present, and fixed, and the drawer sides are fitted to these stops. It is a good practice to make the drawer sides as long as possible, even when the drawer itself is short. This is some insurance against a drawer being pulled out too far and falling on the floor, and the wear from the sides on the front rail is more even.

So now we have a perfectly fitting drawer front, a back exactly as long as the front but lower than the front, and two sides with straight bottom edges and square ends. Before putting these pieces aside, restore the pairing marks on the top edges where necessary. If the piece of furniture has more than

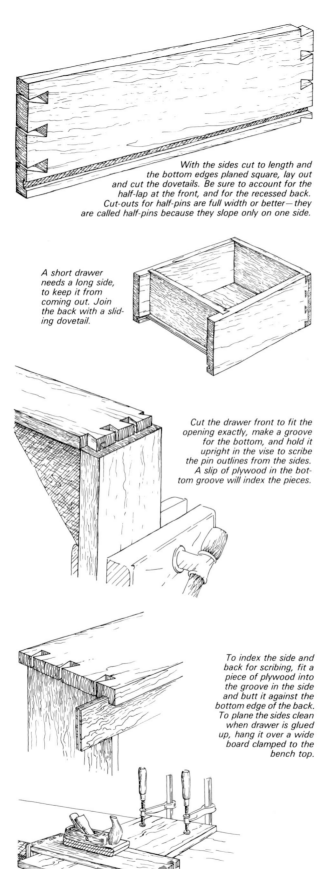

With the sides cut to length and the bottom edges planed square, lay out and cut the dovetails. Be sure to account for the half-lap at the front, and for the recessed back. Cut-outs for half-pins are full width or better—they are called half-pins because they slope only on one side.

A short drawer needs a long side, to keep it from coming out. Join the back with a sliding dovetail.

Cut the drawer front to fit the opening exactly, make a groove for the bottom, and hold it upright in the vise to scribe the pin outlines from the sides. A slip of plywood in the bottom groove will index the pieces.

To index the side and back for scribing, fit a piece of plywood into the groove in the side and butt it against the bottom edge of the back. To plane the sides clean when drawer is glued up, hang it over a wide board clamped to the bench top.

one drawer, repeat the whole procedure for each drawer.

One more thing remains to be done before the drawers can be assembled. A groove must be made in the drawer fronts and sides to receive the bottom. The reference line for this groove is the bottom edge of the drawer fronts and sides, that is, take measurements from this edge. The depth of the groove must not exceed half the thickness of the sides, and enough wood must be left between the groove and the bottom edge of the drawer to allow clearance and to support the bottom without danger of splitting the sides.

The next step is making dovetails at both ends of each side. The half-blind dovetails joining the drawer sides to the front should not present any difficulties ("Hand Dovetails," pages 14 through 18). On the other hand, the joint I use at the back might appear unconventional to some. The sides extend approximately .5 cm. (¼ in.) beyond the back for a drawer as deep as the cabinet.

Because the dovetails extend beyond the back of the drawer, they look best when the tails are wide—almost touching each other—and the pins on the drawer back are small. The illustrations should make this clear. Dovetails are not practical at the back of shallow drawers with long sides. It is better to join the sides and the back with a sliding dovetail, in which the back is slipped into place from below, or let the back into a dado in the sides.

When all the dovetails have been cut, the location of the pins is marked on the drawer fronts and on the back. The bottom edges must be used again for reference, but because the grooves for the drawer bottom have already been made with the bottom edge as reference, the grooves can now be used to align the drawer sides, fronts and backs. Take a small piece of the plywood you intend to use for the bottom, insert it in the grooves of both the drawer front and its mating side, and the two pieces will be correctly aligned and will stay that way while you scribe the pin locations. The drawer back has no groove but it can be held against the piece of plywood to align it with the sides.

I do not dry-fit dovetail joints. They are too easily damaged in fitting, with a subsequent loss in accuracy in the final joint. By holding one piece on top of the other it is not difficult to judge the fit, and it is entirely possible to obtain perfect results without actually assembling the joint first.

One more observation before we return to making drawers. Many workers divide a space in equal parts when laying out dovetails. This results in half-pins that are often too small. Dovetails depend for their strength on a wedging action. If the two outside dovetails are too close to the edge, not enough wood is left to keep the joint tight and closed under all conditions. Severe strains on the joint may even cause a split to start at the half-pins. The answer is wider half-pins. They can be achieved either by making the two outside dovetails a little narrower than those in the center, or by setting out the half-pins first and then dividing the remaining space evenly.

With all the dovetails made and ready to be glued up, now is the time to clean up the insides of all the pieces, and varnish or paint them if you are so inclined. Finally the drawers can be put together. Care must be taken to keep them square while the glue is drying

If you take a board or a piece of plywood, 2 cm (¾ in.) or more thick and a little bit longer than the width of your bench, and put this across your bench, you have a good support for the drawer when you are planing the outsides clean. The board must be secured to the bench, and if the inside of the drawer is already finished, the overhanging end of the board must be covered with cardboard or cloth. Clean up the outside of the drawer, and you are ready for the bottom. Some workers like to have the bottom in the drawer when they work on the sides, but leaving the bottom out is more satisfactory because it allows much better support. The drawer looks best when the bottom is just long enough to extend to the outside of the drawer back, or maybe 2 mm or 3 mm (about ⅛ in.) beyond that. It should not be quite as long as the drawer sides. When the bottom has been sanded and finished, it should be inserted and screwed to the back of the drawer. This is a first-class drawer and nails simply won't do. If the bottom is plywood, use two or three flathead screws, countersunk. If it is solid, use screws in slots to allow for movement.

Some workers like to put glue blocks on the underside of the bottom along the drawer front and sides. Glue blocks are made out of square material about 8 mm (⅜ in.) on a side and are approximately 5 cm (2 in.) long. Two of the long surfaces are coated with glue, and the block is rubbed back and forth a few times in the desired location. The rubbing will distribute the glue evenly, and if you do it right, there will be so much suction that it quickly becomes impossible to move the block. Clamping is not necessary. I believe that glue blocks are not necessary when the stock is dry and free from defects. But if there is any doubt that the drawer front or sides will stay flat and straight, glue blocks provide peace of mind.

The sides of the drawer are still too high. The height of the drawer front should be scribed onto the sides, and the top edges should be planed down to make them even with the drawer front. If you did everything right, you now have a drawer that fits tightly in the opening, more so in height than in width. This is because the height has not been changed since fitting the drawer front, but the width has been slightly reduced by cleaning off the outside dovetail joints. The reduction is hardly noticeable, but it provides just the clearance the drawer needs across its width. Clearance in height is obtained by taking one shaving off the top edges of the front and the sides. This is probably all you need to produce a drawer that fits well and moves freely. If you think the drawer is still too snug, take off one more, very light, shaving, but only after you have rubbed a candle along all the edges and tried the drawer once more. Paraffin is also good to make the drawer slide better, but beeswax or other sticky substances should not be used because they attract dust.

The length of the sides can now be checked. Where the drawer front is going to be in relation to the front of the cabinet is determined by the length of the drawer sides, because the drawer stops are already in place. The front of the drawer can be flush with the cabinet, in which case you should not have to do anything to the drawer sides. A front recessed not more than 1 mm (a fat 1/32 in.) often looks better than a perfectly flush front.

If a recessed front is desired, the sides must be shortened by 1 mm, or less. For those who have not yet been exposed to the impending metric system, your thumbnail is about 1 mm thick. As a finishing touch, slightly break the sharp edges of the drawer, give the last 2 cm or 2.5 cm (1 in.) of the top edge of the drawer sides a slope to correspond to the slope of

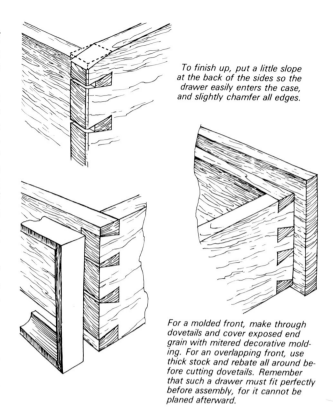

To finish up, put a little slope at the back of the sides so the drawer easily enters the case, and slightly chamfer all edges.

For a molded front, make through dovetails and cover exposed end grain with mitered decorative molding. For an overlapping front, use thick stock and rebate all around before cutting dovetails. Remember that such a drawer must fit perfectly before assembly, for it cannot be planed afterward.

the dovetails, and chamfer the protruding dovetails at the end of the drawer sides.

A drawer with a molded front is made as described above, with one difference: The dovetails joining the sides to the front are through dovetails, and the length of the sides is equal to the depth of the cabinet minus the thickness of the molding. The molding is not applied until the drawer has been fitted and all adjustments have been made. The molding covers the exposed dovetails in the drawer front. This type of drawer is reserved for more traditional work.

A drawer with an overlapping front must fit perfectly when assembled, because the oversized front makes subsequent planing impossible. The rabbeted part of the drawer front must fit in the cabinet with just the right degree of clearance, and the drawer sides must also be the right height before the drawer may be assembled. They can be planed and checked in the opening before assembly. It is somewhat more difficult to give this drawer a perfect fit because of its construction. On the other hand, the very feature that makes fitting difficult, that is, the overlap, also conceals a less-than-perfect fit. The stock for this drawer front should be thick enough to permit dovetails 12 mm to 15 mm (½ in. or more) long, with enough left for an overhang that is not going to break the first time the drawer is closed. Although this type of drawer does not seem to need stops, it is highly recommended that the ends of the sides, not the overlapping edges of the front, take the impact on closing.

A completely different way of making an overlapping drawer is to make a flush-front drawer first. The overlapping front is a separate piece attached after the drawer has been fitted. When this method is used it is imperative to have stops behind the ends of the drawer sides. If this is not done, chances are that the separate front will sooner or later become a separate front in a very literal way. □

Glues and Gluing

Woodworking adhesives, used correctly, are stronger than wood

by R. Bruce Hoadley

The general term "adhesive" covers any substance that can hold two materials together by surface attachment. Those most commonly used for wood are called "glues," although materials described as "resins," "cements" and "mastics" are equally important in the assembly of wood products. Today's woodworkers use adhesives in a number of ways: to make pieces larger than available stock (such as carving blocks or laminated beams), to create combinations or composites for physical or esthetic improvement (such as plywood, overlays or marquetry) and to join parts to create a final product (as in furniture, sporting goods or structures). Certain basic considerations which may be overlooked or misunderstood are too often the cause of serious gluing problems and are worthy of systematic review.

A logical starting point is to wonder why glue sticks at all. It is sometimes assumed that adhesion results from the interlocking of minute tentacles of hardened adhesive into the fine porous cell structure of the wood surface. However scientific research has shown that such **mechanical adhesion** is insignificant compared to the chemical attachment due to molecular forces between the adhesive and the wood surface, or **specific adhesion.** The assembled joint, or bond, is often discussed in terms of five intergrading phases, each of which can be thought of as a link in a chain. The weakest phase determines the success of the joint. Phases 1 and 5 are the pieces of wood, or adherends, being joined. Phases 2 and 4 are the interpenetrating areas of wood and adhesive, where the glue must "wet" the wood to establish molecular closeness for specific adhesion. Phase 3 is the adhesive itself, which holds together by **cohesion**.

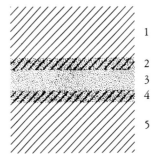

Fundamentally, then, gluing involves machining the two mating surfaces, applying an adhesive in a form which can flow onto and into the wood surface and wet the cell structure, and then applying pressure to spread the adhesive uniformly thin and hold the assembly undisturbed while the adhesive solidifies. The typical adhesive is obtained or mixed as a liquid but sets to form a strong glue layer, either by loss of solvent, which brings the adhesive molecules together and allows them to attach to one another, or by a chemical reaction that develops a rigid structure of more complex molecules.

A wide and sometimes confusing array of adhesive products confronts the woodworker. A common pitfall is the dangerous belief that some glues are "better" than others; the notion that simply acquiring "the best" will ensure success tempts disastrous carelessness in using it. With certain qualifications, it can generally be assumed that all commercially available adhesives will perform satisfactorily if chosen and used within their specified limitations. An important corollary is that no adhesive will perform satisfactorily if not used properly. Within the specified limitations, most woodworking adhesives are capable of developing a joint as strong as the weaker of the woods being joined; that is, the wood, rather than the glue or its bond, is the weak link in the chain.

Wood

Wood is a complicated material. Due to the cellular arrangement within the wood and, in turn, the reactive cellulose within the cell, adhesive bonding is maximum at side-grain surfaces, and minimum at end-grain surfaces. This is especially important to realize in view of the large longitudinal-to-transverse strength ratio we are accustomed to in solid wood. Thus end-grain attachment should be considered only in conjunction with appropriate joints or mechanical fastenings. With side-to-side grain combinations, lamination of pieces with parallel grain arrangement is most successful. With cross-ply orientation, the relative thicknesses of adjacent layers must be considered in relation to the dimensional changes the composite will have to restrain.

Different woods have different gluing properties. In general, less dense, more permeable woods are easier to glue; for example, chestnut, poplar, alder, basswood, butternut, sweetgum and elm. Moderately dense woods such as ash, cherry, soft maple, oak, pecan and walnut glue well under good conditions. Hard and dense woods, including beech, birch, hickory, maple, osage orange and persimmon, require close control of glue and gluing conditions to obtain a satisfactory bond. Most softwoods glue well, although in uneven-grained species, earlywood bonds more easily than denser latewood. Extractives, resins or natural oils may introduce gluing problems by inhibiting bonding, as with teak and rosewood, or by causing stain with certain glues, as with oaks and mahogany.

Since most adhesives will not form satisfactory bonds with wood that is green or of high moisture content, wood should at least be well air-dried. Ideally wood should be conditioned

---

R. Bruce Hoadley is associate professor of wood science and technology at the University of Massachusetts in Amherst. His book Understanding Wood *is available from The Taunton Press.*

to a moisture content slightly below that desired for the finished product, to allow for the adsorption of whatever moisture might come from the adhesive. For furniture, a moisture content of 5% to 7% is about right. For thin veneers, which take up a proportionately greater amount of moisture, an initial moisture content below 5% might be appropriate.

Machining is especially critical. In some cases, especially for multiple laminations, uniform thickness is necessary for uniform pressure. Flatness is required to allow surfaces to be brought into close proximity. The surfaces to be glued should have cleanly severed cells, free of loose fibers. Accurate hand planing is excellent if the entire surface, such as board edges, can be surfaced in one pass. On wide surfaces, peripheral milling (planing, jointing) routinely produces adequate surfaces. Twelve to twenty-five knife marks per inch produce an optimum surface. Fewer may give an irregular or chipped surface; too many may glaze the surface excessively.

Dull knives that pound, heat and glaze the surfaces can render the wood physically and chemically unsuited for proper adhesion even though it is smooth and flat. Planing saws are capable of producing gluable surfaces, but in general (with exceptions, like epoxies) sawn surfaces are not as good as planed or jointed ones.

Surface cleanliness must not be overlooked. Oil, grease, dirt, dust and even polluted air can contaminate wood surface and prevent proper adhesion. Industry production standards usually call for "same-day" machining and gluing. Freshly machining surfaces just before gluing is especially important for species high in resinous or oily extractives. Where this is not possible, washing surfaces with acetone or carbon tetrachloride is sometimes recommended. One should not expect a board machined months or years ago to have surfaces of suitable chemical purity. If lumber is flat and smooth, but obviously dirty, a careful light sanding with 240-grit or finer abrasive backed with a flat block, followed by thorough dusting, can restore a chemically reactive surface without seriously changing flatness. Coarse sanding, sometimes thought to be helpful by "roughening" the surface, is actually harmful because it leaves loose bits. In summary, wood should be surfaced immediately prior to gluing, for cleanliness and to minimize warp, and should be kept free of contamination to ensure a gluable surface.

Time

Shelf life is the period of time an adhesive remains usable after distribution by the manufacturer. Unlike photographic films, adhesives are not expiration dated. Beware the container which has been on the dealer's shelf too long. Out-dated package styles are an obvious tip-off. It is wise to mark a bottle or can with your date of purchase. It is amazing how fast time can pass while glue sits idle in your workshop.

The adage, "when all else fails, read the instructions," all too often applies to glue. It is unfortunate that instructions are so incomplete on retail glue containers. Manufacturers usually have fairly elaborate technical specification sheets but supply them only to quantity consumers. Too often, many critical factors are left to the user's guesswork or judgment. Mixing proportions and sequence are usually given clearly; obviously they should be carefully followed.

Glues with a pH above 7 (alkaline), notably casein resins, will absorb iron from a container and react with certain woods such as oak, walnut, cherry, and mahogany to form a dark stain. Coffee cans or other ferrous containers can contribute to this contamination. Nonmetallic mixing containers such as plastic cups or the bottoms of clean plastic bleach jugs work out nicely.

Once glue is mixed, the pot life, or working life, must be regarded. Most adhesives have ample working life to handle routine jobs. The period between the beginning of spreading the glue and placing the surfaces together is called open assembly time; closed assembly time indicates the interval between joint closure and the development of full clamping pressure. Allowable closed assembly time is usually two or three times open assembly time. With many ready-to-use adhesives, there is no minimum open assembly time; spreading and closure as soon as possible is recommended, especially in single spreading, to ensure transfer and wetting of the other surface. If the joint is open too long, the glue may precure before adequate pressure is applied. The result is called a dried joint. In general, assembly time must be shorter if the wood is porous, the mixture viscous, the wood at a low moisture content, or the temperature above normal. With some adhesives, such as resorcinol, a minimum open assembly may be specified for dense woods and surfaces of low porosity, to allow thickening of the adhesive and prevent excessive squeeze-out.

Whereas commercial operations usually have routine procedures for clamping, the nemesis of the amateur is not having his clamps and cauls ready. In the scramble to adjust screws or find extra clamps, parts may be shifted and assembly time exceeded. It is worthwhile to clamp up an assembly dry to make sure everything is ready before spreading the glue.

Spreading

Glue should be spread as evenly as possible, even though some degree of self-distribution will of course result when pressure is applied. Brush application works well with thinner formulations. A spatula, painter's palette knife or even a flat stick can be used as a spreader. A small rubber roller for inking print blocks does a great job in spreading glue quickly and evenly. Paint rollers and paint trays can be used with some adhesives.

Proper spread is difficult to control. Too little glue results in a starved joint and a poor bond. A little overage can be tolerated, but too much results in wasteful and messy squeeze-out. With experience the spread can be eyeballed, and it is useful to obtain some commercial specifications and conduct an experiment to see just what they mean. Spreads are usually given in terms of pounds of glue per thousand square feet of single glue line, or MSGL. A cabinetmaker will find it more convenient to convert to grams per square foot, by dividing lbs./MSGL by 2.2. Thus a recommended spread of 50 lbs./MSGL, typical of a resorcinol glue, is about 23 grams per square foot. Spread it evenly onto a square foot of veneer for a fair visual estimate of the minimum that should be used. Usually, the recommended spread appears rather meager.

Double spreading, or applying adhesive to each of the mating surfaces, is recommended where feasible. This ensures full wetting of both surfaces, without relying on pressure and flatness to transfer the glue and wet the opposite surface. With double spreading, a greater amount of glue per glue line is necessary, perhaps a third more.

Clamping

The object of clamping a joint is to press the glue line into a continuous, uniformly thin film, and to bring the wood surfaces into intimate contact with the glue and hold them undisturbed until setting or cure is complete. Since loss of solvent causes some glue shrinkage, an internal stress often develops in the glue line during setting. This stress becomes intolerably high if glue lines are too thick. Glue lines should be not more than a few thousandths of an inch thick.

If mating surfaces were perfect in terms of machining and spread, pressure wouldn't be necessary. The "rubbed joint," skillfully done, attests to this. But unevenness of spread and irregularity of surface usually require considerable external force to press properly. The novice commonly blunders on pressure, both in magnitude and uniformity.

Clamping pressure should be adjusted according to the density of the wood. For domestic species with a specific gravity of 0.3 to 0.7, pressures should range from 100 psi to 250 psi. Denser tropical species may require up to 300 psi. In bonding composites, the required pressure should be deter-

mined by the lowest-density layer. In gluing woods with a specific gravity of about 0.6, such as maple or birch, 200 psi is appropriate. Thus gluing up one square foot of maple requires pressure of (12 in. x 12 in. x 200 psi) 28,800 pounds. Over 14 tons! This would require, for an optimal glue line, 15 or 20 cee-clamps, or about 50 quick-set clamps. Conversely, the most powerful cee-clamp can press only 10 or 11 square inches of glue line in maple. Jackscrews and hydraulic presses can apply loads measured in tons. But since clamping pressure in the small shop is commonly on the low side, one can see the importance of good machining and uniform spread.

But pressure can be overdone, too. Especially with low-viscosity adhesives and porous woods, too much pressure may force too much adhesive into the cell structure of the wood or out at the edges, resulting in an insufficient amount remaining at the glue line, a condition termed a starved joint. Some squeeze-out is normal at the edges of an assembly. However, if spread is well controlled, excessive squeeze-out indicates too much pressure; if pressure is well controlled, undue squeeze-out suggests too much glue. Successful glue joints depend on the right correlation of glue consistency and clamping pressure. Excessive pressure is no substitute for good machining. Panels pressed at lower pressures have less tendency to warp than those pressed at higher pressures. Additionally, excessive gluing pressure will cause extreme compression of the wood structure. When pressure is released, the cells spring back and add an extra component of stress to the glue line.

The second troublesome aspect of clamping is uniformity, usually a version of what I call "the sponge effect." Lay a sponge on a table and press it down in the center; note how the edges lift up. Similarly, the force of one clamp located in

To find out just how much pressure typical woodworking clamps could apply, Hoadley attached open steel frames to the crossheads of a universal timber-testing machine. With a clamp positioned to draw the frames together, the load applied was indicated directly.

The clamps are described in the table, with the last column giving the average of three trials by average-sized Hoadley, tightening as if

he were trying to get maximum pressure in a gluing job. The quick-set clamp listed first in the table was used to calibrate the setup: A secretary squeezed 330 lbs., a hockey player squeezed 640 lbs., and Hoadley squeezed 550 lbs. Repeated trials by each person yielded readings that agreed to within 10%. An asterisk indicates that the clamp began to bend and the test was stopped at the value listed.

Brand, size, handle style	Screw dia., thread type	Load, pounds
Lust, 5-in. jaw, straight handle	.645 in., square	550
Hartford, 4-in. jaw, straight handle	.370 in., square	400
Jorgenson, 4-in. jaw, straight handle	.375 in., V	420
Stanley, 6 in., T-bar handle	.375 in., V	355*
S.H. Co. bar, crank handle	.625 in., square	2060
Sears 3/4-in. pipe, butterfly crank	.625 in., square	1120*
Jorgenson, 4 in., T-bar handle	.610 in., square	2110
Jorgenson 8 in., butterfly handle	.750 in., square	1100
Pony, 8 in.	spring	25
Craftsman, 10 in., straight handle	.435 in., square	920
Unknown C-clamp 2-in. jaw, T-bar	.310 in., V	560

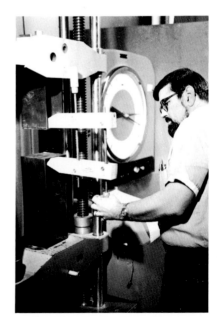

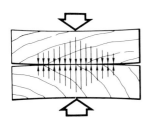 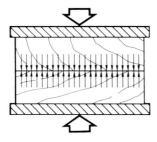

the middle of a flat board will not be evenly transmitted to its edges. It is therefore essential to use heavy wooden cover boards or rigid metal cauls to ensure proper distribution of pressure.

Clamp time must be long enough to allow the glue to set well enough so that the joint will not be disturbed by clamp removal. Full cure time, that is, for development of full bond strength, is considerably longer. If the joint will be under immediate stress, the clamp time should be extended. Manufacturer's specified clamp times are established for optimum or recommended shelf life, temperature, wood moisture content, etc. If any of these factors is less than optimum, cure rate may be prolonged. It's best to leave assemblies overnight.

Most glue specifications are based on "room temperature" (70° F). Shelf life is shortened by storage at above-normal temperature, but may be extended by cold storage. Normal working life of three to four hours at 70° F may be reduced to less than one hour at 90° F. Closed assembly at 90° F is 20 minutes, against 50 minutes at 70° F. A curing period of 10 hours at 70° can be accelerated to 3-1/2 hours by heating to 90° F.

Finally, cured joints need conditioning periods to allow moisture added at the glue line to be distributed evenly through the wood. Ignoring this can result in sunken joints. When edge-gluing pieces to make panels, moisture is added to the glue lines (1), especially at the panel surfaces where squeeze-out contributes extra moisture. If the panel is surfaced while the glue line is still swollen (2, 3), when the moisture is finally distributed the glue line will shrink (4), leaving the sunken joint effect.

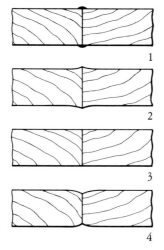

Adhesives

No truly all-purpose adhesive has yet been manufactured and probably never will be. A general-purpose adhesive cannot hope to attain all the individual capabilities and attributes of closely designed ones. Although any of the standard commercial glues will do a satisfactory job if the moisture content of the wood is below 15% and the temperature remains within the human comfort range, there is an increasing trend toward development of special adhesives. Adhesive selection must therefore take into account factors such as species, type of joint, working properties as required by anti-

cipated gluing conditions, performance and strength, and, of course, cost.

One interesting adhesive is water. It is easily spread, wets wood well and solidifies to form a remarkably strong joint. It is delightfully inexpensive. However, it is thermoplastic and its critical maximum working temperature is 32° F. At temperatures at which it will set it has a very short assembly time. But due to its temperature limits water will never capture a very important position among woodworking adhesives.

Glues made from natural materials have been used from earliest times. Although synthetic materials have emerged to the forefront, traditional natural adhesives are still in use.

Hide glue (LePage's Original Glue, Franklin's Liquid Hide Glue) is made from hides, tendons, and/or hoofs of horses, cattle and sheep. It is available in granules which must be soaked in water, but more commonly in ready-to-use form. Hide glue sets by evaporation and absorption of solvent. It has a moderate assembly time and sets in a matter of hours at room temperature. It develops high strength but is low in moisture resistance. Hide glue is used mainly for furniture. Its popularity in recent years has declined drastically with the development of synthetic glues.

Casein glue is primarily a milk derivative although it contains lime and other chemicals in various formulations. It is purchased as a powder that is mixed with water; after mixing, it must be allowed to set for about 15 minutes. Casein glue has the advantage of fairly long assembly time (15 to 20 minutes) but cures rather slowly (8 to 12 hours at room temperature). The glue line is neutral in color but may stain many woods and is somewhat abrasive to cutting tools. The claim of being a good gap-filling adhesive seems somewhat doubtful. Casein has moderately good heat resistance and bonds show significant short-term moisture resistance, but it is not recommended for exterior use. Casein is used extensively for laminating and large carpentry jobs.

Polyvinyl resin emulsions are probably the most versatile and widely used wood adhesives. These are the white glues (Elmer's Glue-All, Franklin's Evertite white glue, Sears' white glue), also called PVA because of their principal constituent, polyvinyl acetate. White glues have a long shelf life and can be used as long as the resin remains emulsified. Setting is by water absorption and quite rapid at room temperature; clamping time of less than one hour may suffice if the joints are not to be stressed immediately. The white glues are non-staining and dry clear. The glue does not dull tools but excess squeeze-out may clog or foul sandpaper under frictional heating because the adhesive is thermoplastic. These glues develop high strength but have low resistance to moisture and heat. An important characteristic is their "cold flow," or creep under sustained loading. This is an asset where dimensional conflict is involved, as in mortise and tenon joints. However, in edge gluing and lamination, "shifting" of adjacent pieces may in time produce visible unevenness at joints. In chair seats, joints may open along end grain due to drastic moisture change.

Numerous modified PVA glues give greater rigidity and improved heat resistance. The so-called **aliphatic resin glues,** commonly called yellow glue (Franklin's Titebond, Elmer's Carpenter's Wood Glue) fall into this group. The low viscosity of the white glues was always troublesome in furniture assembly, since any dribble of glue from joints caused difficulty in later finishing. The aliphatic glues are much more viscous and greatly reduce this problem. Some consider these glues as representing an intermediate position between the white glues and the urea-formaldehyde glues. However, yellow glues are not sufficiently weather-resistant to replace urea resins in carpentry.

The development of modern plywood and laminated products that have outstanding durability under extremes of outdoor exposure was possible only with the thermosetting resin adhesives. Several of these types are available to the woodworker.

Resorcinol-formaldehyde (Franklin or U.S. Plywood Resorcinol Waterproof Glue, Elmer's Waterproof Glue) are the woodworker's mainstay because of their high strength and resistance to heat and moisture. The most common form is a dark reddish liquid resin with a tan powdered hardener, paraformaldehyde. The mixed resin has four or more hours of working life at room temperature and its ample assembly time allows for complicated clamping operations. With high-density woods, double spreading with open assembly of 10 or 15 minutes is recommended to prevent starved joints. The adhesive will set at room temperature; cure periods are 8 to 12 hours, but can be drastically shortened by elevating temperature, which also ensures maximum durability. Use of the adhesive below 70° F is not recommended. Resorcinols are invaluable for room-temperature bonding of laminated timber and of assembly joints that must withstand severe conditions, such as marine and outdoor use. Phenol-formaldehyde adhesives have the superior durability of resorcinols but require heat for curing and are thus not readily suited to the average cabinet shop. They are used mainly for commercial production of plywood and particleboard.

Urea-formaldehyde glues (Weldwood or Craftsman Plastic Resin Glue), often marketed as "plastic resin adhesive," have become extremely important for the woodworker. The ureas represent perhaps the most versatile resin type, capable of bonding at room or elevated temperatures and curable with electronic gluing equipment. They are widely used in cabinetmaking, veneer work, plywood, interior particleboard and furniture. They can be modified with filler to form excellent gap-fillers. They commonly come as a tan powder consisting of both resin and hardener, activated by mixing with water. Liquid ureas are also available. Working life of mixtures is 3 to 5 hours at 70° F. Use with wood at moisture contents below 6% is not recommended, because of the rapid rate of water absorption from the glue. Assembly time of 15 minutes is allowed and the inconspicuous white-to-tan glue lines cure in 6-8 hours at room temperature. Glue bonds are highly water-resistant but lack durability at temperatures above 120° F.

Melamine adhesives are similar in appearance and mixing properties to ureas. They are very strong and resistant to water and heat. They are especially useful where the dark glue line of phenolic or resorcinol resins is undesirable. However, they require heat for curing, and find greatest use as a fortifier for urea in industrial applications and for high-frequency edge gluing.

Hot melts (Sears Glue Gun, Franklin's hot melt) are thermoplastic synthetics marketed as solid sticks that are softened in an electrically heated gun. These glues are applied hot, the assembly quickly closed, and rapid setting effected as cooling takes place. Hot melts are not a new concept, for great-grandfather's double boiler glue-pot used hot animal glue in just this way. Modern hot melts are new chemically, however, and include polyvinyl esters, acetals, cellulose esters or polyamides. Their principal advantage is the rapid development of initial strength upon cooling; a disadvantage is the very brief open assembly time. Hot melts are convenient for applying edge banding, furniture reinforcement, blocking, toy parts, and the like. They are easier to use if the wood is heated to extend assembly time.

Epoxy glues (Elmer's epoxy, Devcon clear epoxy) are among the modern "miracle" adhesives. There are several chemically different types, but all involve two liquids, a resin and hardener, which are mixed in equal amounts to initiate curing. The rate of cure varies widely. In the rapid-set types (Devcon 5-minute epoxy) open assembly is limited to a couple of minutes, but stiffening takes place quickly and a high percentage of full-bond strength is developed in less than ten minutes. Other formulations have up to an hour of working life but take up to 24 hours or more to cure. Epoxy resins will bond to glass, ceramics, tile, brick and many plastics (but not polyethylene, polypropylene and Teflon). They cure by chemical reaction rather than loss of solvent, and are excellent gap fillers. It has been reported that epoxy bonds better on clean, sanded surfaces or even sawn surfaces than on smoothly planed wood. Most glue lines are clear or nearly clear and waterproof. The major disadvantages of epoxy are relatively high cost and rather short pot life.

Contact cements (Goodyear Pliobond, Weldwood Plus-10, Elmer's Acrylic Latex Cabinetmaker's Contact Cement) are thermoplastics applied by double spreading and allowed to dry until no longer tacky. When the adhesive layers are touched together, cohesive bonding forms up to two-thirds of the ultimate strength immediately, hence the term contact cement. They will bond to many materials in addition to wood. Although contact cements have lower strength than conventional adhesives they are suited to many applications where clamping pressure would be difficult to apply and sustain and where high strength is not a requirement. Contact cements are perhaps best known for applying plastic laminates to counter tops. They are liable to fail about 120° F. Water-soluble formulations are available but have relatively low moisture resistance. A major disadvantage is the zero closed assembly time: surfaces bond immediately and cannot be repositioned once contact is made.

Mastics include a variety of thick, pasty cements. They are commonly marketed in caulking cartridges and many are termed "construction adhesives," intended for use in bonding subflooring to joists or plywood wall paneling to studs. They vary widely in rate of cure, usually developing slowly and retaining some flexibility in the adhesive layer. Their gap-filling capability is an additional advantage.

Acrylic adhesives (Franklin's Rexite) are used by applying the thick resin to one adherend, the activator to the other. Within minutes after bringing the surfaces together, amazingly high strength develops. I bonded together two maple dowels 1 in. in diameter and 4 in. long, end-to-end. After allowing a full half-hour for curing, no one was able to break the joint apart by hand. Another outstanding feature of the adhesive is that it cures by polymerization, and so it is a great gap filler. On the other hand, this adhesive so far has only about a six-month shelf life and has therefore not been made available for retail distribution. □

Making Your Own Hardware
Hand-worked brass beats the store-bought stuff

by David Sloan

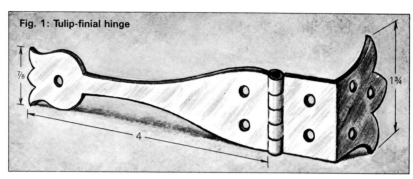

Fig. 1: Tulip-finial hinge

W hy let a limited selection of brass hinges force you to compromise the design of a project? You can have any style hinge you like if you make it yourself. The work is not difficult, even if you have no metalworking experience. All you need, in addition to regular woodworking tools, are a jewelers' saw and blades, a set of needle files, a propane or an acetylene torch, silver solder and flux.

The example here is a simple brass strap hinge with tulip finials, but the techniques I'll describe apply to any kind of brass hardware. Hinges can be constructed with a pin inserted through looped knuckles, or with a simple pivot pin. You can devise all manner of hinges, locks, pulls and handles, each tailored to your project.

The color and workability of brass make it the right metal for hardware making, though copper, silver, aluminum and steel are certainly acceptable. Brass is sold in dozens of different alloys, but one called CA-260, which is 70% copper and 30% zinc, offers the combination of strength and workability demanded for hand-working. It buffs to a rich, yellow luster. Brass comes in five hardness ranges: dead-soft, quarter-hard, half-hard, hard, and spring. Like most metals, brass work-hardens, that is, it gets tougher as you bend and hammer its crystalline structure into smaller, tighter patterns. To soften it again, you anneal it by heating it to a cherry-red

Sources of Supply

Cardinal Engineering Inc., RR 1, Box 163-2, Knoxville, Ill. 61448. Brass, steel and aluminum sheet; rod and bar stock.

Paul H. Gesswein & Co., 255 Hancock Ave., Bridgeport, Conn. 06605. Jewelers' tools and supplies, including saws, files, scribers, solder, and polishing material.

Kitts Industrial Tools, 22384 Grand River Ave., Detroit, Mich. 48219. Metalworking tools, including taps and dies, measuring and marking instruments, and drills.

Small Parts Inc., PO Box 381736, Miami, Fla. 33138. Brass sheet; rod and bar stock; small fasteners.

glow with a torch, followed by a quick quenching in cool water. Picking a hardness range depends on how much cutting and shaping your design requires. Quarter-hard is a good grade to start with, since you can anneal it or work-harden it as required, but don't hesitate to use any available piece of brass whose hardness is unknown.

Brass sheet stock comes in various sizes, and in thicknesses measured by gauge numbers:

$$24 \text{ ga.} = 0.020 \text{ in.}$$
$$20 \text{ ga.} = 0.032 \text{ in.}$$
$$16 \text{ ga.} = 0.051 \text{ in.}$$
$$11 \text{ ga.} = 0.091 \text{ in.}$$

Rod, tube and bar stock are available in all sizes and shapes as well, usually in increments of $\frac{1}{16}$ in. or $\frac{1}{8}$ in. See the supplies box at left for mail-order sources.

I start my hinges by transferring a drawing of the shape to a piece of annealed 16-ga. sheet stock, allowing about $\frac{5}{16}$ in. extra length for the fingers, which later will be looped into the knuckles of the hinge. Draw the fingers directly on the metal with a jewelers' or machinists' scriber and square. It's important that the fingers be square and accurate, or gaps between the knuckles will result.

A jewelers' saw—a small, adjustable-frame saw similar to a fretsaw—is used to saw out the hinges. Jewelers' blades are very fine and easily broken, but they're cheap and sold by the dozen, so it's best to purchase at least that many for one job. For cutting sheet brass, a fine-tooth No. 2 blade is good to start

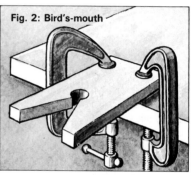

Fig. 2: Bird's-mouth

with. The saw should cut on the pull stroke, so when you insert the blade, make sure that the teeth are pointed toward the handle. The blade needs plenty of tension, too. To accomplish this, adjust the frame's blade opening so it's $\frac{1}{4}$ in. to $\frac{1}{2}$ in. larger than the length of the blade or piece of blade (broken blades of sufficient length may be reused). With the blade mounted in the front clamp, press the front end of the frame against the bench, bending it toward the handle enough to catch the blade in the rear clamp. When you release the pressure, the frame will spring back, tensioning the blade. A properly tensioned blade responds with a clear, musical "ping" when plucked.

Clamp the work to the benchtop so that the section being sawn projects over the edge, or else make a bird's-mouth, as shown in figure 2, to better support the work. This makes cutting somewhat easier, particularly with thin stock or where a piercing cut is made in the middle of a piece. When sawing, keep the blade perpendicular to the surface of the

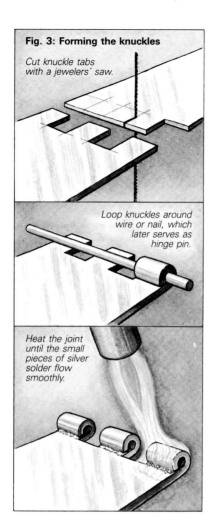

Fig. 3: Forming the knuckles

Cut knuckle tabs with a jewelers' saw.

Loop knuckles around wire or nail, which later serves as hinge pin.

Heat the joint until the small pieces of silver solder flow smoothly.

stock. After sawing, clean up the hinge with files, checking the fingers carefully for square.

I bend each finger separately to form the knuckles. A nail or a wire about $\frac{1}{16}$ in. in diameter makes a good bending form. This will later become the hinge pin. Start each bend with a pair of pliers, wrapping the finger around the pin (figure 3), completing the bend by squeezing the knuckle in a vise whose jaws have been covered with wood or aluminum to protect the brass from marring. You should be able to make all these bends without having to anneal the brass again. When all the fingers are bent around the pin, a final clamping of all knuckles in the vise at once draws them up tight.

With the knuckles bent, I remove the pin and then silver-solder the ends of the knuckles to the back of the hinge, for appearance and strength. Silver-soldering differs from soft-soldering in that the solder has a much higher melting point. You also heat the part and the solder at the same time, instead of heat-ing the part and melting the solder into the joint. Soldered joints are well up to the loads most furniture hardware must bear, and you can solder small pieces together to form whatever shapes you want. First, clean the parts thoroughly with fine steel wool. On the hinge shown here, I held the knuckle ends in the right position for soldering by simply bending the metal into place. If you are soldering separate parts together, clamp or wire them in their proper position. Then brush on silver-solder flux—usually a borax compound that chemically cleans the metal and promotes adhesion and flow—being careful to wet only the parts of the joint that you want to solder. Cut the silver solder into tiny pieces and arrange them along the joint, as close to the mating surfaces as possible. Play your torch quickly over the joint at first, until the parts heat up. Then concentrate the flame right on the joint. When it reaches the melting point, the solder will flow all at once, and you're done. When the solder has cooled, a drill passed through the knuckles will clear the pin hole of any excess solder.

Next, true up the soldered hinge halves with files and fit them together. This is a trial-and-error procedure and it helps to hold the two pieces up to a light to see where material must be removed. Once the pieces fit, you may still have to drill or bend the knuckles slightly to get the pin in. Oiling the pin helps. Once you've inserted the pin, you can close up slight gaps between the knuckles by gently tapping at either end with a small mallet.

When the two halves fit satisfactorily, use a fine file to smooth out the knuckles, and make sure that the outer surfaces are parallel. Make any additional bends your special hinge may require, but keep in mind that you can't anneal after soldering, so don't overwork the metal. Cut the hinge pin to length and peen the ends slightly to hold it in place. Finally, drill and countersink holes for the mounting screws.

To clean away the residue left from annealing and soldering, polish up your work with progressively finer grits of wet sandpaper and steel wool, and, if you want a high polish, finish up with rouge on a buffing wheel. □

David Sloan is on the editorial staff of Fine Woodworking *magazine.*

A catch, three hinges and a lock

Door catch: This spring-loaded catch, which I smithed for a fall-flap door, is essentially a three-sided box soldered to a flat mounting plate. I made the box by engraving V-grooves in flat brass stock and then folding the metal along the mitered grooves. A bead of silver solder reinforces the miter joint. The catch bolt is soldered to a piece of brass rod drilled to accept the steel pivot pin, which fits loosely so that it can be driven out for disassembly. I soldered a pin to the bottom of the box to anchor the spring; the top of the spring nestles in a dimple drilled in the underside of the catch bolt. The wooden activating button, which slides in a mortise, is beveled for leverage on the catch bolt. The strike plate is sawn from the same stock as the mounting plate.

—Ian J. Kirby, Cumming, Ga.

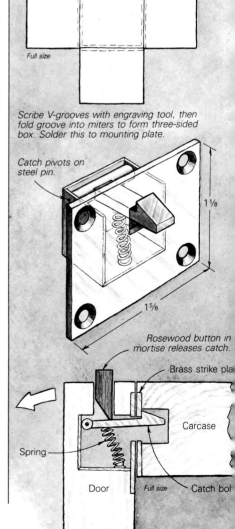

Full size

Scribe V-grooves with engraving tool, then fold groove into miters to form three-sided box. Solder this to mounting plate.

Catch pivots on steel pin.

1 1/8

1 5/8

Rosewood button in mortise releases catch.

Brass strike pla

Carcase

Spring

Door   *Full size*   Catch bol

Knife hinges: These knife hinges, which I made for a drop-front desk, can be tailored to fit any door where a small, unobtrusive hinge is wanted. I start with 1/8-in. thick, rough brass blanks slightly larger than the finished size of the hinges. I locate the holes in one knife with a scriber and center punch, drill the holes and then use this as a master template to transfer hole locations to the other knives. A #2/0 steel taper pin, available from industrial supply houses, serves as the pivot. Once I've drilled all the holes, I clamp the knives together, using 4d finish nails as locators, and then file the hinge to its final shape.
—*Tim Simonds, Chico, Calif.*

Fall-flap hinge: Good fall-flap hardware is always hard to find, so I made a pair of these hinges for a desk I designed. I sawed the hinge parts out of 3/16-in. by 1½-in. brass bar stock, cutting, fitting and test-pinning the angled knuckles before shaping the rest of the hinge. The 55° angle on the flap-side knuckle is critical, to keep the hinge from binding when the flap is closed. I encountered one problem in soldering: small parts, the pivot brackets for example, floated out of position on a river of molten solder. When clamping isn't possible, I just tack the parts in place with brass pins and then solder the joint.
—*Randall Torrey, Scottsville, N.Y.*

Cam lock: When I built grandfather clocks for each of my 12 grandchildren, I designed this cam lock to hold the pendulum door closed. The parts can be of brass or steel, silver-soldered together. I turned the shank on a lathe and cobbled the bearing block from a single piece of metal. The lock is operated from the side rather than the front of the case. I made my own brass key, but you can size the square part of the shank to fit the same key that winds the clock. A small section of brass tubing driven into the keyhole serves as an escutcheon. —*Raymond H. Haserodt, Lyndhurst, Ohio*

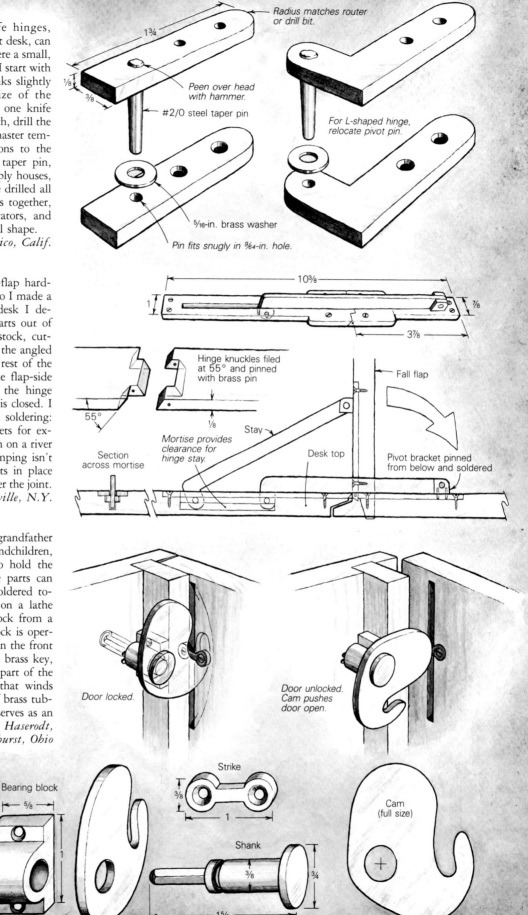

Radius matches router or drill bit.

1¾

1/8

3/8

Peen over head with hammer.

#2/0 steel taper pin

For L-shaped hinge, relocate pivot pin.

5/16-in. brass washer

Pin fits snugly in 9/64-in. hole.

10⅜

1

⅞

3⅞

Hinge knuckles filed at 55° and pinned with brass pin

55°

1/8

Section across mortise

Mortise provides clearance for hinge stay.

Stay

Desk top

Fall flap

Pivot bracket pinned from below and soldered

Door locked.

Door unlocked. Cam pushes door open.

Snap ring holds shank in bearing block.

Brass tube escutcheon

Bearing block

5/8

1

Strike

3/8

1

Shank

3/8

3/4

1⅝

Cam (full size)

Purchased in sheets and worked with unpretentious joinery, plywood lends itself to straightforward furniture projects such as this child's loft bed, plans for which appear on pages 58 and 59.

Plywood Basics
The ideal material for box furniture

by Ann Taylor

If you want to store something, put it in a box. If you want to store something in particular, turn the box up on one of its ends and fit it with shelves, dividers, drawers and/or doors. The basic box is basic furniture. It can stand on its own as a bookcase, hang on the wall as a cabinet, line up in rows as a wall system, or stretch out into a loft bed with plenty of room for storage. For fast, easy construction, nothing beats a box: it's simply four panels joined at the corners, with a back added on for strength or for appearance. And it can be built, without apology, out of plywood.

Cabinet-grade hardwood plywood is the perfect material for furniture-box construction. It's sold in 4x8 sheets, so you can simply cut box parts from a sheet, without having to mill and glue up as with solid wood. Because it's made up of a stack of thin veneers, plywood doesn't swell and shrink with seasonal moisture changes. This makes for some interesting design possibilities. You can, for example, decorate the end of a plywood panel with a contrasting wood without fear of the cross-grain construction cracking. I've found plywood to be economical, too. Even at a cost of between $20 and $100 per sheet, depending on grade and species, it's less expensive than hardwood bought for $3 and more a board foot (1984 prices).

Designing with plywood—Because plywood comes in big sheets, there's a temptation to build hulking, ill-proportioned monoliths that fill every inch of the available space, or use up every bit of the plywood purchased. Just because all the space under the stairs could be filled with plywood boxes doesn't mean it should. I plan my furniture-boxes by first measuring the space they will occupy, then making a scale elevation drawing, which helps me visualize how my design will fit in with the rest of the room's furniture and architectural elements. If the drawing doesn't tell me enough, I make a scale mockup out of cardboard.

A box with classic proportions has a short-side to long-side ratio of 5:8. Adhering to this so-called golden mean is likely to produce a well-proportioned box, but you must also consider real-world dimensions: the room where your boxes will live, and the doorways and staircases through which you'll have to maneuver them. If the boxes must contain specific things, measure these objects, make allowances for clearance, and keep the numbers in front of you as you plan. Multi-box furniture—such as a wall system—compounds the design decisions. What are the best dimensions for each box? How many boxes should there be? Working out the relationships on graph paper, I try to size the boxes so that they'll work in many different configurations, thus increasing the versatility of my designs.

Plywood is marginally more rigid along the grain of the face veneer than across it, but decisions about grain direction still can be more aesthetic than structural—a plywood shelf will bear the same weight regardless of grain direction. Grain does affect the visual size of a box, though. If you run the grain in a box's sides horizontally, the box will look shorter. Drawer fronts with vertical grain look deeper. This is most noticeable with oak and other vividly figured woods.

Plywood will sag if it must span too great a distance, vertical or horizontal. Besides drooping shelves, this also causes the sides of tall carcases to bow outward under their own weight, making it impossible to fit them with smooth-working doors and drawers. For ¾-in. plywood, I've found that 36 in. is the maximum horizontal span unless support is provided by a vertical divider or a face frame. For storing heavy objects, such as big books, 30 in. is better. The long sides of a tall bookcase can span 48 in. or so; if taller, the sides should be tied together with a horizontal member.

After I've designed and drawn the boxes, I make a cutting list that names each part, its thickness, width and length. The length is always along the grain, the width always across. To reduce waste, it's sometimes helpful to draw each piece to scale on graph paper, and after drawing an arrow to indicate grain direction, to cut out the panels and arrange them on a rectangle scaled to represent a 4x8 sheet. Once you have determined how to cut the plywood, decide which cut to make first and mark it with a numbered arrow, indicating grain direction, on the drawing. Then label each piece as you cut it.

Cutting and joining

Cutting and joining—Plywood rips cleanly along the grain, but the face veneer of the sheet splinters when crosscut. Minimize the damage by using a good-quality plywood-cutting blade. On my 10-in. tablesaw, I prefer a 40-tooth carbide-tipped blade with a triple-chip tooth pattern. The 100-tooth steel blades sold in most hardware stores will work, though, if kept very sharp. Get in the habit of positioning what will be the show side of your plywood up when you tablesaw; that way, any splintering will be hidden later. If you're using a radial-arm saw or a portable circular saw, position the good side down. A strip of masking tape applied along the line of cut before sawing will also reduce chipping. Since my basement shop is cramped, I usually have the lumberyard make

Taylor crosscuts panels on her Sears tablesaw, using a shopmade cutoff box. For larger cuts, she feeds sheets against a Biesemeyer fence, which permits cuts to the center of an 8-ft. sheet.

the first rip cut. I ask them to allow at least ¼ in. extra, and then I square the panel on my tablesaw, using the factory edge against the fence.

It makes sense to rough-rip full sheets first, cutting the panels about ⅛ in. oversize, then trimming them to the final size when they're smaller and more manageable. For accuracy, trim all panels of the same width at the same rip-fence setting. Since most box parts are too large to saw with the tablesaw's miter gauge, I use a homemade cutoff box to trim them square. Panels that are too cumbersome to tablesaw can be cut with a portable circular saw or a saber saw guided against a wooden fence clamped to the work. Clean up any ragged edges by cutting the panel a bit oversize and trimming cleanly to the line with a router guided against the wooden fence.

The parts of a basic plywood box can be joined in many ways, ranging from a simple nailed butt joint to dowel or plate joinery. I use four joints for plywood: the rabbet-and-groove (offset tongue), double rabbet, tongue-and-groove, and rabbet—all cut on my tablesaw with a sharp dado

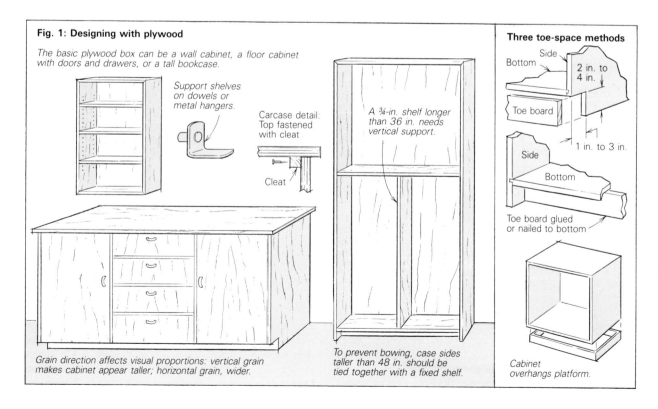

Fig. 1: Designing with plywood

The basic plywood box can be a wall cabinet, a floor cabinet with doors and drawers, or a tall bookcase.

Support shelves on dowels or metal hangers.

Carcase detail: Top fastened with cleat

Cleat

A ¾-in. shelf longer than 36 in. needs vertical support.

Three toe-space methods

Side
Bottom
2 in. to 4 in.

Toe board

1 in. to 3 in.

Side
Bottom

Toe board glued or nailed to bottom

Cabinet overhangs platform.

Grain direction affects visual proportions: vertical grain makes cabinet appear taller; horizontal grain, wider.

To prevent bowing, case sides taller than 48 in. should be tied together with a fixed shelf.

How to buy hardwood plywood

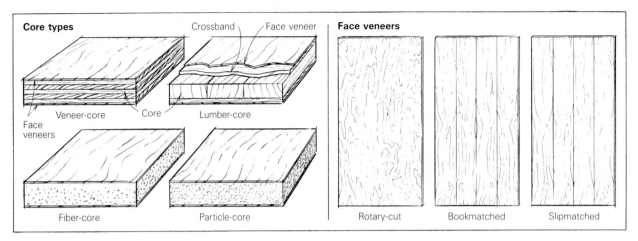

Core types — Face veneers — Crossband — Face veneer — Veneer-core — Core — Face veneers — Lumber-core — Fiber-core — Particle-core — Rotary-cut — Bookmatched — Slipmatched

Most local lumberyards sell a big selection of fir structural plywoods and paneling, but far fewer stock cabinet-grade plywoods. You may have to look around to find what you need. Yards that support busy millwork and cabinet shops, are a good place to start. These yards usually keep a good supply on hand, and they're familiar with the hardwood-plywood grading system, if what you want needs to be special-ordered. In most cities, a check of the "Plywood & Veneers" heading in the Yellow Pages will turn up wholesale suppliers. Wholesalers won't always sell small quantities to amateurs, but it doesn't hurt to ask. At worst, they'll refer you to a well-stocked retailer, or to one who can order for you.

Hardwood plywoods are graded by the quality of their face or surface veneers and by the way these veneers are arranged on one of four kinds of cores, as shown in the drawing. The chart shows the six veneer grades. Typically, one side of a sheet will be premium or A grade, the other side will be a lower grade; thus a sheet might be graded A-1, A-2, and so on. Most suppliers stock grades A-1 through A-3, and will also have on hand something that they call "shop grade." This grade, which doesn't appear in the official rule book, refers to seconds, or sheets that have been damaged in transit or storage. Defects in these sheets are often hardly noticeable, and the lower price makes this grade a good buy.

In addition to the letter-number grade, a sheet will be identified by how the face veneer is cut and laid. Rotary-cut veneer is peeled off the log in one big sheet and glued to the core. It's usu-ally cheaper, but the figure tends to be pronounced. Plain-sliced (also called flat-cut) veneer is usually bookmatched or slipmatched and has a more subdued (and usually more interesting) figure.

Face veneers of any grade or type can be applied to a veneer, lumber, fiber or particle core. Veneer is the most common core and consists of an odd number of veneer sheets or plies, frequently fir or a cheaper hardwood, built up to the required thickness. The face veneers are then glued on top. Veneer-core plywood may contain interply voids, but these usually don't cause much of a problem. Lumber-core—strips of a solid, stable lumber such as mahogany glued up into a large sheet and veneered over—is the most expensive, but the nicest to work with. Fiber-core, similar to Masonite, is made up from sawmill waste ground to a powdery consistency and pressed into sheet form. Particle-core is similar, but is made of larger fibers.

Which grade and core should you buy? That depends on what you're building. Mostly I make children's furniture, so I buy shop-grade (A-1 or A-2 seconds) ¾-in. veneer-core oak and birch. This grade is also excellent for kitchen cabinets and wall units. If I were investing more time in a piece of furniture, I might consider an A-1 lumber-core plywood.

Another thing to keep in mind when buying is that wholesale plywood prices, like lumber prices, are commonly given in dollars per thousand square feet. So if you ask the price on A-2 rotary-cut oak, for example, the salesman might quote $1,380. To find the per-sheet price, move the decimal point three places to the left and multiply by 32, the number of square feet in a 4x8 sheet. In this case, the price is $1.38 per square foot, or $44.16 per sheet.   —A.T.

HARDWOOD PLYWOOD GRADES

A Premium grade	Whether veneer is one piece (rotary-cut) or several (plain-sliced), it's free of defects and discoloration. If the veneer is sliced, the grain is bookmatched or slipmatched for figure and color.
1 Good grade	Face veneers are smooth and tight, but, if sliced, may not be figure- or color-matched.
2 Sound grade	Face veneers are smooth and tight, but not matched for color or figure. Sound knots up to ¾ in. and discoloration are allowed.
3 Utility grade	Veneer can have tight knots up to 1 in., discoloration and slight splits.
4 Backing grade	Open splits and knots up to 3 in. are allowed in face veneer. This grade is rarely found in off-the-shelf plywood.
SP Specialty grade	Custom-made to buyer requirements. Most architectural paneling is of this grade.

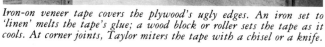

Iron-on veneer tape covers the plywood's ugly edges. An iron set to 'linen' melts the tape's glue; a wood block or roller sets the tape as it cools. At corner joints, Taylor miters the tape with a chisel or a knife.

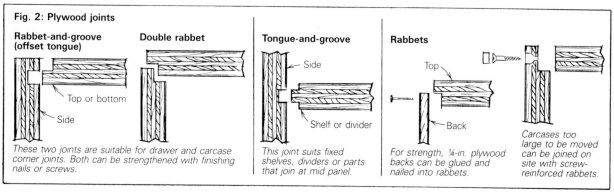

Fig. 2: Plywood joints

Rabbet-and-groove (offset tongue)

Top or bottom
Side

Double rabbet

These two joints are suitable for drawer and carcase corner joints. Both can be strengthened with finishing nails or screws.

Tongue-and-groove

Side
Shelf or divider

This joint suits fixed shelves, dividers or parts that join at mid panel.

Rabbets

Top
Back

For strength, ¼-in. plywood backs can be glued and nailed into rabbets.

Carcases too large to be moved can be joined on site with screw-reinforced rabbets.

set. Figure 2 shows which joint is used where. A box with four flush corners, for example, might hang on the wall, or sit on the floor atop a platform that forms a toe space. I join flush corners with a rabbet-and-groove or, if the box is large and must be delivered knocked down, with a rabbet that I screw together on site. Pilot holes will prevent screws from splitting the plies, and if the screws show, they should be counterbored and plugged. I use No. 8 or No. 6, 1½-in. wood or drywall screws to join ¾-in. plywood. The bed project on pages 58 and 59 shows another knockdown joint.

For fixed shelves and dividers where the end of one plywood panel joins the face of another, use either a tongue-and-groove or a rabbet-and-groove. Brace a box against racking by adding a back. I find that ¼-in. plywood glued and nailed into a rabbet milled into the back edges of the box is fine for this purpose. Make the rabbet for the back the last joint cut, however, since it determines which panels become the left, right, top and bottom of a carcase. And in case of splintering or cutting errors, you can put mistakes at the back of the box.

As a rule of thumb for ¾-in. plywood, I make grooves ⅜ in. wide and ⅜ in. deep. I size the tongues accordingly, but leave a ¹⁄₆₄-in. space between the groove bottom and the end of the tongue for glue clearance. To prevent chipping, I cut cross-grain dadoes in two steps. First, I set up the dado blades and rip fence, and lower the blades so that they just cut through the face veneer. Then I raise them and mill the cut to final depth. Before I pass good plywood through a setup, I always

try it first with scraps of the same stock that I'll be using. A test tongue should be deliberately too thick to fit the groove so that you can raise the blade in tiny increments until it fits exactly, or it can be trimmed by hand with a plane.

Adjustable shelves can be supported by ¼-in. dowels tapped into ⅜-in. deep holes bored into the case sides before the box is assembled. I space shelf-pin holes about 1 in. apart, and locate them about 1½ in. in from the back and front edges of the case. Be very accurate in laying out these holes, else the shelf will teeter when it's installed. A template of ¼-in. Masonite pegboard will ensure consistent hole location. To keep the drill bit from wandering out of line, I dimple each hole with an awl and use a brad-point drill bit in a Portalign tool. Make sure the bit has a depth stop to keep you from drilling through the plywood. Another way to support shelves is with metal or plastic shelf standards let into grooves milled in the case sides, or with steel shelf hangers that plug into ¼-in. holes.

Gluing up—To check the accuracy of the joinery, assemble the box without glue. Examine each joint, and trim away tight spots and ridges with a chisel or a plane. Fix a sloppy-fitting joint by gluing a strip of veneer to the tongue, sanding it smooth after the glue has dried. Since plywood faces are easily marred by clamps, and because there's no other way to apply pressure to a long joint in the middle of a big box, I use 2x4 cauls for each assembly job. If you plane the edge of

Plans for a child's loft bed

Like all the furniture I build for children, this loft bed is durable enough for the small child who plays under the desk and runs his toy cars along the shelves, but spacious enough for the older child whose stereo sound system spreads over the desk behind his computer. And because the bed is up high in a box, it doesn't need to be made each morning. The project was designed for a six-year-old whose room in the family's newly restored Victorian house had a high ceiling but no closet and only one wall long enough for a bed.

The bed consists of four basic boxes—one each for the bed, storage cabinet, desk and bookcase. All but one are made of ¾-in. shop-grade veneer-core birch plywood. To keep the size down, I used a 30-in. wide cot mattress (no box springs) rather than a standard twin-size mattress. Whichever you use, measure it before you begin cutting. Drawers are made of ⅝-in. fir plywood, to keep costs down, but if you prefer, use hardwood plywood. The desk top can be hardwood plywood, let into a rabbet, instead of laminate-covered fir plywood.

The drawing shows a refined version of the piece shown in the photo on page 54, so it differs in some details. For extra strength, for example, the stretcher connects the center of the leg support to the storage cabinet, instead of fastening at its back edge. The desk can be longer or shorter to suit the child's room, or to more economically use what plywood you have available. *—A.T.*

CUTTING LIST

Amt.	Description*	L x W
	Storage cabinet	
2	Cabinet sides	60 x 32
1	Cabinet top	31¼ x 31¾
1	Fixed shelf	31¼ x 31¾
1	Cabinet bottom	31¼ x 31¾
1	Toe board	30½ x 2
1	Cabinet back (¼-in. fir plywood)	60 x 31¼
2	Cabinet doors	18¼ x 14¾
2	Door pulls (¾-in. solid birch)	18¼ x 1½
1	Top drawer false front	30⅜ x 4½
3	Middle drawer false fronts	30⅜ x 7
1	Bottom drawer false front	30⅜ x 8½
5	Drawer pulls (¾-in. solid birch)	30⅜ x 1½
5	Drawer bottoms (¼-in. fir plywood)	29⅝ x 21⅝
10	Drawer runners (¾-in. hardwood)	31 x 5/16
	Drawer parts listed below are ⅝-in. fir plywood:	
1	Top drawer front	29⅝ x 4½
3	Middle drawer fronts	29⅝ x 7
1	Bottom drawer front	29⅝ x 8½
2	Top drawer sides	22 x 4½
6	Middle drawer sides	22 x 7
2	Bottom drawer sides	22 x 8½
1	Top drawer back	29⅝ x 4
3	Middle drawer backs	29⅝ x 6½
1	Bottom drawer back	29⅝ x 8

Amt.	Description*	L x W
	Bed box	
2	Bed sides	78 x 12
2	Bed ends	31¼ x 12
1	Bed bottom (¼-in. fir plywood)	77¼ x 31¼
5	Bed supports (fir 2x4)	30½
2	Mattress boards (½-in. fir plywood)	76⅜ x 15⅛
	Desk box	
1	Desk top (⅝-in. fir plywood)	72¼ x 29¾
1	Top surface (plastic laminate)	73 x 30½
2	Long sides	73 x 3
2	Ends	29¾ x 3
4	Desk crossmembers (¾-in. pine)	29 x 2⅜
2	Leg uprights (¾-in. solid birch)	27⅞ x 3
2	Leg crossmembers (¾-in. solid birch)	29 x 3
1	Stretcher (1-in. solid birch)	72¼ x 3
	Bookcase box	
1	Front side (¾-in. solid birch)	60 x 12
1	Back side	60 x 12
1	Bottom	31¼ x 12
1	Top	31¼ x 12
4	Toe boards	30½ x 2
2	Adjustable shelves	30½ x 11⅞
1	Fixed shelf	31¾ x 12
3	Bookstops (¾-in. solid birch)	30½ x 1½
1	Roll of iron-on plywood edge tape	

**Parts are ¾-in. birch plywood, except where noted. Dimensions allow for joints.*

each caul slightly convex, it will bear down harder on the middle of the joint, pushing the joint home more effectively.

Once the box is dry-assembled, check it for square by measuring diagonally from corner to corner. Both diagonals should measure exactly the same, but for practical purposes a 1/16-in. tolerance is good enough. Another way to check for square is with an accurate framing square, but it isn't as reliable, especially if the box parts bow a bit under clamp pressure. Correct small out-of-square errors by adjusting the clamps; if this won't work, disassemble and check each panel for square.

Before gluing up, sand the box parts with at least 100-grit, finer if you want. Be careful when sanding plywood, particularly with a belt sander. It's surprisingly easy to sand right through the face veneer, resulting in a blemish that's impossible to repair. If the wood appears to darken, the sander is going through the veneer into the next veneer layer. I finish after assembly, but some woodworkers finish before, so that glue squeeze-out won't stick. Don't dribble finish into the joints, however, or the glue won't hold. Let squeeze-out dry completely, then slice it off with a sharp chisel, scraper or razor blade. Wiping the glue, even with a damp cloth, will only force it into the grain, where it will show up when you finish.

Before the glue is dry, I attach the back, which helps square the box. If the back won't be seen, as in a chest of drawers, make it out of ¼-in. Masonite or fir plywood. Open bookcases and cabinets should be backed in plywood that has the same face veneer as the rest of the box. In either case, size the back so that it fits snugly into the rabbets. Don't measure between the rabbets—the clamps may have bowed the carcase in a little, and your measurement will give you a back that's too small. I put a light bead of glue in the rabbet, and nail the back in with 1-in. ring-shank paneling nails, first on one side and then along the top or bottom. If the sides bow, pull them in gently with a pipe clamp before nailing.

Finishing up—There are two ways to hide the ugly exposed edge of plywood: by edgebanding it with thin strips of wood before assembly, or by covering it with iron-on veneer tape or a solid-wood face frame after the cabinet is put together. Some people argue that edgebanding is more durable and a

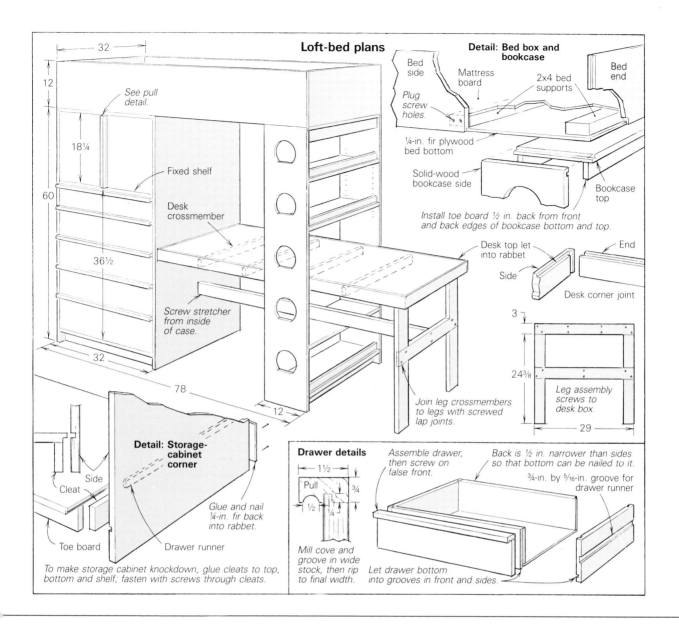

Loft-bed plans

32

12

See pull detail.

18¼

Fixed shelf

60

Desk crossmember

36½

Screw stretcher from inside of case.

32

78

12

Detail: Storage-cabinet corner

Side

Cleat

Toe board

Drawer runner

Glue and nail ¼-in. fir back into rabbet.

To make storage cabinet knockdown, glue cleats to top, bottom and shelf; fasten with screws through cleats.

Detail: Bed box and bookcase

Bed side

Mattress board

2x4 bed supports

Bed end

Plug screw holes.

¼-in. fir plywood bed bottom

Solid-wood bookcase side

Bookcase top

Install toe board ½ in. back from front and back edges of bookcase bottom and top.

Desk top let into rabbet

End

Side

Desk corner joint

3

24⅜

Leg assembly screws to desk box.

29

Join leg crossmembers to legs with screwed lap joints.

Drawer details

1½

Pull

¾

½   ¼

Mill cove and groove in wide stock, then rip to final width.

Assemble drawer, then screw on false front.

Back is ½ in. narrower than sides so that bottom can be nailed to it.

¾-in. by ⁵⁄₁₆-in. groove for drawer runner

Let drawer bottom into grooves in front and sides.

---

face frame stronger. While this may be true, I find iron-on veneer tape faster and a lot easier to handle. Bought in 250-ft. rolls (from The Woodworkers' Store, 21801 Industrial Blvd., Rogers, Minn. 55374, or from some lumberyards), it costs about 15¢ per linear foot. You can cut it with scissors and apply it with an ordinary household iron. If incorrectly positioned, the tape can be reheated and moved.

To apply the tape, cut a strip about ¼ in. longer than you need and iron it in place with the iron set on "linen." While the tape is hot and the glue melted, press it down with a block of scrapwood; the pressure of the iron is not always sufficient to set the tape. Although plywood corner joints are rabbet-and-groove, the veneer tape looks best if it's mitered at the corner (photo, page 57). These miters can be cut with a 1-in. chisel, but a straightedge and X-acto knife makes a neater cut. With two layers of tape overlapping at the corner, I place a straightedge diagonally from the outside corner to the inside, then knife through both thicknesses of veneer at once. Reheat the tape, then pull the joint tight and press down. Since the tape is ¹³⁄₁₆ in. wide, I trim it flush with a

chisel, and then sand the outside of the box with 100-grit and finer belts. I round the taped edges and corners slightly with 120-grit sandpaper. This helps bond the tape to the edge, and prevents it and the face veneer from being snagged and chipped.

A completed box can be fitted with drawers or doors using the construction methods shown in the drawings above. You can buy metal drawer slides or make your own out of hardwood. Doors can be hung on butt or knife pivot hinges, or on adjustable concealed hinges like those discussed on page 79.

Plywood boxes can be finished with just about any wood finish, or even covered with plastic laminate. A clear, fast-drying finish such as shellac or lacquer, or an oil finish is the easiest to apply. If the box is stained, discolorations from glue and uneven sanding, and ripples and other imperfections in the plywood will become more obvious, as will variations in grain. Paint will hide all these and any mistakes that you've had to fill or patch. □

Ann Taylor makes furniture in Winnetka, Ill. Photos by the author.

Hardwood Plywood
Modern 'glued-up stuff' saves work, money and wood

by Tage Frid

There is great confusion about how to buy hardwood plywood, about the different grades and qualities, and about its advantages and disadvantages against solid wood. Having a good knowledge of these things makes it easy to decide when to use plywood and when to use solid stock.

The advantage of plywood is that it's more stable and won't change its dimensions, except in thickness. It's easier to make machine joints using veneer-core plywood because the alternating direction of the plies makes for about 50% long-grain to long-grain gluing surfaces. It would be impossible to make much modern furniture without plywood.

The advantage of solid wood is that it can be shaped and carved. Its color is usually darker and its figure more pronounced because it's not cooked and steamed like veneer. The joints in solid-wood constructions can be exposed, making an attractive addition to the design. Solid-wood surfaces are also easier to repair, something to consider when making a piece that will receive lots of wear and possible abuse.

The greatest disadvantages of solid wood are that it doesn't have much strength across its width, and its dimensions never stabilize—it's always moving in width and thickness. The disadvantages of plywood are that it's difficult to repair, its joints usually have to be hidden and its edges have to be faced with either veneer or strips of solid wood.

Many people talk about plywood and veneer as "that modern glued-up stuff." Actually there's nothing modern about it, except the glues used today. Veneering, the basis for plywood construction, was known to the Egyptians 3,500 years ago. The ancient Greeks and Romans used the technique also, but during the Middle Ages the technology was lost, and solid-wood furniture was joined with pegs rather than glue. In the 15th century the Italians rediscovered the technique of veneering and the art spread throughout Europe, reaching its climax of skill and artistry in 18th-century England and France. With the introduction of machinery and the decline in craftsmanship during the 19th century, the art of veneering again suffered. After World War I, the first fumbling experiments were made to use plywood in furniture construction, and since then it has become indispensable.

The flush corners and edges of modern furniture and the development of panel constructions into plain unbroken surfaces would have been impossible without the dimensional stability of plywood. Architecture has been revolutionized by the availability of standard-size sheets of wood that are stronger than ordinary lumber. Exterior-grade plywood made with weather-resistant glue and used for decking and siding has changed our conception of house framing. And with the shortage of wood today, manufacturing veneer for plywood, unlike sawing boards from logs, produces little waste. Almost 100% of the log is made into plywood, except for its center, which is put to other uses.

Plywood means less waste for the craftsman too—there are no knots, checks or other natural defects that must be cut out. Also, more expensive species of woods, such as rosewood and teak, can be purchased in plywood form for about half the cost of an equal amount of solid stock. Generally though, the cost of one square foot of good quality ¾-in. hardwood plywood is about the same as one board foot of solid stock of the same species. Using plywood saves labor as well as material because it's not necessary to glue up large panels from narrow boards or to construct frames to hold the panels. Woodworkers should not rule out using plywood because they think it costs too much.

Plywood veneers are cut in one of four ways, depending on the species of the lumber and the use to which the veneer will be put. Most veneer is rotary cut. This method requires first cooking the log and removing its bark. Then it's placed between centers in a big lathe and revolved into a knife. As the log turns, the knife automatically advances into the stock at a controlled rate, which determines the thickness of the veneer. A cylinder of wood six or seven inches in diameter is left over. Veneer that has been rotary cut does not have the fine figure of sliced veneer, because when rotary cut, the veneer is peeled off the log like a sheet of wrapping paper being pulled from a roll. Because the cuts are always parallel to the annual rings, the grain of the veneer looks unnaturally stretched and doesn't have much character.

For face veneer the finest hardwood logs are used, and the veneer is sliced instead of rotary cut. Whether cut tangentially or quarter-cut, there are several ways to slice veneer. Usually the log is rammed into a fixed knife and automatically advanced between cuts so each slice is the exact same thickness, usually ⅟₂₈ in. The pieces are kept in order as they come from the machine so they can be matched. Sliced veneers are sold in flitches, bundles containing all the stock from one log or from a section of a large log. This makes it possible to panel a whole room with face veneer from the same tree.

Somewhat similar to sliced veneer, but cut instead on a

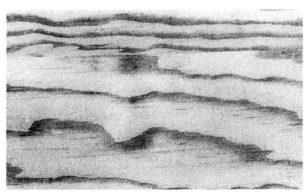

Rotary-cut veneers often lack natural-looking figure because they're cut parallel to the growth rings.

lathe, is half-round veneer. The log is bolted to a stay and mounted to the lathe in eccentric chucks. As the log revolves, it presents only a small arc of its circumference to the knife. Another method of getting veneer is by sawing on a band saw with a thin blade, which makes a narrow kerf. Even so, as much wood is wasted as is saved. Because this way produces so much waste, it is little used.

Though most plywood is made for the building industry, there are several good products available to the craftsman, who can buy them with the face veneer already glued on or with no face veneer at all (so he can veneer it himself). The plywoods commonly used by the craftsman are veneer core, lumber core, particle-board core and fiber-board core. All plywood is built up of an uneven number of plies of various thicknesses, depending on the finished thickness of the sheet itself. But whatever the thickness and the species of lumber used, the grain direction of any ply must be at right angles to that of the adjacent plies. This crossing of the grains gives plywood its great strength and dimensional stability.

The most used and best-known plywood is veneer core. The thinner the veneer used to build up the core, the greater the strength of the plywood. I would never use, for example, three-ply ¼-in. plywood. In most cases such plywood is made of cheap materials, especially the core, so any imperfection in the core telegraphs right through the face veneer. Assuming that the face veneers are 1⁄28 in. thick, this makes the core about 1⁄5 in. thick, and because the grain of the core must cross the grain of the face veneers at right angles, the plywood is weak along its length and easy to break. If ¼-in. plywood is made out of five plies, the center ply and the face veneers run in the same direction, and with the two crossbands, it's stronger and more stable.

The quality of veneer-core plywood varies greatly. Cheaper plywood contains voids and unsound knots in its inner plies. Voids in the crossband, the plies directly below the face plies, make the face veneers weak in those places because there's nothing to back them up, and they can break through. A better veneer-core plywood is a Russian product called Baltic birch. The quality of the wood is good, but the plywood itself tends to twist, and lately I've found that the layers sometimes separate. Most Baltic birch plywood is made to metric dimensions—standard sheets are 150 cm by 150 cm (roughly 5 ft. square) and the thickness also is in millimeters. Another very good veneer core is made in the Philippines and is sold under the general commercial name lauan. It is very stable and the core is good. Its color is close to mahogany.

Lumber-core plywood is made up of two face veneers, two crossbands and a solid-wood core. Because the core is much thicker than the crossbands and its grain runs in the same direction as the face veneers, it has great strength lengthwise. Most lumber-core plywood is made up of edge-joined strips in its center; poplar and basswood are common, though mahogany is better. These strips vary in width, but 3 in. is usually the maximum. The strips are glued together and then dressed to the necessary thickness. Next the crossbands and face veneers are glued on. Lumber-core plywood can twist because the glued-up core acts like one piece of wood.

Imported lauan plywood is also available in lumber core. The difference between the lauan lumber core and the ordinary commercial kind is that the core strips in the lauan are not glued up into one solid sheet. They're held together by the crossband plies with small spaces between the strips. This

The three-ply material, top, is weaker than the more expensive five-ply material, bottom. Defects in the three-ply core will telegraph through the face veneer.

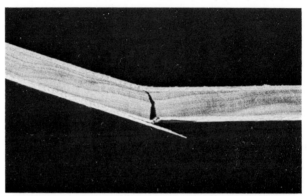

Three-ply ¼-in. plywood breaks easily, especially if it is used in narrow strips.

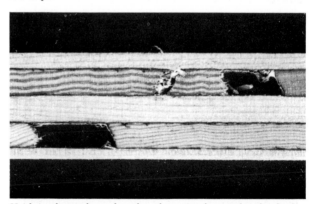

Voids in cheap plywood weaken the entire sheet and make the face veneers vulnerable because there's nothing to back them up.

Baltic birch plywood, a Russian import, contains no voids and has exceptional strength and good working properties. Though it sometimes twists and delaminates, it's generally a superior product.

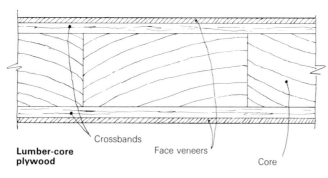

Lumber-core plywood

Crossbands
Face veneers
Core

Two bookmatched veneers. When taken from the flitch, one piece is flipped over, as you would open a book.

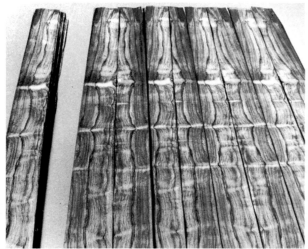

An entire panel can be made up of bookmatched veneers by flipping every other piece as it comes from the flitch.

Slipmatched veneers have a different look because there's no mirror-image effect.

allows each core strip to move independently, making the plywood more stable and more suitable for cabinetmaking. This lumber-core plywood is available without face veneers in 4x8 sheets that the craftsman himself can veneer.

When veneering plywood yourself, take the pieces of veneer from either the top of the flitch or the bottom. Don't pull them out of the center or any other place in the bundle because that splits up the flitch and makes it impossible to match the figure later on. There are two ways to match veneer on a panel. One is called bookmatching, because the piece on top is flipped over, as though you were opening the cover of a book. Bookmatching can be done with more than two pieces of veneer, and this is usually how good-quality sheets of plywood are faced. The other way of matching is to use veneers in the order they come from the flitch, only without flipping them. This is called slipmatching.

When working plywood of any type, the cardinal rule is that what you do to one side you must do to the other. Whether you veneer your own plywood blanks or buy them with the face veneers already glued on, make sure that the face ply and the back ply are the same species. If two different face veneers are used, for example, walnut on the front and poplar on the back, the two will expand and contract at different rates. There are plywoods available with plies of the same species on the front and back, though usually the quality of the front veneer is better and allows for fewer defects.

There are other materials that can be veneered or that come already faced with veneer. These are sold under the commercial names of particle board and fiber board and are usually less expensive but not nearly as strong as plywood. The greatest advantage in using these materials is that because they're

made out of sawdust or fibers they don't have any grain direction, so the veneer can be applied with its grain going in any direction. The greatest disadvantage of this type of material is that it doesn't have much strength and that it's not easy to join together, because the joints must be reinforced with splines made of some other material. Another disadvantage of particle board is that it will bow if it's used to make doors that slide in a track on the bottom. This is because there's no grain direction to support the weight. To prevent this from happening, either put a wide facing on the edges of the doors or hang them from a frame at the top.

The U.S. Department of Commerce has established voluntary product standards for grading hardwood plywood. This grading system is different from the one used to grade softwood plywood, and the two should not be confused. Premium-grade veneers are given the symbol *A*, while other quality veneers are designated by a number: good grade—1, sound grade—2, utility grade—3, backing grade—4, and a specialty grade—*SP*. Any combination is possible, the first symbol representing the quality of the face veneer and the second the quality of the back veneer. Plywood grade *A*-3, for example, has a premium-quality face veneer and a utility-grade back veneer. The absolute best would be *A-A*. Often the back veneer is a different species from the front veneer, so it's a good idea to ask about this when ordering because the grading system doesn't take this into account. For more information, write the Hardwood Plywood Manufacturers Association, Box 2789, Reston, Va. 22090. □

Tage Frid is a cabinetmaker, author, and professor emeritus at Rhode Island School of Design.

Tapered Sliding Dovetails
Router jig and masking-tape shim make for easy fit

by Brian Donnelly

For carcase construction the sliding dovetail is a strong, attractive joint. With a router it is also easily made. Its problem, especially in wide boards of dense hardwoods, is that it tends to bind when being slid home. The solution is to taper one side (usually the bottom) of both the male and female sections so the joint is loose until the final inch or so, when firm hand pressure completes the job. To taper a sliding dovetail I use a router table, first with a straight bit to make a slotted plywood jig used in cutting the female section, then with a dovetail bit to cut the male section. Both the slot in the plywood jig (and thus the female section it produces) and the male section are given the same taper on one side by way of a masking-tape shim. My method is adaptable for any size work or joint. The bits, bushing and shim specified below yield a joint in ¾-in. stock that tapers from ¹¹⁄₁₆ in. to ⅝ in. over 12 in. Here's how I do it:

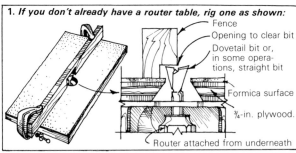

1. If you don't already have a router table, rig one as shown:
- Fence
- Opening to clear bit
- Dovetail bit or, in some operations, straight bit
- Formica surface
- ¾-in. plywood.
- Router attached from underneath

2. Use router table to make ¼-in. plywood jig for cutting female section:

Mark top left-hand corner and, directly underneath, mark another X.

Drill ⁹⁄₁₆-in. hole in center, 2 in. from end (for use with ⁷⁄₁₆-in. router bushing and ½-in. dovetail bit in ¾-in. thick stock — sizes are adaptable).

2"

5 in. longer than width of stock

~8"

¼-in. thick plywood

⁷⁄₁₆"

Set fence so that cutting edge of straight router bit (smaller than diameter of hole) just touches left-hand edge of hole.

Rout straight slot parallel to edge of jig.

Router table

Feed

Stop 2 in. before end of plywood.

Fence

Flip jig over

Cutting edge of straight bit again just touches left-hand edge of hole.

Feed

Place 4 or 5 pieces of masking tape on jig to provide ~¹⁄₁₆-in. taper over 12 in.

Rout slot tapered on one side, opposite X. (Taper exaggerated for illustration.)

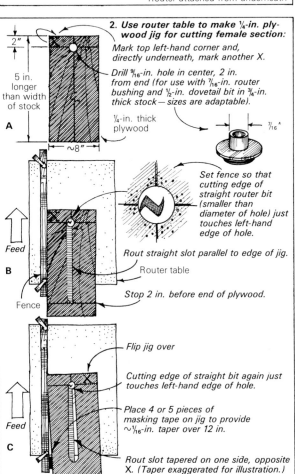

3. Mark cabinet parts with triangle:

Top

Left outside

Right outside

Bottom

Carcase sides

Shelves

Illustration: Bob Crosby

4. Lay out and rout female sections on carcase sides, using measuring stick, jig, router bushing and dovetail bit:

A

Mark top of both measuring stick and carcase sides with X.

Centerlines on jig and carcase side correspond.

B

Coordinating Xs ensure that top edge of slot is parallel to top of carcase side, the result: level shelves.

Dovetail router bit, with bushing guiding against insides of slot, enters work here. Set depth to ½ thickness of stock.

To avoid tearout, place scrap piece where bit will leave work, or shift jig and cut stopped dado.

Note: For large cuts, it is best to rout first with smaller straight bit to remove most of the waste.

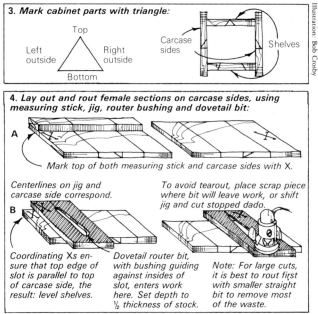

5. Cut male section of dovetail on router table:

A

Set depth of cut from female section.

Test piece

Fence

B

Carcase side (cut in step 4)

Router table

Lay out male dovetail on test piece with measurements from narrowest end of tapered female section.

Align cutting edge of bit with layout of dovetail. Set fence. Cut and check fit with test piece before cutting actual stock.

C

Feed

Adhere masking-tape shim (same thickness as used to cut jig) to bottom face of shelf stock high enough to clear router bit.

Scribe shoulder line with marking gauge to prevent tearout.

Note: Only bottom face of shelves (check triangle mark, step 3) gets masking-tape shim; top face gets untapered dovetail shoulder, no shim.

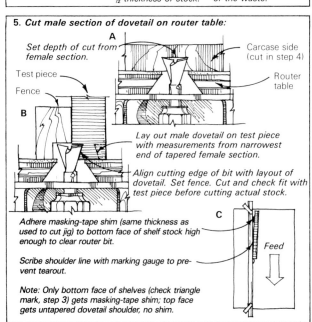

Man-Made Boards
Working with particleboard and fiberboard

by Simon Watts

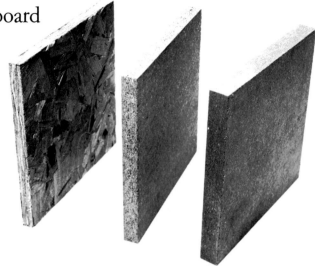

Three man-made boards: left, waferboard, used only in construction; center, furniture-grade particleboard, showing characteristic layered structure (fine particles for the faces, coarse particles for the interior); and right, medium-density fiberboard, with uniformly dense edges. Photo: Forest Products Laboratory.

However solid wood is used to make furniture, its fibers, the actual strands of ligno-cellulose, remain arranged much as they were in the living tree. If the wood is sliced into sheets and then glued together so that the grain of adjacent layers runs at right angles to one another, we get plywood, a composite material with some of the properties of the original wood plus some new ones—it won't split easily and it's more stable. In spite of this, it is easily recognizable as wood, and the fibers in each veneer are still aligned almost as they were in the tree.

Instead of making plywood, suppose we grind the original piece of wood into flakes, chips or sawdust, coat the particles with glue and press the result into sheets. We have a new material—particleboard—with properties somewhat different from both plywood and solid wood. It is equally strong in both directions, for example. Although particleboard is barely recognizable as a wood product, if we inspect it under a hand lens we can see the individual elements still organized as they were in the tree.

We could go one step further and reduce the wood to its component fibers by steaming or with solvents. This technique opens up a new range of possibilities. Fibers can be mixed with water to form a slurry, which is deposited on moving, porous belts to make paper, or they can be dried, blown into forming machines and then pressed into fiberboard. Whatever the final result—tissue paper, cardboard, soft insulation board or hardboard—these products all have one thing in common. The arrangement of the individual fibers is now random, and has no relation to how they grew in the tree. Its fibers have been reorganized.

These processes of modifying the structure of wood do not end with fiberboard. The cellulose portion can be liquefied by solvents and used to make such new materials as rayon, cellulose lacquer and cellophane. But furniture-makers have not yet turned to cellophane, and plywood has been around long enough to be well understood. Particleboard and fiberboard, on the other hand, have developed so rapidly that the techniques of working with them and designing for them have not yet caught up.

It is time to take a fresh look at the new generation of sheet materials and to stop thinking of them as substitutes for solid wood. After manufacturing out of the tree all the irregularities that make it a unique material, it seems perverse to then reconstitute it to look like old barn boards or wormy chestnut. This practice only encourages people to think that man-made board and solid wood have a lot in common. Although they can be worked with the same tools, the fact is that they don't have much in common. Man-made board has large, smooth surfaces; although generally weaker, it is uniform and dimensionally stable, compared to solid wood, moving minimally and predictably in response to humidity changes.

Even woodworkers excited by these new materials have difficulty making the switch. This is because there is such a weight of accumulated experience where solid wood is concerned—much of which has to be discarded when working with man-made board. It is structurally incongruous, for instance, to use particleboard for frame-and-floating-panel construction, a design developed to allow for the seasonal movement of a solid-wood panel.

Solid wood, for practical reasons of weight and drying, has traditionally been worked in thicknesses under 2 in. But using man-made boards, it is possible to choose your own thickness by means other than lamination—hollow-core construction, for instance. The dimensional stability of man-made board makes it possible to organize the architecture of the piece—the interplay of solids and voids—in ways that are simply not possible in solid wood. Also, the large, smooth surfaces invite the use of color and texture in coverings that can produce a wide range of visual effects. These may have little or nothing to do with the underlying structure.

Particleboard, the oldest of the new man-made boards, first appeared in Europe after World War II. The forests had been depleted, and after the widespread destruction of the war there was a desperate need for building materials. Particleboard utilized low-grade raw materials—trees too small or crooked to be sawn into lumber, as well as sawdust and shavings. Particleboard panels were soon being produced in quantity, but America, with its vast timber resources, was slower to adopt its manufacture. In the past ten years this situation has changed dramatically—America produced 3.3 billion square feet in 1979, enough to cover 80,000 acres.

Particleboard can be made from almost any species of wood, hard or soft, from large trees or planer shavings. The wood does not have to be new, and even old railroad ties have been used experimentally. Starting with round logs, the first step is to remove the bark. The wood is then reduced to ¾-in. to 2-in. chips and fed into a ring-flaker, which yields thick shavings. It's then dried, graded by size and blown into large storage bins. As needed, the particles are sprayed with glue and shaped into mats in vacuum-forming machines where they are deposited, like snowflakes, on moving metal plates. These mats then enter a precompressor, which reduces them to a height of 10 in. or less. Next they are trimmed and sent to the main press for a 1,600-PSI squeeze.

After pressing, the panels must be immediately cooled or else the glue bond deteriorates. They are slowly pivoted on one edge, like the leaves of a giant book, trimmed again, then fed through a series of drum sanders to remove about 1/32 in. from each side, reducing them to uniform thickness.

Virtually all particleboard sold, both construction and furniture-grade, is made by pressing like this, but it can also be made by extrusion. Extruded particleboard begins with dry wood, which is splintered by grinding or hammer-milling and then sprayed with glue as before. The glue/particle mix is squeezed through a heated die and emerges as a continuous ribbon, like toothpaste. By changing the shape of the die, different sections can be made, and some experimenters have made 2x4s and even I-beams.

Extrusion is the cheaper process because no forming press is involved. But it cannot produce "layered boards" having a surface composition different from the interior. Particleboard intended for the furniture industry is different from construction-grade particleboard commonly sold in building-supply stores and used for sheathing and floor underlayment. It has this layered composition: fine particles on the surfaces and coarser ones in between. A board composed entirely of fine particles would be heavy and wasteful of glue; one made only of large particles would soon lose its smoothness as the surface absorbed moisture with changes in humidity. For this reason trying to cover construction-grade particleboard with wood veneer is a lost cause. The coarse surface particles will swell and soon show through the veneer until the surface has the texture of oatmeal.

Most furniture-grade particleboard goes directly, in large quantities, to furniture factories. It is therefore difficult to obtain at retail, though some of the larger outlets are beginning to stock it. It's easily recognized by its size: 4 ft. 1 in. by 8 ft. 1 in., instead of the standard 4x8 sheets used in the building trade. If your local lumber dealer doesn't carry it, ask him to order it for you from his wholesaler.

Fiberboard is not layered but still retains its smooth surface in spite of changes in humidity. The manufacturing process begins by softening and loosening the wood fibers. Raw sawmill wastes are first fed into large boilers, where they are subjected to intense steam pressure for several minutes. When the pressure is suddenly released, the particles explode into a pulpy mass. This thick batter is then forced through a ring-refiner where the shearing action between two rotating discs tears the particles to fibers. From here it goes to flash-tube driers where, in less than three seconds, its moisture content is reduced to 2% or 3%. Then it is sprayed with a fine mist of glue and stored in large bins until needed. The glue is activated under the heat and pressure of pressing.

This process is similar to making particleboard except that the fiberboard material is much fluffier, and a mat 23 in. high will squeeze down to make a 3/4-in. board. After pressing and cooling, boards are sanded and cut to order on a variety of computer-controlled equipment.

A typical fiberboard plant uses 300 tons of sawmill wastes—sawdust and shavings—each day, and 30 tons of

A knife-ring flaker reduces wood to chips on its way to becoming particleboard. Raw material enters the chute and is thrown against the rotating knives by centrifugal force. This machine is about 10 ft. high and contains 56 knives, each 2 ft. long. Photo: Pallmann Pulverizer Co.

A typical particleboard press. The largest of these presses, in Brazil, can produce 26 4x8 panels every six minutes—more than a million square feet per day. Photo: Washington Iron Works.

urea-formaldehyde glue. One of the striking features of such a plant is that it not only feeds on waste but also produces practically none itself. Offcuts prior to final pressing go back to the storage bins, subsequent trimmings fire the flash driers, and dust from the sanders is collected to heat the boilers.

Depending principally on the amount of pressure applied and the thickness of the original mat, the product of a fiberboard plant may be a lightweight insulation board, with a density of 15 lb. to 20 lb. per cubic foot; medium-density fiberboard (MDF) 44 lb. to 55 lb.; or a high-density fiberboard (HDF) weighing approximately 60 lb. per cubic foot. Known as hardboard or Masonite, high-density board can be toughened (tempered) and made weather resistant by hot-rolling with oil.

For making furniture, fiberboard is superior to particleboard in every respect except availability. It has a better surface quality that stays smooth regardless of changes in humidity, which makes it an excellent substrate for veneers. Its edges are tighter, making them easier to mill, mold and finish, and somewhat better able to hold fasteners. It is easier to glue because there are no voids. Its lower glue content makes it less abrasive to tools and, very likely, less of a health hazard to the woodworker. As its advantages become more

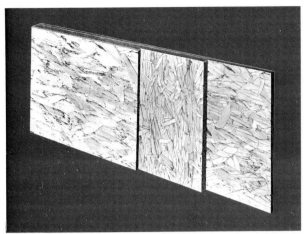

The newest type of man-made board is OSB (oriented-strand board), in which the face strands are aligned with the length of the board, while the interior strands run the width. Experiments are being conducted to produce boards with surfaces smooth enough to be used in furniture. Photo: Elmendorf Corp.

widely known, fiberboard could eventually supersede particleboard altogether. Again, the most likely way to obtain it at present is to ask your local retailer to order it for you from his wholesaler.

Oriented-strand board (OSB) has a layered construction, like furniture-grade particleboard, but the particles are not placed at random. It has a distinct "grain" because the fibers in the top and bottom surfaces are aligned lengthwise while the middle layer runs across the width of the board like plywood. Unlike plywood, however, it does not require scarce and expensive veneer logs but can be made from low-grade cordwood. The first U.S. manufacturer, Elmendorf Board Corp., has started production in Claremont, N.H.

Working with man-made boards—All these new sheet materials depend on glue, fiberboards less than particleboards because the interweaving of the fibers gives strength and also because the lignin remaining from the tree acts somewhat as a natural adhesive. The two common glues are urea and phenol formaldehyde, which release formaldehyde vapor both before and after manufacture.

When a Seattle research team exposed laboratory rats to this vapor at residual levels often found in mobile homes, whose interiors are sealed tight with man-made boards, the animals developed an abnormally high rate of nasal cancer. It is known also that with heat, as generated when machining man-made boards, these glues decompose, releasing formaldehyde. Without further research it is impossible to know what the health hazards of living and working with products made from these glues really are. The Federal Consumer Products Safety Commission has proposed a ban on urea-formaldehyde foam insulation (which also releases vapor), and industry is looking into alternative adhesives. In the meantime it seems prudent to work with these materials in well-ventilated areas, to wear a respirator with an organic-vapor cartridge when machining them, and to seal raw surfaces to reduce vapor emission in finished products.

Formaldehyde glues are highly abrasive and soon take the edge off even a high-quality steel blade, requiring frequent resharpening. Particleboard is worse than fiberboard in this respect because of its higher glue content. Carbide-tipped sawblades are now used almost exclusively, and special tooth configurations have been developed. The features that everyone wants in a blade are long tool life, clean cutting and minimum tear-out. However, these requirements conflict, and no single tooth form or combination entirely satisfies them.

The common rip tooth (or flat-top) is not recommended for cutting particleboard because it takes such a big bite that

Structural properties of some man-made boards

This table compares the structural properties of ¾-in. particleboards and fiberboards typically used for furniture. As one would expect, the denser the material the stronger it is and the better able to hold fasteners. Expansion and contraction as a result of changes in humidity, although small, cannot always be disregarded. An 8-ft. panel of MDF, for example, would increase about ¼ in. in length as the relative humidity rose from 50% to 90%. Change in thickness due to changes in humidity depends too much on the species, size and geometry of the particles to be listed, but it is roughly ten times the linear expansion. Thickness movement is of little consequence, except that surface particles swell unevenly and produce an "orange peel" surface.

	Modulus of rupture (min. avg.) PSI	Modulus of elasticity (min. avg.) 10^6 PSI	Internal bond (min. avg.) PSI	Linear expansion (max. avg.) Percent	Screw holding (min. avg.) lb. Face	Screw holding (min. avg.) lb. Edge
¾-in. particleboard, interior grade						
Low density (37 lb./cu. ft. and under)	800	0.15	20	0.30	125	—
Medium density (37 to 50 lb./cu. ft.)	1,600	0.25	70	0.35	225	160
High density (50 lb./cu. ft. and over)	2,400	0.35	200	0.55	450	—
¾-in. fiberboard, medium density (48 lb./cu. ft.)	4,000	0.40	100	0.35	350	275
Eastern white pine (*Pinus strobus*)	8,600	1.24				
White oak (*Quercus alba*)	15,200	1.78				

Modulus of rupture: the load necessary to break a panel.
Modulus of elasticity: a measure of the resistance to deflection.
Internal bond: the force two faces of a panel will withstand before pulling apart.
Linear expansion: the change in length that occurs when relative humidity of surrounding air rises from 50% to 90%.
Screw holding: the force required to extract a 1-in. #10 type A or AB sheet-metal screw.

Data adapted from the National Bureau of Standards' Commercial Standard CS 236-66 and literature from the Plum Creek Lumber Co., Columbia Falls, Mont.

the large cutting pressures tear out the fibers at the point of exit. It also has a tendency to choke on its own waste, generating heat and requiring more power. The alternating-top-bevel tooth (ATB), often used for crosscutting, makes a smoother cut with minimum tear-out, but its sharp tips are vulnerable to shock loads and will wear quickly. If quality of cut is not crucial, the triple-chip design is the best to buy. But if you want a smooth cut and plan to use particleboard extensively, buy a blade specifically designed for man-made boards. Such blades usually combine an alternating face bevel with ATBs and sometimes beveled lead teeth as well. These are expensive blades—both to purchase and to maintain. (Winchester Carbide Saw, 2635 Papermill Rd., Winchester, Va. 22601 is one supplier.)

Other factors that affect the cutting of particleboard are hook angles, clearance angles, the thickness of the saw body and tooth approach angles. The first three of these are built into the saw but the last one can be changed by altering the height of the saw above the table, as shown at right.

With hard, abrasive materials like particleboard, cutting edges can dull quickly. For this reason a relatively large chip load, achieved by feeding the stock fast, is best. For the same reason, bandsaw blades for cutting ¾-in. particleboard should not have more than three teeth per inch. Carbide-tipped router bits are more effective because high-speed steel bits soon dull, overheat and become useless.

Fiberboard has a tendency to flow back, which means that the material recovers slightly after its fibers are compressed by, say, a drilling or routing operation. This can result in a smaller hole than intended, sometimes an advantage when doweling or splining.

Joining man-made boards—Man-made board is weaker than solid wood in every respect except possibly resistance to splitting. Because of this inherent weakness it is seldom used in small sections, and most joining is of one surface to another. The trick is not to weaken the material further by using the wrong joint. Avoid shouldered tenons and continuous slots. This is particularly important when using furniture-grade particleboard because of the material's hard, dense surface and relatively weak interior. Cutting through the skin exposes the more loosely connected interior particles, which have little resistance to shearing forces. Both particleboard and fiberboard are too weak to be dovetailed, and corners must be joined in other ways. Various methods, including methods for lipping, are illustrated on the next page.

A joining system rapidly gaining popularity in this country is the Lamello. Invented in Europe about 20 years ago, it uses a machine that looks like a small router. It cuts a curved slot in the two surfaces or edges to be joined. Into this slot is glued a lens-shaped beech spline cut on the bias. Each spline is compressed in manufacture so it swells on contact with glue and produces internal pressure on the glueline. This ensures a strong joint. It can join boards edge to edge or edge to surface, and can also be used in miters, working equally well for particleboard, fiberboard (MDF) and solid wood. It is imported by Colonial Saw, Inc., 100 Pembroke St., Kingston, Mass. 02364.

Another method for joining particleboard and fiberboard is to use knock-down (KD) fittings. A wide variety is available, as well as hinges and hardware specially designed for use in man-made boards. Generally they involve letting a plate or

Tooth approach angles

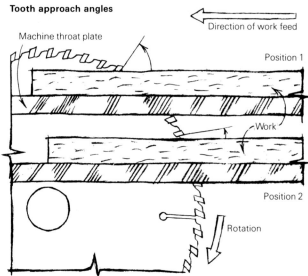

One of the factors determining smoothness of cut, particularly significant in cutting man-made boards, is the height of the blade in the work. Thin stock should be cut with the blade barely projecting above the work (position 1). Although it takes more power to cut this way, the uncut material acts as a backing and minimizes tear-out. Position 2, with the saw raised almost to its arbor, has the smallest approach angle, and blunt tooth forms like the triple chip work best this way because they can exert maximum shear. However, because the tooth makes its exit almost at right angles to the work, it tends to chip out the bottom surface.

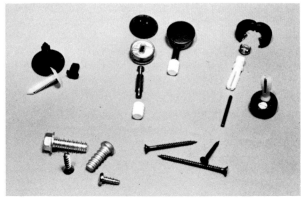

Typical particleboard fasteners, clockwise from top left, include face-joining Christmas-tree fasteners, butt-joining inserts, right-angle-joining inserts, twin-start screws and hi-lo screws.

cylinder into the board to increase the surface area of the attachment. Some of the more useful designs are shown in the photo above, and suppliers include Furntek Corp., PO Box 26792, Charlotte, N.C. 28213, and Fastex, 195 Algonquin Rd., Des Plaines, Ill. 60016.

No hardware is any better than its attachments. Screws and other fastenings used with man-made boards have to be selected with care. When joining panels face to face, all the fastenings used for wood will work for particleboard and fiberboard. Fastening into the edge is the problem because there the material is weak. Smooth nails are useless, and barbed ones not much better. Machine-driven staples coated with epoxy resin are popular. They are driven at such speed that the friction melts the epoxy and creates a glueline. When attaching particleboard face to edge, use 2-in. staples with a ⅜-in. bridge. They hold well with virtually no splitting.

When screwing conventional hinges or other load-bearing hardware to the edge of particleboard, it is good practice first to rout for and then glue in a wood insert. Sheet-metal screws

Joining man-made boards

Figure 1

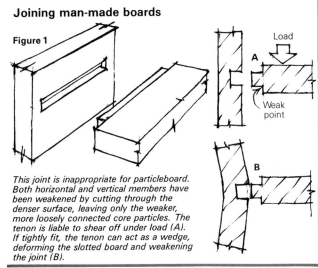

This joint is inappropriate for particleboard. Both horizontal and vertical members have been weakened by cutting through the denser surface, leaving only the weaker, more loosely connected core particles. The tenon is liable to shear off under load (A). If tightly fit, the tenon can act as a wedge, deforming the slotted board and weakening the joint (B).

Figure 2

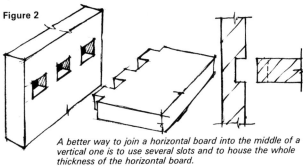

A better way to join a horizontal board into the middle of a vertical one is to use several slots and to house the whole thickness of the horizontal board.

Figure 3

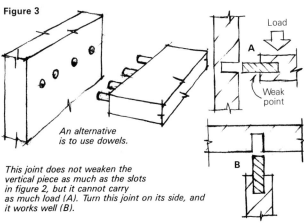

An alternative is to use dowels.

This joint does not weaken the vertical piece as much as the slots in figure 2, but it cannot carry as much load (A). Turn this joint on its side, and it works well (B).

Figure 4

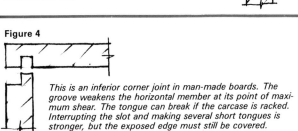

This is an inferior corner joint in man-made boards. The groove weakens the horizontal member at its point of maximum shear. The tongue can break if the carcase is racked. Interrupting the slot and making several short tongues is stronger, but the exposed edge must still be covered.

Figure 5

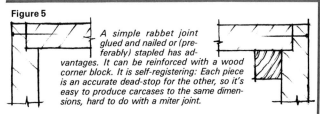

A simple rabbet joint glued and nailed or (preferably) stapled has advantages. It can be reinforced with a wood corner block. It is self-registering: Each piece is an accurate dead-stop for the other, so it's easy to produce carcases to the same dimensions, hard to do with a miter joint.

Figure 6

Miter joints are difficult to position precisely and worse to clamp. They can be doweled or splined, but drilling a round hole a short distance in particleboard is difficult. To be strong, a splined miter must be interrupted, and it has been made obsolete by the Lamello fastening (see figure 10).

Figure 7   Figure 8

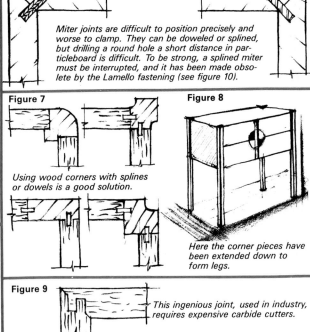

Using wood corners with splines or dowels is a good solution.

Here the corner pieces have been extended down to form legs.

Figure 9

This ingenious joint, used in industry, requires expensive carbide cutters.

Figure 10

Beech inserts are glued into curved pockets made by the blade for a Lamello machine. For maximum strength they should be placed 5 in. on center.

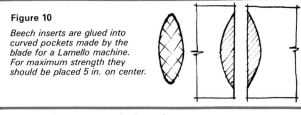

Lippings for man-made boards
Figure 11

Lippings can be simply butt-glued with yellow (aliphatic-resin) glue. A tongue or plywood spline does not add much strength, but does prevent the lipping from sliding when clamping pressure is applied.

Figure 12

A lipping wider than is needed can be attached and then ripped down after gluing.

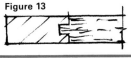

Rip here.

Figure 13

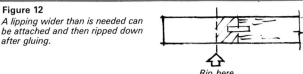

This is an inferior lipping construction because the tongue is weak.

Using flexible films as structural members

Figure 14

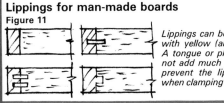

This joint is made by first covering the particleboard with vinyl or Mylar, then V-grooving, folding and gluing the edge. The flexible film acts as a hinge.

Figure 15

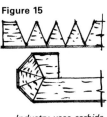

Industry uses carbide cutters to make ingenious folds like this.

Drawings: Ian J. Kirby

have more holding power than regular wood screws, but better still are twin-start, bugle-headed dry-wall screws (available from Equality Screw Co., PO Box 292, El Cajon, Calif. 94022) or the hi-lo screws (available from Shakeproof, St. Charles Rd., Elgin, Ill. 60120). Both these styles have two sets of threads, the hi-lo style with one major and one minor set. This combination severs rather than compresses the stock and increases the holding power of the screw. The twin-start screws were designed for power driving, and are sharp and slender enough to be driven without pilot holes.

Covering man-made boards—Furniture manufacturers often cover particleboard with sheets of printed vinyl, embossed and even "distressed" to give the appearance and texture of actual wood. This only encourages the erroneous notion that these panel products are suitable substitutes for traditional wood. A better approach is to consider them simply as structural vehicles to carry other materials. There is nothing wrong about covering one material with another—leather, gold leaf, mosaic—it's been done at least since Egyptian times. Wood veneers were used in the 18th century to achieve decorative effects that simply could not have been accomplished with solid wood.

The fault lies in the attempt to deceive. When we see a piece of painted furniture, we know very well that it is not made of paint. When we look at the same piece covered in plastic which has the grain and texture of wood, we are confused as to its real nature. Our eyes tell us one thing, our hands another and our noses a third. Slate floors are often only ¼ in. thick. What is underneath them does not matter. The surface of the floor looks like stone, it is cold to the touch and no glass survives a fall. There is a world of difference between this and even the finest imitation.

Both particleboard and MDF make excellent substrates for wood veneers. If you are using furniture-grade particleboard with a well-sanded surface (composed entirely of fine particles) it is not necessary to use an underlayment or base veneer. However, for thin veneers using a base veneer will produce a better final surface, helping to prevent telegraphing through of the particles underneath. The base veneer should be about the same color as the face veneer or it will show at the edges.

A recent development is paper underlayment instead of wood. Yorkite, available from the N.V.F. Co., Box 38, Yorklyn, Del. 19736, is one such product. It is very tough and is made in several thicknesses and colors to match the lippings and face veneers. If underlayment is used on one side it must also be used on the other side, to keep the panel in balance.

The easiest and usually the cheapest finish for man-made boards is paint. Fiberboard, with its smooth, stable surface, can be painted directly. Particleboard should first be filled by priming it thoroughly. Latex paint works well but should be allowed to cure for three or four days and then sanded. If the surface is still not smooth, repeat the process. Once the surface is primed, it can be painted in any of the usual ways—brushed, rolled, sprayed or silk-screened. You can save yourself work by buying the board factory-primed.

For indoor signs and posters, you can seal the raw surface with polyurethane and then stencil or silk-screen directly on it. This is one way the basically bland color of the board can be used as a background.

There are several types of flexible film. The thin, vinyl sheets that industry prints with wood-grain patterns to disguise man-made boards can also function as structural members. The panel can be grooved, folded on itself and glued, using the vinyl as a hinge. Intricate shapes are possible, but the process requires complex machinery carefully adjusted since the particleboard must be cut right through while leaving the vinyl film intact. This technique can be adapted for small shops by using a plastic tape such as Mylar. The tape can be applied either before or after cutting the board. The edges are then glued, the board folded and the tape removed after the glue cures.

Another flexible film is polyvinyl chloride, of which Naugahyde is best known. You can buy it in a variety of colors and textures and get it either unsupported (not reinforced), or with a woven or knitted back. The latter may be glued to the substrate, but the former is only for thermoplastic welding. One common variety of PVC has a thin layer of foam between the film and the cloth back to give it a better feel (known in the trade as "handle"). The PVCs with a backing of cotton cloth glue better than those with synthetic backing. In either case, use white glue, and apply it to the substrate with a roller. Then lay the PVC on and rub over it with a rounded block or rolled-up cloth (not with your hands).

You can also cover man-made board with leather. It too is applied with white glue, which is spread over the board. The leather is then covered with heavy brown wrapping paper, shiny side down, and pressed flat on the board with a warm iron. Don't use the soft kind of paper. It will draw moisture from the leather and stick to it.

There is also cloth. Thicker cloth can be glued on, but there is no need to press it hard like leather. If you do, the glue will be forced into the fibers and spoil the texture. You can often just stretch cloth over the board and staple the edges, using no glue at all.

Semi-rigid materials suitable for small-shop application include Formica and metals such as copper, aluminum and stainless steel. These can be purchased from most building-supply outlets in large sheets and as stamped tiles about 4 in. by 4 in. Visually pleasing, these tiles are easy to apply. They have a lot of technical advantages such as resistance to chemicals and physical abrasion as well as to wet heat, dry heat and pressure. Stainless-steel tile bends easily around corners and comes in a variety of patterns and textures. You can also apply metals in the form of foils. These come backed with adhesive or can be put on with contact cement. Formica is best applied with urea-formaldehyde glue and a veneer press. It can also be put on with contact cement.

Rigid materials include opaque or colored glass, slate, stone and ceramic tile. These are attached to the panel by a special adhesive. There is a large variety of these adhesives available today for gluing almost any material to any other— wood to concrete, for example, or leather to glass. These special adhesives can be ordered through building-supply retailers, if you know what you want. For a listing of the various products made, with a description of their use and working properties, write Gulf Adhesives and Resins Consumer Products, PO Box 10911, Overland Park, Kans. 66210. All-purpose panel adhesives are stocked in most hardware stores, but don't choose these if you can get a formulation specially suited for the materials you're using. □

Simon Watts is contributing editor of this magazine.

Two Sticks

Ancient method simplifies layout of big jobs

by Hank Gilpin

The stick method of measuring and drawing is by no means new. I'm certain it predates all other methods used in designing furniture, since the availability of large pieces of paper is a relatively recent luxury. Prior to the introduction of S-curves in the late 17th century and the multiple-angle joinery of the Chippendale period, most furniture was joined very simply and readily adaptable to stick layout. The introduction of complex joinery and curved forms in furniture has not diminished this method's usefulness because even today most wooden objects are based on rectangles and squares. Contemporary English cabinetmakers use this method for nearly all construction except chairs, which are difficult to lay out on a stick. However, the simple Carver chairs of colonial America and the delicate chairs turned by the Shakers are obvious results of the stick method. In reproduction work the stick is very handy. If you are asked to duplicate a Sheraton bow-front chest, all you have to do is hold a stick to the front and scribe all the elements of the chest onto the sticks. Then you need only a full-scale drawing of the front curve.

I was introduced to the stick method by Tage Frid during the construction of a library circulation desk that measured 15 ft. by 18 ft. Frid grabbed the scale floor plan we'd drawn up, took a few measurements and covered two sticks with mysterious pencil lines. He made a cutting list, somehow related to those marks on the stick, attacked a 24-sheet pile of plywood, cutting, grooving and tonguing and in less time than it would have taken to execute a full-scale drawing (I'd still be hunting for an 18-ft. table) all the parts for the desk were cut to size,

Hank Gilpin makes furniture in Lincoln, R.I., and teaches woodworking at Rhode Island School of Design.

tongued and grooved, and ready to be glued together.

None of this really sank in until I had my own shop and was faced with my first big job. But, once I had adapted to the sticks as a substitute for full-scale drawings and devised my own method of marking, I wondered how I ever worked without them. Every element of a job can be drawn on just two sticks: doors, drawers, carcases and frames, drawer sides, bottoms, pulls, hinges, edge-banding and shelves.

In this article I'll use a kitchen to illustrate the stick method of layout, but everything I'm going to discuss can be applied to any large job that is to be constructed in your shop and installed elsewhere. I'm focusing on a kitchen because it is a job you are likely to obtain; everybody needs one. Undoubtedly this will be a larger job than you've ever done, possibly including fifty feet of cabinets. No problem. If proper attention is paid to measuring, layout and some standardization, things will progress with staggering swiftness.

The first step is careful measurement of the room with sticks, two pieces of wood 3/4 in. square (it's a handy size), each at least 18 in. longer than half the largest dimension of the room. In an 8-ft. by 12-ft. room with an 8-ft. ceiling, two sticks each 7-1/2 ft. long will suffice for all necessary measuring, with a face of the pair of sticks used per wall. For large or complicated rooms I use two sets of sticks, one for the horizontals and one for the verticals.

Assuming walls B and D are to receive cabinets we'll proceed to measure, or "stick off," the room. Facing B, hold the sticks horizontally at chest height and push them apart until they meet walls A and C. Mark the two sticks appropriately and check for variations at floor and ceiling level, noting any differences on the sticks. This noting of variations in length

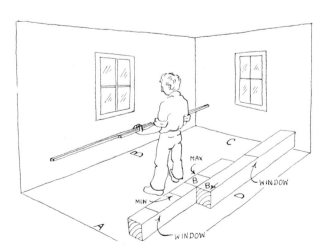

Gilpin sticks off room, noting window position. Stick marks (left) establish scribing allowances for fitting cabinets.

will prepare you to make the necessary allowances for scribing the cabinets upon installation.

If there is a constant, such as the window in wall B, the sticks must be marked to indicate its extreme dimensions, including moldings. Use a straightedge to carry the window lines to the floor and ceiling and again check for variations in the length of wall B. Any other permanent elements in the room should also be marked on the sticks. This might include radiators, electrical outlets, pipes, doors, ducts, etc. This process, if carefully done, gives you an exact, full-scale horizontal cross section of wall B.

To obtain a vertical cross section follow the same basic procedure, but use one of the unmarked faces on the sticks or two new sticks and push them from floor to ceiling, once again marking windows and such. Check and mark variations in height by moving the sticks all along the wall. If the floor has a truly dramatic pitch, not unusual in older buildings, I like to set a level line on the wall 36 inches above the highest point in the floor's rock and roll. With this line acting as an imaginary counter top, and thus a necessary constant, I set my sticks accordingly. This is important for fitting the cabinets around appliances such as stoves and dishwashers, which require a specific counter height.

The process of sticking off should be repeated on all the walls and in any other areas, such as the middle of a large room, that are to receive cabinets. After measuring the whole room and returning to the shop I transfer all the information to clean sticks cut to length, and often to a new stick for each marked face of the old ones. Since a 16-foot stick isn't easy to come by, I use short lengths overlapped and nailed together.

Now you must design the kitchen around the available dimensions. It is at this point that you discuss entrances and approaches: cabinet styles, paint, light, heat, type of wood, sinks, tiles, floors, everything, but most importantly, appliances. A real nuisance these refrigerators, stoves, ovens and dishwashers, but these are the fixed elements in the evolving picture. So they are where you start. It is imperative that you have all the dimensions of each and every appliance your customer desires and that once a decision has been reached you state firmly but diplomatically that no changes can be allowed without increase in cost. When considering all the other aspects of the room, remember that the final appearance of your work, which will dominate the room and thus be most open for criticism, depends to a great extent on forethought and coordination of details. This usually means working with a number of subcontractors who may not be as concerned with esthetics as you are.

Once all of this preliminary discussion is completed you have to sit down and design the job. Referring to the sticks for overall dimensions, make a rough floor plan that includes all the appliances and various cabinet, drawer and counter combinations. Be careful to consider function with the esthetics.

It is helpful to make this floor plan to some scale, and 3/4 in. to the foot is easy to read and not overly cumbersome. Many cabinetmakers draw scale elevations to accompany the floor plan, but I find most customers just cannot project two-dimensional elevations into a vivid picture of the finished project. I've scrapped the elevations and instead present perspective sketches incorporating as much detail as possible. These sketches, along with the floor plan and a wood sample, give the customer a fairly good picture of what to expect. After you've done a few jobs it is always possible to take prospective customers to see a finished product, the best way of solving the problem of explaining ideas.

I know all this talk of appliances and plumbers seems contrary to the discussion of woodworking but I've learned that the preliminary planning, though time-consuming and a bore, is absolutely essential to a quick, trouble-free job.

Here is one of the basic structural approaches I use when building a kitchen. This is only *one* way of doing the job, and not *the* way.

I use 3/4-in. veneer-core plywood for all carcases, usually birch for interiors and hardwood-veneered plywood for all visible exterior surfaces. It's wise to check the thickness of the plywood stock you buy as it often comes through a bit under 3/4 in. and this discrepancy might cause joinery problems. The carcases are joined by tongue and groove in two basic forms, each with a 1/4-in. tongue. One uses the standard centered tongue and the second uses an offset tongue. The offset joint is simply a way to add a small amount of strength to what is obviously a less than convincing corner joint. By setting the tongue to within 1/16 in. of the inside you gain enough strength in the vertical member to prevent the short grain from popping while gluing. Always leave a shoulder, no matter how small, as it adds a bit of strength and helps keep things square.

These joints can be cut in a number of ways, but I find it quickest and easiest to run the groove on the table saw with dado blades and the tongue on a shaper with two pattern bits coupled by a spacer made of long-grain wood that has been

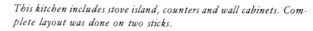
This kitchen includes stove island, counters and wall cabinets. Complete layout was done on two sticks.

fitted to the groove. A new wood spacer should be made whenever you sharpen your blades because the kerf gets smaller each time. I generally find it a good practice to cut the groove first and fit the tongue to it. I also cut the groove about 1/64 in. deeper than the tongue, to allow for glue build-up and any slight inconsistencies in the cutting.

I make the carcases without backs, and the tops need not be solid pieces of plywood—a strip 4 in. or 6 in. wide at the front and back is enough to fasten the counter top to. I make my own counter tops of solid wood, usually 1-1/4 in. or 1-1/2 in. thick, with corners and edges carefully detailed. Sometimes I 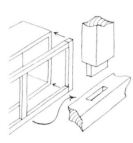 use floor tiles on the surface. After the carcases are glued up I face each with a solid wood frame that has been mortised and tenoned together. Remembering that any given edge of veneer-core plywood is at least 40% long grain, it becomes obvious that nothing more than glue and clamps is necessary to fasten the frame to the carcase. This frame adds the strength that was so menacingly deficient in the tongue-and-groove carcase.

In any case, the weakness of the carcases will become inconsequential once they are screwed to the wall or floor at installation, even if the solid frame is omitted. To do this, I usually glue the edge of a 3/4-in. thick by 1-1/4-in. wide strip to the underside of the top of the carcase, at the back. I mark the location of this strip on the wall and drive nails until I hit a stud, then hold the cabinet in place and drill through for a No. 12 screw. I had a football player chin himself from an upper wall cabinet that was supported by screws into two studs; it held.

Remember that the frame is the element of the cabinet left oversize to allow for scribing as the carcase cannot be cut to match irregularities in the walls. Minor irregularities at floor level can be adjusted by scribing the lower cabinet kickboard supports before fitting the kickboard itself. Occasionally an

independent base must be fitted to a room that is really out of kilter, but this does not occur very often.

Our main concern now is transferring this information to the sticks, concentrating on the carcases, the frames, and the spaces necessary for fitting appliances. (Doors and drawers should also be laid out, but style preferences complicate matters and we'll ignore them at this point.) The depth of cabinets is predetermined in most cases, 24 inches or so for floor cabinets and 12 inches plus for upper cabinets. These are only average sizes, not absolutes, and thus, not directly related to the stick layout. As in any full-scale working drawing, the main functions provided are location of all joinery and full-scale measurements for the cutting list.

I'll discuss only the sink cabinet, since it is typical and straightforward, but remember that everything applies to the entire job. After locating the space necessary for the dishwasher, leaving no more than 1/8 in. on each side for fitting, you begin by marking the extreme dimensions of the plywood carcase on the width stick, the one carrying the horizontal cross section of the long wall. The cabinet is to be 36 in. wide so draw two lines, A and A-1, 36 in. apart. Then measure in 3/4 in., or whatever is the actual thickness of the plywood, from each and draw the next two lines. These represent vertical plywood sections. Now mark the height stick. If the height of the cabinet is 34-1/2 in. (without the counter top), draw a line on the stick 34-1/2 in. from the floor mark. Then simply measure down the thickness of the plywood and draw the next line. This represents the carcase top. Assuming a 4-in. kickspace, your next mark should be 4 in. up from the floor level. Again, measure in the thickness of the plywood and draw a line to indicate the carcase bottom. If you have plywood drawer dividers or permanent shelves, they too are marked out at this point. These lines on both sticks represent the carcase elements and locate the joints. I should add that I find it very helpful to color-code the various markings. I use black pencil for plywood elements, red for frames and green for doors and drawers.

Once the carcase elements are laid out you turn to the

Centered and offset tongues join carcase elements, and sliding dovetails fit the sides of this drawer to an overhanging front.

Cabinet at left has large allowance for scribing; it will be surfaced with ceramic tile. Splashboard, right, is carefully detailed.

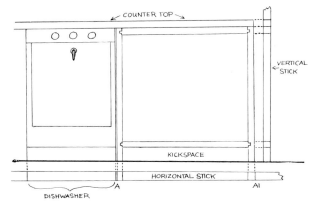

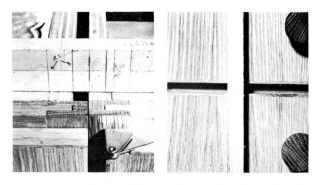

Sink cabinet, left, is marked out on horizontal and vertical sticks. Above, photo at left shows sticks atop finishing cabinet, with marks for plywood carcase and front framing; right, vertical stick locates drawer dividers and finished drawer fronts. Sticks and frames below include a 1/2-in. allowance for scribing to irregular wall.

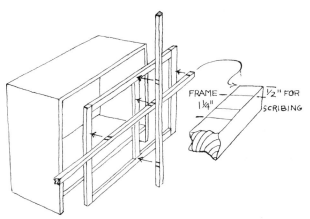

frames that face the carcase. If your design calls for 1-1/4-in. frames throughout, simply measure in 1-1/4 in. from the extreme dimensions on the carcase and, using the red pencil, mark the sticks appropriately. If you are allowing for scribing, this is the time to mark it on the sticks. If the wall to which you are fitting is 1/2 in. off square over the 3 feet needed for the cabinet, mark the frame 1/2 in. beyond the line indicating the outside of the carcase on the length stick and then measure 1-1/4 in. inward from the same line, thus ensuring finished symmetry.

All vertical and horizontal stiles, integral parts of the frames necessary for the division of the doors and drawers, should also be drawn on the sticks. If you have decided to use lipped doors and drawers (3/8-in. square lip) they can be indicated on the sticks by simply measuring 3/8 in. out from

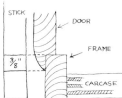

the inside frame marks on both the length and height sticks. With face-mounted doors and drawers you must first determine the spacing that is desired between each and then mark each accordingly, remembering that these marks indicate finished sizes and might include edge-banding.

Now, with all the carcases, frames, doors and drawers marked on the sticks, your next step is to compile cutting lists. One will include all the plywood elements (carcases, shelves, and probably door and drawer fronts). The other will include all the frames. I always follow the same procedure to compile the cutting lists. On the plywood list I include a cabinet designation, what each piece is, the number of said pieces, type of wood and size. I indicate the pieces to be tongued and those to receive edge-banding.

You know the depth of the cabinets, so all the carcase pieces will be 23-7/8 in. deep (or 11-7/8 in. in the case of upper wall cabinets) and because all the floor cabinets stand 34-1/2 in., the vertical elements will be listed as such. In general, horizontal pieces have tongues, and verticals have grooves. The first pieces you must measure are the carcase top and bottom. Measure between the plywood marks on the length stick and add 1/4 in. for each tongue, noting same when you add the dimensions to the list. Example: If you have 37-1/2 in. between the plywood marks with two tongues, add 1/2 in., giving you a piece 38 in. long. This may seem academic but it is not often that the pieces will measure exactly 38 inches. You will more often have to fit the cabinet into a space 37-11/16 in. wide and careful measuring becomes imperative, lest you assume too much. Door sizes are simply measured and noted, although you must remember to

subtract the thickness of the edge-banding if it is an element of the design because the marks on the sticks indicate finished dimensions. I make cabinet doors of solid ply, but they could be frame-and-panel for a more traditional appearance.

The frame list is compiled in the same way. All vertical end pieces will be 30-1/2 in. because all the kickspaces are 4 inches, all the cabinets are 34-1/2 in. high, and the frame does not extend to the floor. All other elements are determined by measuring between the frame sections drawn on the sticks, be they vertical or horizontal components, and adding the length of the tenons. In this case all the tenons are 3/4 in. long and shouldered on four sides (strictly personal choice—two shoulders satisfy many builders). Here again I note those pieces which will receive tenons. It is imperative to measure carefully because a 1/4-in. variation might not show up until you try and fit the frame to the carcase. Also, try to use the same ruler throughout the entire job as it is not unusual to find a 1/8-in. difference between two seemingly identical 6-ft. rules.

Once the cutting lists are complete and you have gathered the necessary stock you actually get to do some woodworking. One point I feel is helpful and hopefully obvious: When cutting plywood and lumber to size always start with the larger pieces and work to the smallest. This means you'll be cutting parts for different cabinets at the same time, which can get confusing, especially if you consider that an average-size kitchen might have 100 or more plywood parts and nearly as many frame parts. So this is not the time for casual conversation and extended coffee breaks. A few hours of uninterrupted concentration will prevent large headaches later. □

Boxes, Carcases and Drawers   **73**

Bookmatched doors hinged on concealed hardware make for clean, uninterrupted kitchen cabinets.

European-Style Cabinets
Frameless carcases, hidden hinges and continuous veneers

by Bill Pfeiffer

About four years ago, I happened upon a dazzling maple kitchen in a New York loft that changed the way I look at kitchen cabinets. The kitchen's sleek, seamless doors and drawer fronts and clever concealed hardware gave it an uncluttered appeal that I'd never seen. When I looked closer, I discovered yet more refinement beneath the pretty shell—the cabinets were of a remarkably simple, direct construction that squeezed the most out of materials and space, both in short supply in the small rooms that become today's kitchens.

The cabinets were built in what has come to be called the European style, a no-nonsense construction that's gaining favor on this side of the Atlantic. Euro cabinets evolved in postwar Germany as tradesmen, strapped by materials shortages, struggled to restore bombed-out housing. To save wood, they turned to man-made materials, often attractively veneered plywood and particleboard trimmed with thin strips of solid wood instead of a bulky face frame. And by joining panels with knockdown fasteners, cabinetmakers catered to the European custom of bringing the kitchen along when moving the rest of the furniture from one home to another.

In the United States, we don't take our kitchens with us when we move. Nonetheless, I find European-style cabinets appealing because of the sophisticated result I get without having to resort to long-winded joinery. You need only master a simple corner joint to build cabinets elegant enough to be adapted as built-in furniture for the living room, or even freestanding pieces for other rooms in the house.

Bill Pfeiffer makes cabinets and architectural millwork in New York City.

Layout and construction—In a nutshell, Euro-style cabinets are simple boxes made of ¾-in. plywood, banded on their front edges with ½-in. by ¾-in. solid wood strips. This banding replaces the wide, solid wood frame that trims traditional cabinets (figure 1). There are two advantages to frameless construction: you can bypass the tiresome job of mortising or doweling the face frame together and, once done, the cabinets are more spacious because there's no frame to encroach. As figure 2 shows, each base cabinet consists of two sides, a bottom, and a ¼-in. back let into grooves. A doweled or mortised frame holds the top of the cabinet square and serves as a mounting surface for counters. Wall cabinets are similarly constructed, but have a plywood top instead of a frame top.

Before I explain construction details, I need to say a word about design. If a kitchen is to be functional as well as attractive, cabinets must be sized and located to encourage an economic work flow. This is a complex subject that's beyond the scope of this article, so I refer you to three books for help: Terrance Conran's *The Kitchen Book* (Crown Publishers), Sam Clark's *Rethinking the Kitchen* (Houghton Mifflin) and Jere Cary's *Building Your Own Kitchen Cabinets* (Taunton Press). I suggest you start your design by selecting appliances, favoring ones whose proportions will relate to the width of the cabinet doors—which, along with drawer fronts, are the single most important visual element. Once you've decided what will go where, draw cabinet and appliance locations on a scale floor plan.

As figure 3 shows (page 77), wall (upper) and base (lower) cabinets should conform to some standard depths and heights, but the width of each cabinet will be set by the appliances and room size. The 36-in. standard countertop height seems to be comfortable for most people. You can vary it to suit, but don't make it too low, else dishwashers and other under-the-counter appliances might not fit. Positioning the lowest shelf of the upper cabinets 52 in. above the floor, with 16 in. between countertop and cabinet, is the best compromise between working room and comfortable access to the upper cabinets.

I try to work out the width of my cabinets so that all the doors will be between 14 in. and 19 in. wide. These dimensions produce the most pleasingly

Fig. 1: Euro-cabinet vs. face-frame construction

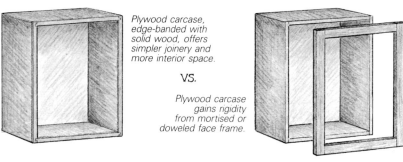

Plywood carcase, edge-banded with solid wood, offers simpler joinery and more interior space.

VS.

Plywood carcase gains rigidity from mortised or doweled face frame.

Fig. 2: Carcase construction

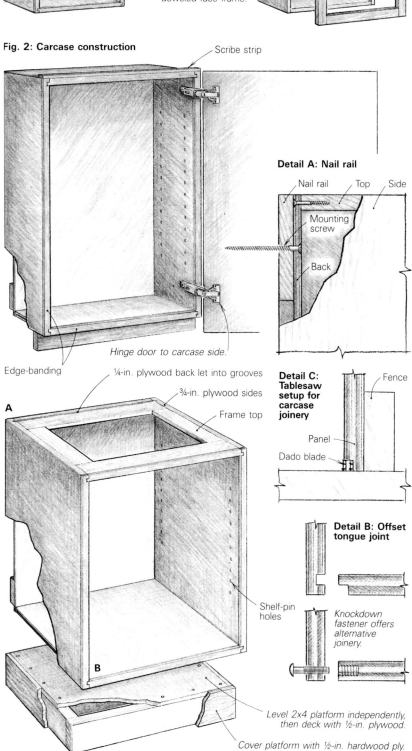

Scribe strip

Hinge door to carcase side.

Edge-banding

¼-in. plywood back let into grooves

¾-in. plywood sides

Frame top

A

B

Shelf-pin holes

Detail A: Nail rail

Nail rail   Top   Side

Mounting screw

Back

Detail C: Tablesaw setup for carcase joinery

Fence

Panel

Dado blade

Detail B: Offset tongue joint

Knockdown fastener offers alternative joinery.

Level 2x4 platform independently, then deck with ½-in. plywood.

Cover platform with ½-in. hardwood ply.

Photos: Carl Takakjian; drawings: Lee Hov

Scribe strip fits bumpy walls

In a new house, kitchen cabinets may be ready to hang as soon as they're finished. But in an older home where extensive renovation is contemplated, wall framing, rough electrical and plumbing work, and drywalling must be done first. Some makers install the cabinets before the walls are painted, but I prefer to wait until afterward, so there's no chance of paint spatters ruining the finish.

If I can offer any cardinal rule of cabinet installation, it's take your time and get at least one other person to help you. Even carefully crafted cabinets will look awful if sloppily hung.

So I won't have to clamber over the base units, possibly damaging them in the process, I install the wall cabinets first, beginning in the corners and working out. They're screwed directly to the wall studs with 3-in. No. 8 screws passed through the nail rails.

Begin by marking out stud centers on the walls. Measure and transfer these marks to the cabinets so you can pre-drill and countersink the screw holes. Taping two levels to the carcase—one vertically and one horizontally—will free up your hands for scribing, as shown in the drawing. Knock together a 2x4 T-brace to help support the load. The scribe should be trimmed to fit the wall as neatly as possible, but minute gaps,

say, ⅛ in. or so, can be filled with a bead of latex caulk and painted over.

A screw at each corner is plenty to hold a small carcase, but a larger one needs fastening in the middle of the cabinet's length. A shim between the nail rail and wall keeps the carcase from bowing back. Base and wall cabinets can be screwed together by driving extra-long screws through the hinge mounting plates.

Screw the base cabinets to a platform made of 2x4s decked over with ½-in. plywood. The platform, which forms the cabinet's toespace, is leveled independently with shims before it's screwed to the floor. Bolts passed through brackets fabricated from angle iron and into lead anchors will fasten the platform to a concrete or masonry tile floor. Once the platform is in place, the base cabinets need be scribed only where their back vertical edges contact the wall.

Setting the countertop completes the job. Plastic laminate is the most popular counter material, although wood, tile, marble, slate and granite are attractive, if expensive, alternatives. After they're scribed to the wall, the laminate, wood and the plywood ground for tile counters are anchored by screws driven up through the base cabinet top frames. Gravity and a bead of mastic will hold stone counters in place. —*B.P.*

rectangular proportions. Also, plywood shelves tend to sag if asked to span more than about 38 in. Carcases can be wider and have three or more doors, but you'll need to install partitions on which to mount shelves and doors. Bigger carcases are hard to keep square during assembly and installation.

As you build a kitchen, you'll discover that square cabinets won't fit into the room as readily as a drawer might fit into a carcase. This is because walls, floors and ceilings, no matter how carefully constructed, are rarely plumb, level and square with each other. The sagging foundation of an older home makes this problem particularly troublesome, so you need a way to fit the cabinets.

Adding a scribe—a small strip of wood attached to the carcase to extend its overall dimensions—is the simplest way to do this. The scribe strip is first marked with a compass, then trimmed to match the contour of the wall or ceiling (see box at left). Usually a ⅜-in. by 1-in. scribe strip screwed to the carcase is enough, but badly out-of-plumb walls may need more. Before you calculate precise carcase sizes, check the walls and ceilings with a level, then decrease the overall carcase sizes to fit the minimum distance in each direction and allow for the scribe you need. For base cabinets, the 2x4 platform serves as a leveling device. It can later be covered by cabinet-grade plywood or by flooring material (figure 2, page 75).

With scribe accounted for, you can calculate the size of each carcase and the parts needed to make it. In figuring the size of each part, don't forget to allow for the solid wood edge-banding when you work up your cutting list. Plywood components for base cabinets, for example, can be rough-cut slightly narrower than their finished sizes, since gluing on the solid wood edge-banding will bring them to the finished width. Wall cabinet sides, which usually get edge-banded on both their front and bottom edges, can be sawn a bit undersize in both width and length.

For an economical plywood cutting list, keep two things in mind: first, figure from large pieces to small, and second, to ensure uniformity, cut all similarly sized pieces at one saw setting. For most kitchens, expect to get six base cabinet sides or twelve wall cabinet sides from a 4x8 sheet of plywood.

I use ¾-in. lumber-core red birch plywood made in Japan. This material is

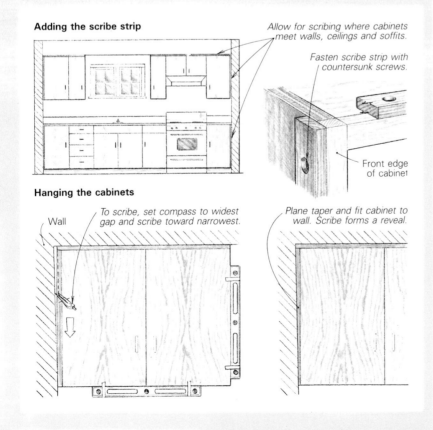

Adding the scribe strip

Allow for scribing where cabinets meet walls, ceilings and soffits.

Fasten scribe strip with countersunk screws.

Front edge of cabinet

Hanging the cabinets

Wall

To scribe, set compass to widest gap and scribe toward narrowest.

Plane taper and fit cabinet to wall. Scribe forms a reveal.

not only cheaper than its American counterpart, it's also of more uniform thickness, thus making for more precise joinery. Cabinet-grade plywoods may be hard to find, but I recommend this material, even if you have to special-order it through a commercial cabinet shop. Interply voids in fir structural plywood make it troublesome to join, and its wild grain is unattractive, even if painted. Cabinet-grade plywoods are sold in dozens of species and several grade ranges. For kitchens, an A-1 or A-2 grade with a lumber, veneer or fiberboard core is suitable.

Fig. 3: Cabinet dimensions

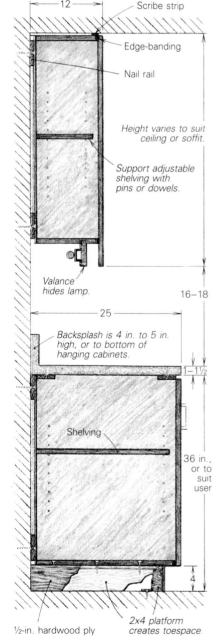

12

Scribe strip

Edge-banding

Nail rail

Height varies to suit ceiling or soffit.

Support adjustable shelving with pins or dowels.

Valance hides lamp.

16–18

25

Backsplash is 4 in. to 5 in. high, or to bottom of hanging cabinets.

1–1½

Shelving

36 in., or to suit user

4

½-in. hardwood ply

2x4 platform creates toespace.

Carcase joinery—Begin construction by cutting the plywood, labeling and stacking each piece as it comes off the saw. Next, glue on ¾-in. thick by ¹³⁄₁₆-in. wide edge-banding, which will later be ripped down to about ½ in. wide when the plywood parts are trimmed to final size. Wall cabinet sides get bands on their front and bottom edges. So end grain won't show at the front of the cabinet, do the bottom edge first, trim a bit off the width of the panel to flush up the joint, and then band the front edge. Once the plywood parts have been banded, trimmed to size (including the top frame for base cabinets) and carefully checked for square, you're ready to cut joints.

Plywood lends itself to production machine joinery. I cut most of the joints on my shaper, but the only essential tools are a tablesaw, a router and the usual hand tools. For lumber-core and veneer-core plywood, the offset tongue joint shown in figure 2, detail B, is strong and quick. Plate joints (see pages 19 through 21) or dowels are better for particleboard and fiberboard. Knockdown fasteners are suitable for either material, if you prefer that method.

Whether you machine the offset tongue on a tablesaw fitted with a dado blade or on a router table, plywood that varies in thickness will cause some joints to be loose. One remedy is to machine the tongue slightly oversize and then hand-plane it to a good fit. A second, as shown in detail C of figure 2, is to feed the plywood vertically between the fence and the dado head, with the tongue against the fence. Most ¼-in. plywood seems particularly scanty these days, being only 0.220 in. thick. If you don't have a 0.220-in. cutter but still want the backs of your cabinets to fit snugly, try cutting the groove in two passes with a ⅛-in. wide blade in the tablesaw. Move the fence slightly to widen the groove for the second pass.

With machining complete, you can sand the carcase parts before assembly. Glue-up is straightforward, but check carefully that everything is square, to avoid trouble when fitting the doors and drawers later.

After assembly, clean up the carcases with a hand plane and/or a finish sander and ease the edges with sandpaper. Before you begin drawer and door construction, drill holes for the shelf pins using the template shown in the photo, above right. I use 5mm brass shelf pins,

A plywood template, wedged inside assembled carcases, speeds boring of shelf-pin holes, which should be spaced about 1½ in. apart.

but dowels will also work, or, if you prefer, metal or plastic shelf standards. On narrow carcases, you may want to drill the shelf-pin holes before assembly.

Doors and drawers—I figure door and drawer face sizes at the same time I calculate case dimensions, but if you're uncertain about these sizes, wait until you've completed the cases. If you're using full-overlay doors and drawer fronts, size them so that they will completely overlap the front edge of the carcases. I leave about ³⁄₃₂ in. between two doors or between a door and a drawer front. This clearance is fine-tuned later by planing the doors and/or adjusting the hinges.

Concealed hinges work with plywood or solid panel doors, but they're also fine on frame-and-panel doors, provided that the hinge stile is wide enough for the cup flange, usually a 2¼-in. minimum. I make my doors of ¾-in. fiberboard edge-banded with solid wood and veneered on both sides. To allow for trimming later, I make the edge-banding ½ in. wide.

Choosing the veneer with the customer is the highlight of the job for

After glue-up, the fiberboard and edge-banding assembly shown above will be veneered then crosscut to yield a cabinet door and drawer front with continuous grain. Figure 4, below, shows a similar setup for a bank of drawers.

Fig. 4: Drawer face cores

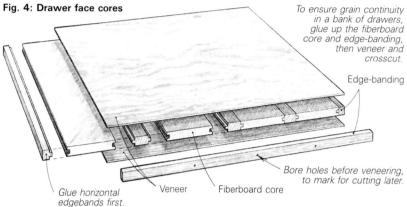

To ensure grain continuity in a bank of drawers, glue up the fiberboard core and edge-banding, then veneer and crosscut.

Edge-banding

Bore holes before veneering, to mark for cutting later.

Glue horizontal edgebands first.

Veneer

Fiberboard core

Fig. 5: Drawers and guides

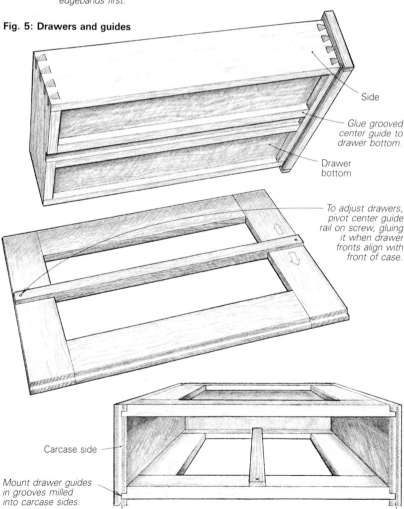

Side

Glue grooved center guide to drawer bottom.

Drawer bottom

To adjust drawers, pivot center guide rail on screw, gluing it when drawer fronts align with front of case.

Carcase side

Mount drawer guides in grooves milled into carcase sides.

me. We usually pick veneers from the same flitch, and it's fun to flip through the stack, envisioning how the raw log was sliced into so many thin sheets. We organize the veneers to be bookmatched or slip-matched in sequence for each door and drawer face. To assure grain continuity between a drawer face situated above a door or in a bank of drawer faces, I glue up a sandwich core (figure 4 and photo at left) which is then cut into components after it's veneered.

If I've got only a few doors to make, I veneer them myself on a shopmade press. Otherwise, I job out the work, sending the matched, taped veneers and cores to a local architectural millwork house, preferably one equipped with hot presses. If you don't want to bother with veneered or frame-and-panel doors, fiber-core hardwood plywood edged with solid wood is a stable alternative. To hang the doors, refer to the box on the facing page.

I like the whisper of a well-fitted wooden drawer sliding on a wooden track, so I use the drawer scheme shown in figure 5. The drawers slide on bearing rails grooved into the sides of the carcase. A grooved member glued to the drawer bottom slides on a center guide rail, making for smooth, accurate travel. But practically any method for hanging drawers is okay for kitchen cabinets, including metal ball-bearing slides, which are quicker to install than wooden tracks. Most metal slides require at least $\frac{1}{2}$ in. of clearance between the inside of the carcase and each side of the drawer, so be sure to allow for it.

Honduras mahogany router-dovetailed together makes strong, attractive drawers, but poplar, maple and Baltic birch plywood are excellent, less expensive alternatives. In fact, I recommend making drawers deeper than 10 in. out of plywood—they'll be less likely to warp. Once I've hung and fit the drawers to my satisfaction, I install the drawer fronts with screws driven in from the inside of the drawer. Make sure the edges of the drawer fronts align with each other and with the doors.

With all the doors and drawers in place, and before I apply the finish, I make any final adjustments that require planing or cutting. I coat the carcases, doors and drawers with nitrocellulose vinyl sanding sealer, followed by a fine sanding two to three hours later. A coat or two of Flecto Varathane completes the finish. □

Hanging doors on concealed hinges

The trouble with a lot of cabinet hinges—including some expensive ones—is that you can't adjust the doors once they're hung. Some hinges permit a smidgen of adjustability through slotted mounting holes, but these are awkward and liable to work loose in service.

Concealed hinges made by several European firms solve these problems cleverly. Though formidably complicated in design, these hinges are simple to install. Besides remaining out of sight when the doors are shut, they are adjustable in three planes, by as much as ³⁄₁₆ in. for some models. You need only locate mortises to within a fraction of an inch—you can fine-tune *after* the door is hung. Euro hinges work with an elbow action that throws the door's hinged edge slightly sideways, keeping it from banging into the adjacent door. Though invisible when the doors are closed, concealed hinges are big and mechanical-looking when the doors are open.

Most concealed hinges consist of two parts: a baseplate which you screw to the inside of the cabinet carcase, and a metal arm that pivots on a cup-shaped flange which you let into a round mortise in the door, as shown in the top photo at right. To hang a door, mark out and bore the hinge mortises. With a fence clamped to the drill press, use a 1³⁄₈-in. (35mm) Forstner bit (available from hinge suppliers) to bore a ⁹⁄₁₆-in. deep mortise for each hinge. The edges of the mortises should be about ⁵⁄₃₂ in. in from the edge of the door. Push the hinge temporarily into place. Locate the baseplate by holding the door in the position it will be when open, and transfer the center marks. A jig like the one shown in the photo, far right, will speed the mounting of baseplates. Screw the hinge cup into the mortise, then hang the door by sliding the hinge arms onto the baseplates.

Once the door is hung, you adjust it by turning screws in the hinge arm to move the door vertically, horizontally, or toward or away from the carcase.

You can buy spring-loaded, self-closing hinges or else use nylon roller catches to hold the doors closed. I find an Austrian brand of hinge called Grass to be the strongest and most adjustable. Grass hinges are sold wholesale by Kessler Inc. (229 Grand St., New York, N.Y. 10013), and are available retail (about $9 a pair) from Woodcraft Supply; you can get a complete list of local distributors from the importer, Grass America (1377 S. Park Dr., Kernersville, N.C. 27284).   —B.P.

Staff photos

Most European-style concealed hinges have two parts—a baseplate that attaches to the inside of the carcase, and an arm-on-flange that fits into a round mortise in the door. The top hinge opens about 100°; the lower, 176°. Made by Grass, both self-close, and are available for either inset or overlay doors. The bit bores a 35mm round mortise.

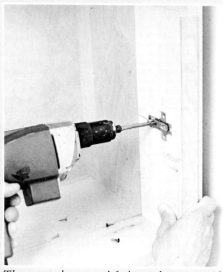

The setup shown at left bores the mortises for concealed hinges. In a production run, the plywood jig pictured above speeds mounting of the baseplates. It positions the plates at the correct depth, and equidistant from the top and bottom edges of each door opening.

In the arm of this hinge, the screw at the right controls the door's lateral position; the middle screw, its distance from the front edge of the carcase. The third screw, when loosened, allows the door to be moved up or down in the vertical plane.

Blanket Chests and Record Cabinets

Contemporary versions of traditional frame-and-panel designs

by Simon Watts

The blanket chest is 52 in. wide and 27½ in. high. Its ends are solid boards; the front, back and lid are paneled frames.

Many of today's craftspeople feel compelled to make each of their designs original, but I think very few of us are truly original, except when aided by the arrival of a new material, such as steel tubing, or a technical innovation. As a designer, I borrow freely from the past and enjoy making contemporary versions of classic pieces. Occasionally I even make exact copies. I see nothing wrong with copying, as long as it is done honestly, the materials and construction of the copy are comparable to those of the original, and no attempt is made to deceive the buyer by antiquing. Besides, furnituremaking is a deliberate craft, not a spontaneous art form. If you don't start with a clear idea of what you want, the result will most likely be a muddle.

I used traditional designs and methods as a starting point for developing my own ideas for the blanket chest and record cabinet shown here. Both pieces utilize panel frames, and today's methods of constructing this type of chest have changed little since medieval times. Other variations are possible. You could make a liquor cabinet, for example, by slightly altering the record cabinet: Adjust the bottom shelf to hold bottles and glasses, add doors, and extend the legs 5 in. to 6 in. Make the top of slate or other impermeable material to provide a good surface for mixing drinks.

The blanket chest combines two traditional methods: its ends are solid boards, and the front, back and lid are paneled frames. The frames and panels can be treated in many different ways. Some 18th-century panels were beautifully carved and inlaid. A molded frame

Simon Watts, of Putney, Vt., has been making furniture for 20 years. This article is adapted from his recently published book, Building a Houseful of Furniture *(Taunton Press, 224 pp.). The book has complete plans for the blanket chest and record cabinet as well as 41 other pieces, including beds, sofas, chairs and tables.*

and raised panels create a subtle interplay of shadows. Medieval chests, on the other hand, often had plain, flat panels and heavily chamfered frames.

For a decorative effect, I used red birch panels with walnut frames and ends. The proportions of each panel and the relation of the panels to each other and to the whole are very important. These proportions are difficult to visualize on a scaled-down drawing, so I always draw the panels and framing full-size on a large sheet of paper, hang it on the wall and live with it for a bit—ungainly proportions soon become apparent.

The ends are 1¼ in. thick to support the tenons of the frame rails. If you can't find boards wide enough, join up several boards. The frame members should be fairly uniform in grain and color so that they don't detract from the panels. Plane the material for all three frames (lid, front and back) to ⅞ in. thick.

Lay out and cut the mortises in the ends, then cut the bare-face tenons (tenons with one face flush to the rail) on the rails of the front and back frames. The bare-face tenon allows you to leave as much wood as possible between the mortise and the edge of the chest end. Even so, be careful not to lever the rails from side to side when fitting the tenons, because you could break out the mortises.

Next cut the mortises and tenons that join the stiles to the rails on the front

and back frames. When you lay them out, make sure that one side of the mortise cheeks and tenon cheeks will line up with the groove, as shown in figure 1. This way, you can be sure that the grooves for the panels will fall within the thickness of the mortises and tenons.

You can now push the carcase together dry while you work on the lid. Because the lid is held only by hinges along its back edge, it must be flat, so it's important to cut the joints accurately. The intermediate stiles are tenoned into the rails as for the other frames; the end stiles and rails are bridle-joined.

I make bridle joints using the tablesaw and a good carbide blade. Lay out the bridle joint for one corner (the saw will be set to this layout, so you needn't mark the other pieces). Use a marking gauge, or knife, and a square to mark the tenon shoulders on the stile—the tenon should be 1/16 in. longer than the width of the rail. The width of the tenon equals the width of the stile minus the depth of the groove for the panel. The thickness of the tenon is customarily two-fifths the thickness of the stock—⅜ in. here. You can mark the cheeks of the mortise and the tenon with one setting on a mortise gauge; remember to gauge both pieces from the outside face.

Cut the tenons first, holding the stiles vertically against the rip fence. I use a homemade wooden table insert with a blade opening just a sawkerf wide, so

Fig. 1: Assembling the chest

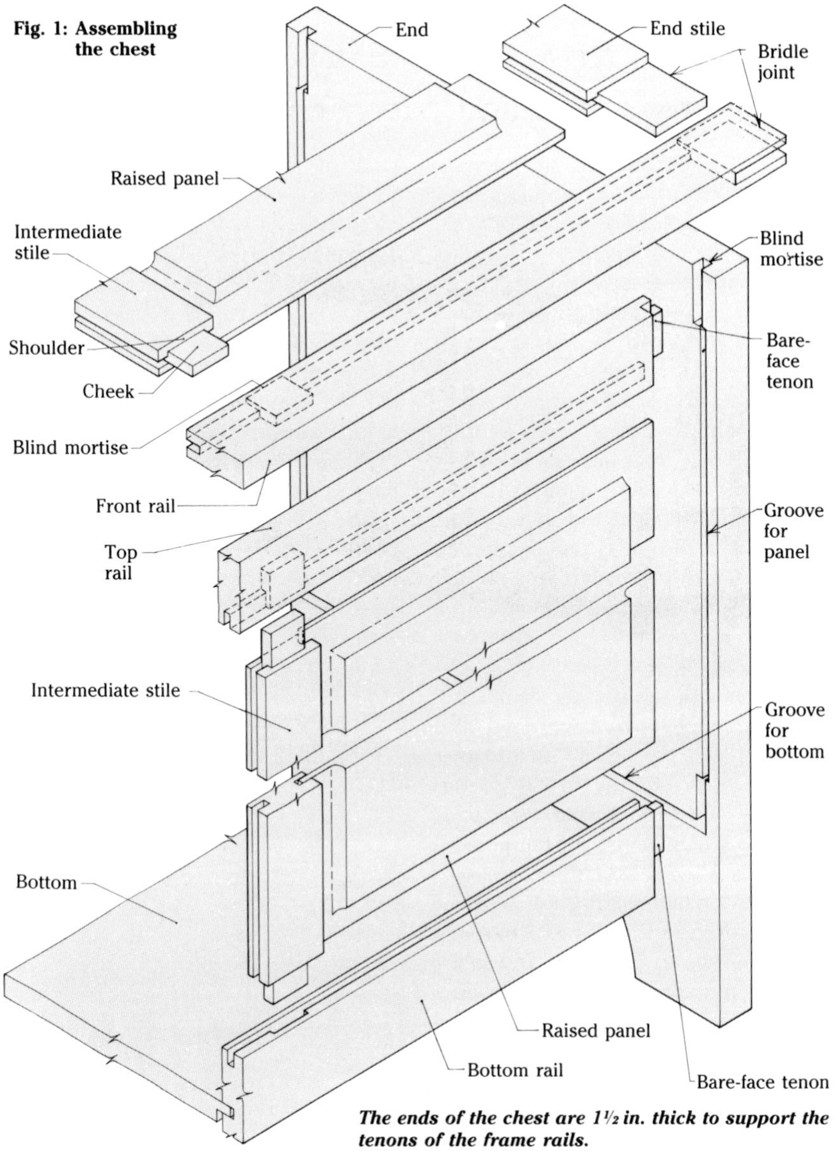
End
End stile
Bridle joint
Raised panel
Intermediate stile
Shoulder
Cheek
Blind mortise
Front rail
Top rail
Blind mortise
Bare-face tenon
Groove for panel
Intermediate stile
Groove for bottom
Bottom
Raised panel
Bottom rail
Bare-face tenon

The ends of the chest are 1½ in. thick to support the tenons of the frame rails.

Fig. 1A: Chest dimensions

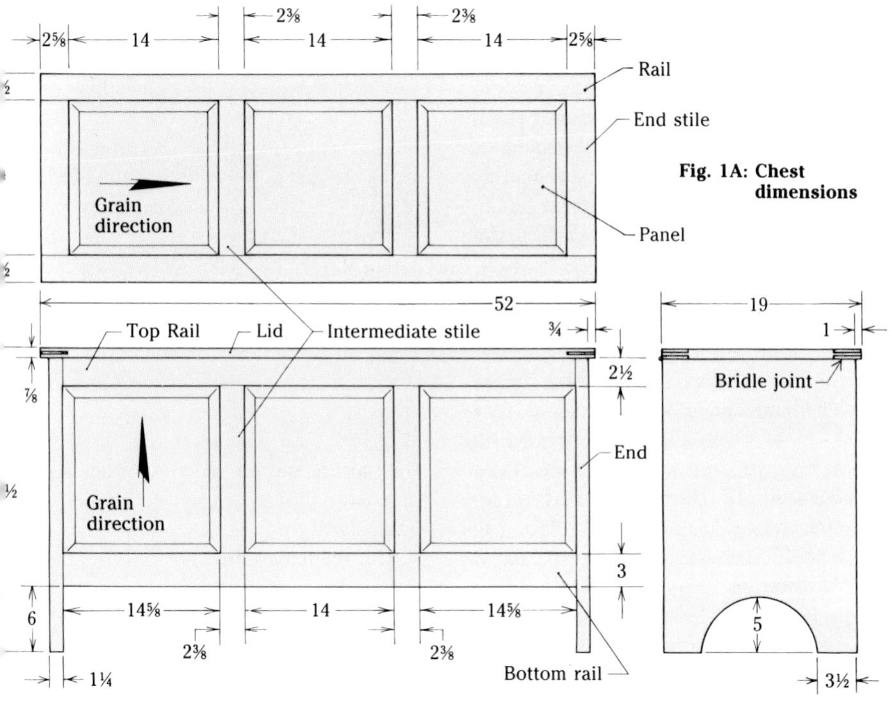
2⅝
14
2⅜
14
2⅜
14
2⅝
Rail
End stile
Grain direction
Panel
52
Top Rail
Lid
Intermediate stile
¾
2½
End
Grain direction
3
6
14⅝
14
14⅝
2⅜
2⅜
1¼
Bottom rail
19
1
Bridle joint
5
3½

that the pieces will be supported right next to the blade, and I screw an 8-in. high wooden fence to the rip fence. Set the saw ⅛ in. below the shoulder lines, and adjust the fence to cut right to the cheek lines. Saw the shoulders next, using an accurately set miter gauge. You can use the rip fence as a stop block, but don't saw through the waste or it will come whistling back at you. The remaining waste is easily cleaned up with a chisel or a shoulder rabbet plane.

Next saw the cheeks of the mortises in the same way as the tenon cheeks. Saw a scrap piece to reset the rip fence—the tenons should fit into the mortises snugly, without force. Remove the waste by boring a hole in from both edges, or by cutting it out with a coping saw. Chisel to the gauge mark to complete the mortises.

To lay out the grooves for the panels, I assemble the frames without glue and mark the four inside edges of each panel opening with a crayon—a groove in the wrong place, even when repaired, looks terrible. Disassemble the frames and cut the grooves. I use the tablesaw and dado head, though you could rout. Set the rip fence so that the outside face of the rail or stile will run against it. This method is possible because one side of the groove lines up with one cheek of the mortises and tenons on all but the bare-face tenons, as shown in figure 1. I make the grooves about ½ in. deep to allow for movement of the panels. Using the same setting, cut the panel grooves in the ends—but here you must remember to stop the grooves at the mortises—and trim square with a chisel.

Make the panels next. The grain of rectangular panels should run parallel to the panel's longest dimension to minimize the effects of shrinkage. The grain of the square panels on the lid runs along the length of the top, which is customary for paneled chest lids.

It's best to make all the panels at one time. I make the three panels for each frame from a long board, for consistency in grain and color. A single, wide board would be ideal, but I usually have to edge-join two or three boards.

Plane the long piece flat and ⅝ in. thick, then saw the panels to size. Their widths and lengths depend on the size of the frame openings and the depth of the grooves. I leave about ⅛ in. of clearance between the edges of the panels and the bottoms of the grooves, allowing shrinkage to be taken up inside the

Cutting panels with a router

The center on the face of each panel on the blanket chest is raised by using a router with a ⅝-in. corebox bit and a tablesaw.

Use a sharp bit and sawblade—you won't have to sand as much later. Mark the outline of the raised center on the panels and on a few pieces of panel scrap with a pencil gauge (a marking gauge with a pencil instead of a metal point—you can make one from an old marking gauge).

Now set the router fence so that the widest part of the corebox bit just touches the line. Check the setting on a scrap piece of panel wood, then rout four grooves in the face of each panel. To avoid burning and chattering, it's best to take a heavy cut initially, almost to full depth, followed by a light final cut, which will leave a clean, burn-free surface.

Saw off the waste on the tablesaw, holding the panel vertically with its back to the fence. Set up the tablesaw for tenoning as described in the text, using the wooden table insert and high fence. Check the setup on a scrap piece to ensure that the panels slip into their grooves without rattling. If a panel is slightly bowed, you can clamp it to a stiff batten while sawing, as shown in the drawing below.

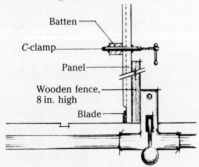

Now sand the panels. The end of an orbital sander will conform to the curve on the raised panel, and will remove any router marks.

It's not a bad idea to finish the panels before you install them, so that any subsequent shrinkage won't expose unfinished wood. Also, glue won't adhere to most finishes, so if you finish the panels before joining up their frames, there will be less chance of the panels sticking to the frames, then cracking with seasonal movement. —S.W.

groove. The ends of the panels should almost make contact with the grooves. Then I raise the panels following the tablesaw and router procedure described in the box at left.

I use aromatic cedar for the bottom, to keep moths at bay. You could attach ledger strips to the rails and rest the bottom on them, but I prefer to rabbet the bottom into grooves in the ends and bottom rails, and glue it to the ends.

Before gluing up the carcase, sand the pieces. You should also sand and put a light chamfer on the frame edges that surround the panels, as this is difficult to do once the panels are in place.

Glue the lid together, pull the shoulders of the joints tight with pipe or bar clamps, and then C-clamp the bridle joints with softwood pads to squeeze the cheeks tight. I glue the whole carcase at once with a plastic resin glue, which has a long assembly time. Center the panels in the openings, and after the clamps are off, peg through the back of the rail into the center of each panel end, so the panels can move equally in each stile groove. I use brass sliding stays and ¾-in. offset brass hinges for the lid.

Frame-and-panel techniques also provide an attractive solution to a modern decorating problem: cabinets are needed to store record albums and to display modern, often elegant, high-fidelity equipment. The 66-in. walnut record cabinet shown in the photo on the facing page is designed to stand behind a couch. The turntable, amplifier and so on are placed on the 15-in. deep top surface, with space for about 300 records below. The lower shelf, 8 in. above the floor, slopes toward the back to keep the records in place and to make it easier to see the name on the spine of each record jacket. Unlike the blanket chest, this cabinet needs its center legs to support the weight of the albums. All the legs are cut from 1¾-in. square stock.

The two ends and center section are frame-and-panel constructions—in each, two 25-in. legs and two short rails surround a solid-wood panel. These three sections are joined by long rails—four 2½-in. wide bottom rails are tenoned into the end and center legs, while two 3-in. wide top rails run from end to end, notched into the center legs. The top, made of narrow random-width slats, is supported on ledger strips screwed to the top rails. The shelf, made of 3-in. wide strips, rests on the front bottom

rails and on ledger strips screwed to the back bottom rails.

Cut the legs and rails to size, then lay out and cut the mortises and tenons. Center all the tenons on the rail ends. I made them ⅜ in. thick, with ¼-in. wide shoulders—a thicker tenon would put the mortises too close to the face of the legs. To avoid misplaced mortises, first mark the faces of the legs that are to be mortised. Then place the legs together, with the marked faces up. Align their ends and mark the mortises with a square. Do the same for the other mortised faces. Make the front and back rails flush with the faces of the legs, but set the end rails back from the faces.

The joints between the rails and center legs are complicated. The top of each center leg is notched twice: one notch takes the long rail, which finishes flush with the face of the leg, and the other forms a bridle joint for the short rail (fig-

Fig. 2: Joining center legs

Rabbet

Top rail, front or back

Top center rail

Ledger strip

Ledger strip

Groove for panel

Rabbet (both faces)

Center leg

Ledger strip (lower back rail only)

Lower rail, front or back

Lower center rail

Cut the notch for the long top rail before cutting the bridle joint for the short rail.

This walnut record cabinet is designed to stand behind a couch. The turntable and other high-fidelity equipment are placed on top.

Fig. 3: Notching the corner legs

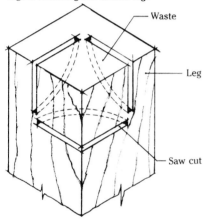

— Waste

— Leg

— Saw cut

Notch the legs by making three cuts on the tablesaw, then chiseling the waste.

ure 2). Both can be cut on the tablesaw, the same way tenons are sawn. The bottom center rail and two long bottom rails are tenoned into each center leg. Make sure the three mortises don't meet inside the leg, as that would weaken it.

When all the mortises and tenons have been cut and fitted, rabbet the top rails. (The rabbets position the ledger strips that support the slat top, and they make the rails appear thinner.) Cut ¼-in. by ½-in. rabbets on the inside faces of the front, back and both end rails; cut a ⅛-in. by ½-in. rabbet on both faces of the center rail. The top center rail butts into the front and back top rails, and its ends must be notched into the rabbets in those rails, or a gap will show.

Dry-assemble the whole cabinet frame. Mark the notches for the slat top on the corner legs. Mark where to cut off the

top ends of the bridle-joined center legs even with the rabbets of the rails. Notch a corner of each leg by making three cuts on the tablesaw, as shown in figure 3. Then clear the waste with a chisel. At the same time, mark with a crayon the position of the panel grooves in the legs and rails. Trim the center legs to length, and saw or rout the grooves, stopping the grooves in the mortises.

Glue up the ⅜-in. thick panels, running the grain parallel to their long dimension and leaving room for seasonal wood movement.

Sand the legs, rails and panels, and chamfer all the arrises of the legs and rails. I finish-sand all the pieces before gluing up. After sanding the rails, align the ledger strips with the rabbet on the top rails and screw them in place. Screw the ledger strips for the shelf along the bottom edge of the back bottom rails. Bore and countersink clearance holes in the center legs for the screws that will fix the long top rails to the notch.

It's easiest to glue the frame-and-panel ends and center section together first. Set the cabinet on a flat surface while gluing and clamping the remaining rails, to prevent twisting. Make sure the openings for the slat top are square. Clamp the long top rails tight to the notches in the center legs, then screw them in place and remove the clamps.

I made the top of narrow slats of solid walnut. A stable wood such as walnut, teak or mahogany, when cut in narrow strips and left loose in a top like this, won't expand enough to destroy

The record-cabinet ends are frame-and-panel construction. Setting the face of the rail about ¼ in. back from the faces of the legs adds depth to the end.

the top. Bevel the ends of all the slats and one edge of each outer slat at 5° for a better fit. Groove the edges of the slats for splines, which will keep adjacent slats even. The splines shouldn't be glued in. After fitting the slats to the openings, put a light round or a small chamfer on all four top arrises of each slat.

Finish all the surfaces of the slats before final installation. I didn't screw the top down, but you can put one screw in the end of each slat.

Cut the shelf slats to dimension and rabbet their front ends to fit over the front bottom rails. These slats are wider than the top slats, and their combined widths run the length of the cabinet. Allow $\frac{1}{32}$ in. to $\frac{1}{16}$ in. per slat for movement. Finish all the slats before final installation. You needn't fasten the slats—the weight of the records will keep them in place. The shelf slats are short and stiff, so splining for alignment is also unnecessary. □

Two Designs for Chests of Drawers

Chest of bags

by Len Wujcik

As a designer and builder of furniture, I find that a most challenging part of my work is problem-solving: experimenting and/or playing with form by manipulating materials and processes to answer a specific need. Having a clear statement of the problem and objectives is important because it focuses design efforts. Here's how I went about developing a piece I call the chest of bags.

I'd noticed that knockdown furniture designs included no chests, particularly chests with drawers. This seemed odd and interesting, so I pursued the idea. The problem was to design and build a chest of drawers that would meet three criteria: One, the chest should be easy to assemble and disassemble, mainly for reduced shipping size. Two, construction should be good-quality, whether the joinery be traditional or non-traditional. Three, the design should lend itself to mass production. Industry can make good products, if only it would stop feeding consumers period-style clones cheapened by dishonest constructions and materials. I wanted to dispel the idea that knockdown furniture necessarily compromises quality.

The chest, despite its contemporary appearance, is based on traditional construction. The only difference is that the elements of frame, panel and drawer have been rethought as skeleton, skin and organ, respectively. This anthropomorphic wording may seem playful, yet it proved helpful in designing the bag chest. In fact our body has a lot to do with the form of many products, from eating utensils to architecture.

Making the chest's components easy to assemble and disassemble was accomplished with a skeletal case composed of pre-assembled frames, which reduces the size of the shipping package without requiring its recipient to fiddle with an excessive number of parts. There are two side frames, the rails of which act as drawer slides and are glued to the stiles using groove-and-tenon joints. These two frames are connected by another set of rails: Rosan inserts receive flat-head Allen screws, making these joints knockdown. A diagonal brace across the back provides rigidity.

Now that the case could be made to collapse, I needed a drawer system that could do the same, since the volume of a chest is determined by its drawers. Thinking of the drawer as just a container was an important breakthrough. Containers are made of metal, paper, plastic, glass, leather and fabric, any of which can be used in a drawer system. I chose fabric because it could be worked easily and folded. With my wife Beverly's skilled assistance, we made our first collapsible bag drawer. It hangs in a double wooden frame, which slides on the side rails. A slatted cedar frame laid in the bottom of the drawer bag prevents sagging and also scents the clothing stored in it.

I'd decided on a skeletal case and a bag drawer; the chest was complete except for an enclosure. Considering the visual and physical lightness of the chest, and its anthropomorphic nature (it already had a skeleton on which its functioning parts hung), it was obvious that if it were to be enclosed, the chest should have a skin. I opted for the same fabric as the drawers are made of, to maintain a unity of materials, and avoid the problems of wood movement and weight. Actually, I can accept the chest

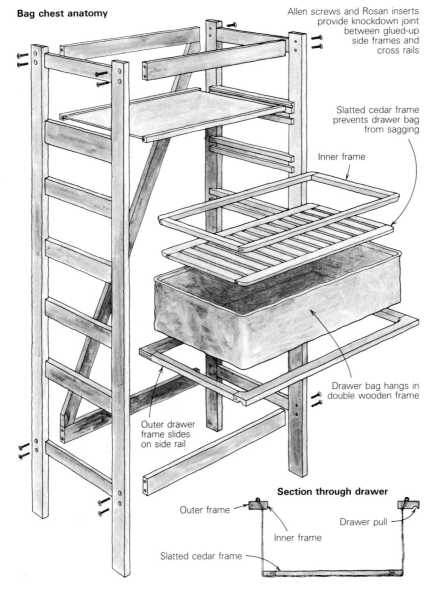

Bag chest anatomy

Allen screws and Rosan inserts provide knockdown joint between glued-up side frames and cross rails

Slatted cedar frame prevents drawer bag from sagging

Inner frame

Drawer bag hangs in double wooden frame

Outer drawer frame slides on side rail

Section through drawer

Outer frame

Drawer pull

Inner frame

Slatted cedar frame

Len Wujcik

as complete with or without the skin. An advantage of cloth is that it is removable, washable, and replaceable in all sorts of colors, patterns and textures.

Since 1977 I have made five types of chests, each with its own character—a "family" of bag chests. They were not an attempt to be different for the sake of difference alone. I arrived at their form and function through strict problem-solving and a little fantasy. There is a misconception that design means different. Good design may be different, but different may not be good design. □

Len Wujcik teaches three-dimensional and furniture design and construction at the University of Kentucky College of Architecture.

Wujcik's family of bag chests have in common a skeletal case that is easily knocked down for shipping. The drawers are frames on which fabric bags hang, making them collapsible too. Chests and drawers can be fitted with fabric of various colors, patterns and textures. Prices of the chests range from $350 to $1200.

Open carcase, musical drawers

by Michael Pearce

Most people like opening drawers—to find out what's inside them, or simply to see how they slide. A chest of drawers invites you to use it, just as a chair entices you to sit down.

In 1973 I built a chest with a skeletal carcase that supported but did not conceal the drawers. The idea was to give a sense of form created by the absence of mass, and also to expose the workings of the thing. Somehow this stylization of function—common to so much contemporary furniture—seemed to make the piece more inviting and kinetic.

Jewelry boxes with the same open construction were a natural spin-off. The smaller scale opened up another possibility. One day, while playing with a music-box movement, it occurred to me that it could work as well in a drawer as in the traditional hinged box. The only difference is that in a standard music box the movement is started and stopped by the shifting of a lever or rod activated by the lid; in a musical drawer the rod remains stationary while the movement is shifted from the stopped position to the released position.

Since people never expect to hear music from the mouths of drawers, it's

fun to see them giggle when a Cole Porter tune jumps out at them. I use Swiss movements by Reuge ($12, 1982); I find them more reliable than cheaper ones. Think beyond boxes and drawers: anything hollow can house a musical movement, and almost anything that moves can start it singing. □

Michael Pearce makes furniture in San Francisco. Reuge music-box movements are sold by Craft Products Music Boxes, 2200 Dean St., St. Charles, Ill. 60174, or Klockit, PO Box 629, Lake Geneva, Wis. 53147.

Music and structure play in Pearce's two open-carcase jewelry boxes, approximately 13 in. high. A musical movement in the bottom drawer of each is activated when the drawer is opened. The box on the left is of chechen, zebrawood and rosewood; the one on the right, rosewood and shedua. A ⅛-in. dowel stops the music when the drawer is closed (above).

Photos: Michael Pearce

Stereo Equipment Cabinets
Take the heat off your audio gear

by Carl Spencer

RCA

This RCA record player/radio combination was a forerunner of modern audio equipment cabinets. This cabinet, constructed of veneers and solid wood, was closed up to hide and protect the electronics.

Housing audio and electronic equipment in specially designed casework is not a new idea. Thomas Edison's first commercially available phonographs came complete with their own wooden cases, and even Marconi's early radio sets had their own boxes. The casework was originally devised to protect the fragile gear from damage, and the consumer from electric shock. Retailers quickly learned that the appearance of the package was often more of a selling point than the sound of the equipment.

Even today there is lively competition at antique shops for the beautiful old AM-shortwave radios from the 1920s and 1930s. That some of the old radios still operate is only a portion of the appeal. Modern stereo furniture—for which there is a growing market—has its roots in the prepackaged high-fidelity consoles first marketed just before World War II. With the advent of FM radio and stereophonic sound, the console became common in the American home. By the 1950s, the console had evolved into a tuner, phonograph, amplifier and two speakers all permanently installed in a single wooden cabinet that fit the decor of the day. Many even incorporated television sets. Consoles remain popular, probably because they combine and conceal, with a minimum of wires and controls, what some people see as unsightly and confusing equipment. The console's advantage, an all-in-one package, proved to be its weakness as well. If the amplifier or the television died beyond repair, one could only replace the entire unit or limp along indefinitely with half of an entertainment system. Some old consoles could be retrofitted with new gear, but variation in case construction and proportions made that remedy costly in money and trouble. The console's shortcoming teaches a valuable lesson to the designer of modern stereo cabinets: good casework will outlast the electronics, so it makes sense to design for equipment changes.

By the 1960s, "component" audio systems confronted consumers with more storage problems. The audiophile could buy separately the best amplifier, tuner, speakers and turntable—each from a different manufacturer. While some people didn't care about the resulting tangle of patch cords, others wanted their systems to look as neat as the old consoles did. Thus the modern stereo cabinet industry was born.

The early 1970s saw a resurgence of the console approach as stereo "racks" began replacing the cinderblock and pine board shelving that had been pressed into service by early

component fans. The racks were supports that organized the equipment with maximum exposure—for better or for worse. Little attention was paid to good equipment placement, tidying up the wires, or dustproofing and ventilating the electronics. The racks were more attractive than boards and bricks but still offered little protection for sensitive equipment. As the "baby boom" kids of the 1950s began having their own children, they found that nothing can so thoroughly devastate a phono stylus or decorate a room with yards of magnetic tape quite like a two-year-old. Audio equipment also needs protection from thieves; it is easily stolen and resold. Equipment racks are simple to spot in a room, and some even have casters. A burglar can just unplug the system and roll it out to the trunk of his car—a perfect 60-second crime.

The problems of designing cabinets for stereo components can be solved in ways that improve the appearance and function of the equipment while protecting it from children and thieves. Wires can be run out of sight, panels can be installed for dustproofing and ventilation, and all of the equipment can be housed in attractive cabinetry that permits quick changes when the system is replaced or updated.

Case design and equipment placement—The shape and style of stereo casework is up to the aesthetic bent of the client and the maker. Vertical designs are generally superior to the traditional horizontal layouts. Few people "drive" their audio gear like a car, nor do they sit in front of it while using it. Adjustments are made after the listener has walked up to the equipment so it is sensible to assume the user will be standing. Vertical formats are also less expensive to build: there is no finished countertop to add to the carcase.

Heat is the bane of electronic gear, and ignoring it can shorten the life of expensive systems. Always locate the receiver, amplifier and other heat-producing components near the top of the case. This keeps the rising heat away from the other units, and also puts the various scales and controls at eye level, easy to read. Other frequently adjusted equipment that can be set by ear or by feel can be mounted wherever convenient. If the system you are housing has both amplifier and tuner, mount the tuner below the warmer amplifier. Some systems use preamplifiers and they ought to be mounted below but as near to the main amplifier as possible. This will ensure short patch cords and a clean signal between the units. Some systems solve this three-component problem by combining all three units in a receiver. If so, the receiver should be mounted above the other units.

Turntables should be as close as possible to waist height. Mounted too low, one's view of the turntable is blocked by the shelf above it, making it difficult to put a record on the spindle. If it's too high, the oblique view makes it equally hard to operate, and the inevitable result is scratched records. Leave enough room for opening the turntable dust cover if you mount it on open shelving. Never put turntables on pull-out platforms. Turntable designers go to great lengths to produce balanced, vibration-free equipment. The sloppiness in even the best ball-bearing drawer slides will defeat this sophisticated engineering for which you've paid so dearly.

Cassette recording decks are available in both front-load and top-load designs. They should be mounted as near to eye-level as the case and amplifier placement permit. If frequent taping of records is anticipated, the deck could be placed on a fixed shelf at the same level as the turntable.

Televisions complicate stereo cabinet design because they compete for the ideal equipment locations, and they are nearly always wider and deeper than stereo components. Usually, it's best to keep the TV elsewhere, but if it must go in the stereo cabinet, the best position seems to be centered at sitting eye level. Horizontal formats favor television-stereo combinations because they permit more spacing between the heat-producing components. Don't mount any equipment above televisions; they generate large amounts of heat.

Mounting, dustproofing and ventilation—Stereo equipment can simply sit on a shelf or it can project through a vertical panel mounted in the front of the cabinet. Shelves should be cut to allow for wire runs and for cooling ventilation, either by leaving a 1-in. space between the back of the shelf and the carcase back or by boring holes in the shelf. To panel-mount equipment, an opening the exact size of the component chassis is cut in the panel and the unit is slid in, supported behind the panel by shelves or cleats to keep the weight of the gear from bulging the panel. Panel mounting looks neat, and the equipment is less available to thieves. What thief has time to extract equipment from something that looks so intimidating? I've had customers who have lost their speakers, televisions and silver to burglars, but so far none have lost stereo components that I've set into panels. Another tip on security: don't bother with locks on stereo cabinet doors. If a burglar encounters a locked cabinet, he'll assume there's something really valuable inside and break the doors with a crowbar, perhaps leaving the equipment anyway.

Besides improving security, panel-mounting aids dust-proofing and ventilation. Dust finds its way into cabinets and settles on equipment heatsinks, reducing cooling efficiency and shortening equipment life. Closely fit panels seal out the dust and actually improve ventilation by suspending the equipment in a cooling bath of moving air. Panels should be mounted so they can be removed from the rear of the case, and modified for new equipment.

Cabinets with open compartments can be fitted with false backs to give a finished appearance. The actual cabinet back should be removable and have an access panel to permit equipment installation and connection.

Cabinets can be ventilated by drilling a row of 1-in. diameter holes in the lower back of the equipment compartment to draw in cool air and to exhaust heated air out the top through a slot. The ventilation flow should be baffled to force the air to turn a corner on its way out—this keeps dust from filtering into the equipment compartment when the system is off. Higher-powered equipment (more than 50 watts per channel)

Vertical cabinets can have shelving for turntables and top-loading cassette decks. Other components are panel-mounted for protection against dust and theft.

may need a "whisper" fan mounted in the top of the case to draw hot air out. A commonly available 55-cfm fan can cool the largest amplifier. Figure on using a fan if the temperature inside the cabinet when the stereo is on is more than 10° warmer than the room temperature.

Books, records or additional equipment can be stored behind doors, on open shelving or in drawers. Store record albums at the bottom of the cabinet where it is cooler. Their weight will add to the stability of the case—an important consideration here in earthquake-prone California.

All of the design requirements I've mentioned can be altered to suit special equipment or the whims of builders and clients. Rapid-fire innovation in electronics quickly changes shapes and sizes of components, so there's a constant demand for cabinet work both for equipment protection and for the convenience and satisfaction of those who use it.

Plans and directions on the next two pages show how to build a basic audio cabinet.

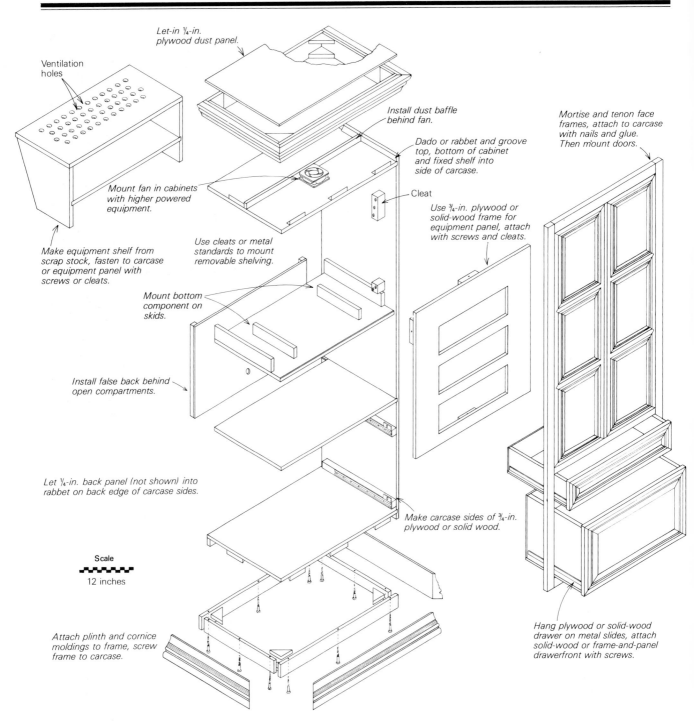

Ventilation holes

Let-in ¼-in. plywood dust panel.

Install dust baffle behind fan.

Dado or rabbet and groove top, bottom of cabinet and fixed shelf into side of carcase.

Mortise and tenon face frames, attach to carcase with nails and glue. Then mount doors.

Mount fan in cabinets with higher powered equipment.

Cleat

Use ¾-in. plywood or solid-wood frame for equipment panel, attach with screws and cleats.

Make equipment shelf from scrap stock, fasten to carcase or equipment panel with screws or cleats.

Use cleats or metal standards to mount removable shelving.

Mount bottom component on skids.

Install false back behind open compartments.

Let ¼-in. back panel (not shown) into rabbet on back edge of carcase sides.

Scale

12 inches

Make carcase sides of ¾-in. plywood or solid wood.

Attach plinth and cornice moldings to frame, screw frame to carcase.

Hang plywood or solid-wood drawer on metal slides, attach solid-wood or frame-and-panel drawerfront with screws.

A basic audio cabinet

Stereo cabinets can be made of solid wood or plywood, with traditional joinery or the simplest knock-up construction. Whatever way, the placement of the equipment governs the cabinet's size and shape. I make five or more cabinets at once in small production runs using what's basically kitchen cabinet construction: plywood carcases with solid-wood face frame and door frames. I measure the equipment that will go into a case, leaving room for accessories that might be added later.

First I cut parts for the face frame from 5/4 lumber planed to 1¹⁄₁₆ in. thick. The frames are mortised and tenoned together, but dowels could also be used. I make the face frame ¹⁄₁₆ in. wider than the plywood case and trim it flush later, so I won't have to sand the veneer. While the face frame is in clamps, I cut the door rails and stiles from ¾-in. stock, and join them with mortise and tenons. I glue ¼-in. plywood to the back of the frames for panels, but you can float the panels in ¼-in. grooves milled in the rails and stiles.

Cabinet access and ventilation

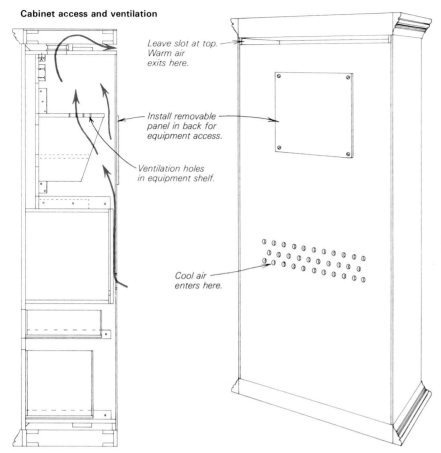

Leave slot at top.
Warm air exits here.

Install removable panel in back for equipment access.

Ventilation holes in equipment shelf.

Cool air enters here.

A removable shelving unit, made from plywood scraps, supports the equipment. The shelf is attached with screws or wedged between cleats. Holes in upper shelf are for amplifier ventilation.

Next, I rip the major carcase components—sides, top, bottom, shelving and equipment panel—from ¾-in. A-2 cabinet plywood. You can use solid wood, or substitute cheaper plywood or even particleboard for unseen parts, like the carcase top and bottom.

I join the top, any fixed shelves, and the bottom to the carcase sides with fully-housed dado joints that are nailed and glued. This joint is quick, and it has proven to be strong enough for the stresses involved. Before assembly, I rabbet the back edges of the carcase sides for the ¼-in. plywood back, which can later be attached with screws.

With the case squarely assembled, I attach the face frame with glue and nails and make certain that the edge of the frame is flush or slightly proud of the plywood. When the face frame is cured and cleaned up, I trim the doors to size before hanging them. These can be lipped, flush or overlay doors. Hang the drawers with metal slides, particularly if they're intended to store weighty record albums. Record drawers need at least 100-lb. slides.

The equipment panel is next, and you must carefully measure the components going into it. Some have front bezels slightly larger than the chassis. If so, cut the panel openings to fit the chassis and slide the gear in from the front. Otherwise, cut the panel openings to fit the exact outside of the bezel. I plunge-cut these openings on my tablesaw, but a saber saw or router would also do the job. I slide the completed panel in from the back of the case so it's 2 in. from the back of the face frame. This leaves clearance for equipment knobs. The panel is held in place with screws so it can be removed for equipment additions. I make a removable shelf unit from scrap wood that supports the equipment inside the case (photo above). The shelf unit slides in from the back and is held in place between two cleats. Shelves must be level, or the equipment will project unevenly from the openings.

Test-fit the equipment by sliding it in. Rubber feet mounted on some chassis may have to be removed. I've found it unnecessary to attach the equipment to the cabinet, but for extra security, it could be blocked or wedged in place. If there's a fan or built-in lighting, install these next. Plan on connecting them to switched outlets on the stereo gear so they'll go on and off when the equipment does; it's a heat-insurance policy for the components.

Next fit plinth and cornice molding. I make up frames to which I can then attach the molding—this allows me to cut the plywood carcase sides shorter, reducing waste. The molding could, of course, be glued and nailed directly to the case. After filling all the nail holes and sanding the case, I spray-lacquer the cabinets, rubbing them by hand between coats. Any finish is suitable, however, including oils and varnishes, whatever suits the needs of the client. Move the cabinet to its location before installing the equipment, to avoid damaging the gear. Make the connections through the removable access panel just before you set the cabinet in the room. □

Carl Spencer owns Presidential Industries, a stereo cabinet manufacturing company in Riverside, Calif. He is the author of Designing and Building Your Own Stereo Furniture, *published by Tab Books Inc., Blue Ridge Summit, Pa. 17214. Photos, except where noted, by Carl Spencer.*

Quick and Tricky Little Boxes

How I bookmatch scrap wood into Christmas gifts

by Jim Cummins

I'm an impatient putterer with thrifty inclinations. Over the past year I've gotten a big kick out of converting my scrap pile into a bunch of Christmas presents. Inspired by Sam Bush's matched-grain box (see figure 1, facing page), I decided to explore variations in the design and construction of small boxes. My intent was to have fun while never making the same box twice. I ended up with a dozen variations, most of them figure-matched in one way or another, with different designs for lids and bottoms, and different joinery details. Some required a little thoughtful planning, some were last-minute adaptations based on chance, and a couple of my favorite details grew out of my efforts to fix mistakes. The elements can be combined in lots of ways, and there isn't a box here that can't be made in an hour or two, not counting the finishing, of course.

The first variation—Sam Bush's box in figure 1 comes out of a board, but my first bookmatched box, shown in figure 2, came from a walnut turning scrap about 2 in. square by 9 in. long. First I bandsawed it into four strips, and planed them smooth on both sides. On one pair of strips, I laid out the

box sides and ends the same way Bush did. The other pair of strips I edge-glued, using masking tape to clamp the joint (page 92). This bookmatched piece was as wide as the ends of the box, and long enough to cut in half to become the bottom and lid. While the strips dried, I rabbeted the top and bottom edges of the sides and ends as shown in figure 2A, then I mitered and glued them, again with tape, adding rubber bands for more pressure. While the sides cured, I rabbeted the lid and the bottom to fit into the rabbets in the sides. I glued the bottom in, using tape clamps, put the lid on and sanded the edges flush.

When I was done, I realized that I'd made three dumb mistakes. First, I hadn't examined the direction of the grain in the turning square. Bookmatching, because of the sawkerf, is never perfect, but if you arrange the grain as shown in figure 2B, it will be close. I had sawn the blank at an intermediate angle to the annual rings, which gave me pretty wood, but a poor match. My second mistake was in jointing and thicknessing the stock before I joined the sides. Bookmatched figure matches best right at the sawkerf, so you want to remove minimum wood from the show surfaces. I should

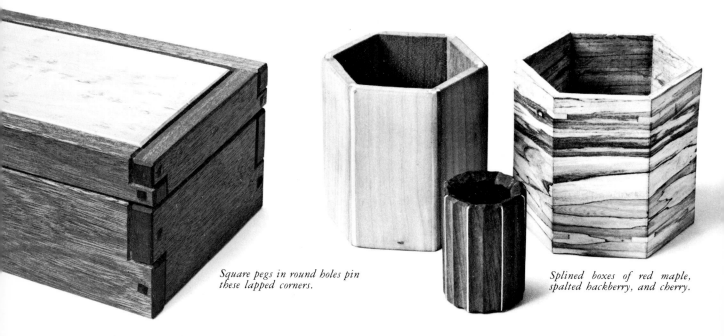

Square pegs in round holes pin these lapped corners.

Splined boxes of red maple, spalted hackberry, and cherry.

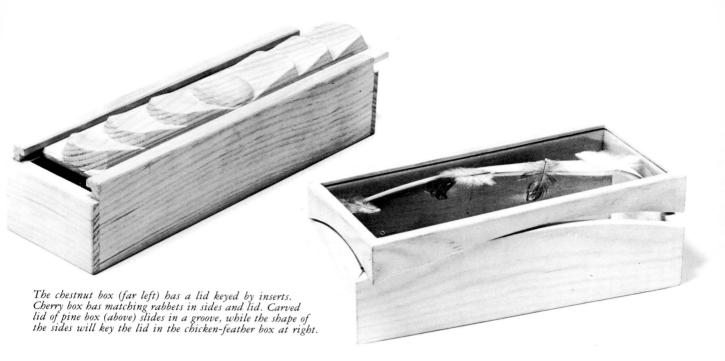

The chestnut box (far left) has a lid keyed by inserts. Cherry box has matching rabbets in sides and lid. Carved lid of pine box (above) slides in a groove, while the shape of the sides will key the lid in the chicken-feather box at right.

have smoothed the inside surfaces only, and waited until the box was joined before sanding the bandsaw marks off the outside surfaces. A more careful workman than I might plane both sides of the stock smooth before bandsawing, and might be sure to resaw exactly in the middle of the thickness. Then he could skim off the sawmarks before gluing up. Others might just tablesaw the stock to thickness in the first place. Since people argue about which resawing procedure wastes the most wood, I tested several tablesaw blades against my bandsaw. I found that by the time I'd planed away the bandsaw marks, I'd lost more wood than to an ordinary ripping blade. Two carbide blades—the Freud thin-kerf and the Forrest/Mr. Sawdust—left surfaces clean enough to sand.

The third mistake was the rabbet for the top and bottom: it left no allowance for wood movement. Even in this small box, the width of the top and bottom could drift 1/16 in. from summer to winter, and sooner or later the glue joint would break, or the lid would stop fitting, or both. I knew all this, but I'd been too interested in the figure match to bother about it. Anyway, it is humid summer as I write, and nothing untoward has happened to my walnut box yet.

Fig. 1: How it all began

This simple bookmatching technique yields a box with perfectly matched grain at all four corners. The rough lumber need be only as long as one side and one end of the box, but thick enough to resaw. First resaw. The inside surfaces match, so reverse them to become the outside of the box. Cut the sides and ends sequentially, keeping all the waste to one end. To assemble, I prefer the dramatic matched effect of mitered corners, with spline reinforcements.   —*Sam Bush, Portland, Ore.*

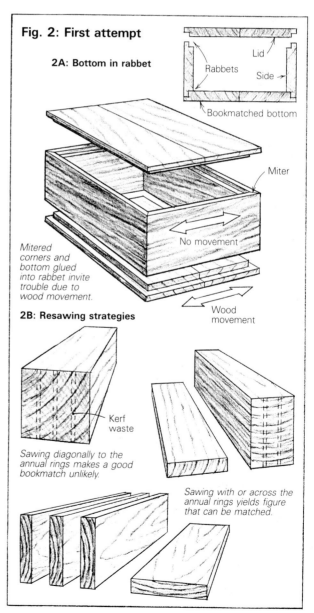

Fig. 2: First attempt

2A: Bottom in rabbet

Lid
Rabbets
Side
Bookmatched bottom
Miter
No movement

Mitered corners and bottom glued into rabbet invite trouble due to wood movement.

Wood movement

2B: Resawing strategies

Kerf waste

Sawing diagonally to the annual rings makes a good bookmatch unlikely.

Sawing with or across the annual rings yields figure that can be matched.

Miters, tape and glue

I use ordinary masking tape to clamp up a bookmatched panel for the lid or bottom of one of my little boxes. To glue up a box's mitered corners, I supplement the tape with rubber bands.

Before gluing up a matched panel, sand, plane or joint the good side of both pieces so that you can see the final figure. Then hold the pieces together in front of a window or a bright light, to make sure the gluing surfaces meet exactly. If they don't, plane them until no light shows through anywhere. You don't have to fret about square edges if you fold the bookmatch good-side-in, clamp the pair of boards in the vise and plane both edges at the same time. If you machine-joint, you'll get the cleanest glueline by skimming off the mill marks with a pass of the hand plane.

Both pieces of wood ought to end up the same thickness, but if at this stage they aren't, you'll have to take care that the good side glues up flat, with the irregularities on the back side only. To do so, lay the pieces on the bench good-side-up, and line up the figure. Run a piece of masking tape across the joint line to keep the figure from shifting. Next, lightly apply a strip of tape along the full length of the joint and flip the assembly over. From the back, press along the joint to stick the tape down firmly.

Bend the joint open and apply glue. Yellow Titebond, as it comes from the jug, is formulated for filling gaps and thus is thicker than it needs to be for long-grain gluing. If your joint is light-tight, such a thick glue will leave a visible glueline. If you thin a tablespoonful of the glue by adding a few drops of water, it will hold better, and the joint will be invisible. To clamp the joint, run a short piece of tape opposite the first one, then similarly tape every 2 in. or so across the joint, taking care to balance the tension on both sides of the panel as you go, else it will curl. You should not need to weight the panel flat.

Miters for box sides are best cut with the wood flat on the saw table, with the blade tilted to 45° and the gauge set at 90° to the blade. I used to set the miter gauge with the aid of a carpenters' square, but a reader, Dustin Davis of Frostburg, Md., sent in a simple device (figure A) that makes the job much easier. It's a shim of ¼-in. plastic that allows you to register the face of the miter gauge against the front edge of the saw table, which on most saws is accurately machined at 90° to the slots in the table. Just drop the shim over the miter-gauge guide bar, push the gauge against the saw table, and tighten the knob. Some saws don't need a shim—you can just turn the gauge upside down for squaring against the table's edge.

The 45° setting is almost as easy. First, tilt the blade to a nominal 45°. To check the angle, take a straight, squared-up length of wood about 2 ft. long, and miter-crosscut it near its middle (figure B). Then recut the miter on the offcut end. Butt the mitered surfaces together and see if the wood lies straight. If it doesn't, the angle is not 45°, and the saw's adjustment wheel needs a twist one way or the other. On my saw, this trick will tell me if I'm as little as a sixteenth of a turn off. Save the test pieces. You can miter them quite a few times before they get too short.

To tape up a box, lay the sides and ends on the bench, outside up, with the points of the miters touching. Run wide tape along the length of each joint (figure C). Press down hard, but don't try to stress the tape so that it will exert pressure across the joint. Just keep the corners touching. When you roll up the box to check the fit of the top and bottom, the tape takes the long way around, automatically pulling taut.

The glued miter is strong enough for most small boxes, except when the sides are so thick that wood movement in the thickness can force the joint to open up, or so thin that there's just not enough gluing surface. To reinforce the corners, I insert a couple of cross-splines in table-sawn kerfs. I saw the slots with my sharpest rip blade (because its kerf has a flat bottom), supporting the box in a simple jig made from a scrap of 2x4, as shown in figure D. The jig runs against the saw's rip fence, and the clamping tape on the box corners is usually enough to prevent chipping.

If the miter angle is correct, you can use tape and rubber bands to clamp almost any number of sides during glue-up—one of my boxes has 15 sides. A possible pitfall: On my first hexagonal box (how I hate to admit this), I unrolled the box and put glue in all the joints, but I forgot to glue the miters at each end, leaving me one joint completely unglued when the tape came off. There might be a plus in that experience some day: If I'd left two joints unglued, the box would still have gone together fine, but later I would have been able to remove one side, and I probably could have figured out some way to make a sideways lid out of it. —J.C.

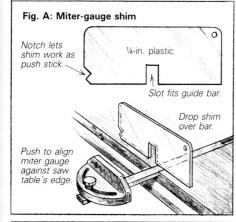

Fig. A: Miter-gauge shim

Notch lets shim work as push stick.

¼-in. plastic

Slot fits guide bar.

Drop shim over bar.

Push to align miter gauge against saw table's edge.

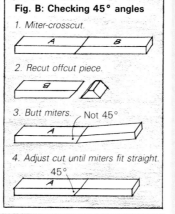

Fig. B: Checking 45° angles

1. Miter-crosscut.

2. Recut offcut piece.

3. Butt miters. Not 45°

4. Adjust cut until miters fit straight.
   45°

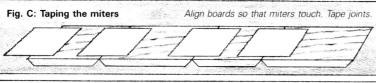

Fig. C: Taping the miters   Align boards so that miters touch. Tape joints.

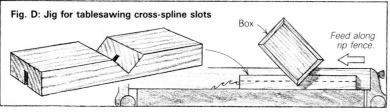

Fig. D: Jig for tablesawing cross-spline slots

Box

Feed along rip fence.

Coping with movement—In the next box, I made room for both the lid and the bottom to move (figure 3). I used some bird's-eye maple picture-frame molding, which was barely thick enough to yield $\frac{3}{16}$-in. thick strips for the sides. I ran the rabbet for the lid and the groove for the bottom, cut the miters, and taped the corners together without glue. Then I cut the bottom and top to fit. I removed the tape from one corner of the box and unfolded the box flat on the bench. I applied glue to the miters, fit the bottom into its groove without glue, and rolled the box up tight, taping the last corner.

Because the sides were so thin, I felt I should reinforce the glue joint at the corners. So while the glue was setting, I grabbed a 2x4 scrap and made a jig (facing page) for sawing a couple of slots for cross-splines through each corner. Then I puzzled over what to do about the lid. As things stood, there was no way of getting it out of its rabbet, short of turning the box upside down.

At first I debated drilling a finger hole through it, but then I remembered that a British designer, Desmond Ryan, had worked out a lever-action lid with a built-in fulcrum. If you pressed one corner of the lid down, the other end would rise out of its rabbet. I used the same idea, and the relief cuts turned out to be decorative as well. To make them, I raised the tablesaw blade $\frac{3}{8}$ in. above the table, and clamped a stop to the fence at about the location of the arbor. Feeding with the stock faced against the fence produced the curved shape, which is simply the profile of a 10-in. sawblade. I cut the detail on both ends and both sides of the lid, so it fits and works no matter which way around it's put (figure 3A).

Two other variations of the lever-action lid are also shown in figure 3. In 3B, the fulcrum is built into the rabbet instead of the lid. Make the relief cuts on the tablesaw before the box is joined, and be sure to relieve the ends as well. In 3C, the fulcrum is in the lid, but it isn't obvious. The lid is symmetrically tapered on both faces of both ends, so that it fits either way, and the projecting lip of the rabbet is shaped to conform to the lid's curve.

It can be perilous to tablesaw box-sized pieces of wood, if you don't take precautions. When you're resawing or making relief cuts, the stock might slither down beside the sawblade, which you can prevent by making a new, tightly fitting table insert. Bandsaw the outline from $\frac{3}{4}$-in. plywood, file or sand it to a good fit in the saw's throat, shim it (or relieve it) so that it sits flush with the table, then raise the blade through it to cut a snug slot. When ripping small pieces to width, be sure that the bottom of the fence is tight to the saw table, otherwise the work can slide under it and bind. Small pieces are notoriously prone to catch and kick back, so push sticks are essential. My favorite is a sharp ice-pick. With it you can hold the work tight on the table at the same time as you feed it forward. Strive to keep the work moving steadily through the blade, to avoid blade-marks and burns.

Frame-and-panel lids—Another type of lid that accommodates wood movement is the frame-and-panel assembly, essentially what I used for the bottom of the box in figure 3. Here are a couple of ways to secure such a lid without hardware. The little cherry box shown at the top of p. 32 has a rabbet in the lid that fits over a matching rabbet in the box. In a large box, it's easy enough to cut the rabbet in the lid before it is joined up around its panel, but in a small box the lid pieces are tricky to handle. It's better to glue up the whole

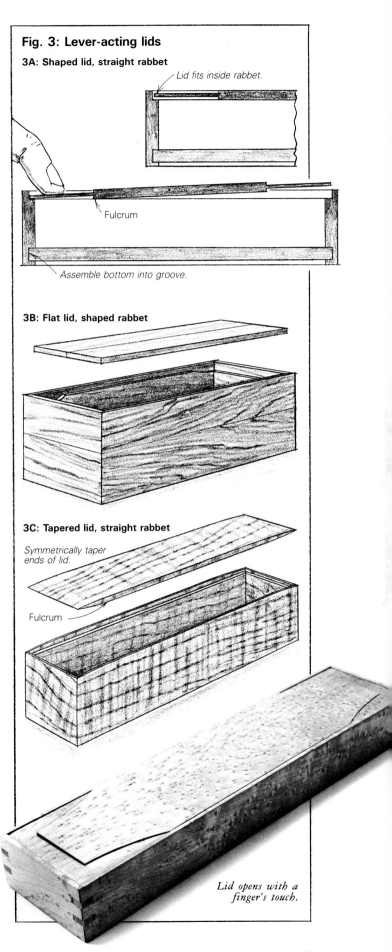

Fig. 3: Lever-acting lids

3A: Shaped lid, straight rabbet

Lid fits inside rabbet.

Fulcrum

Assemble bottom into groove.

3B: Flat lid, shaped rabbet

3C: Tapered lid, straight rabbet

Symmetrically taper ends of lid.

Fulcrum

Lid opens with a finger's touch.

box, then cut the lid off later, complete with rabbet.

The procedure, as shown in figure 4, is to groove the inside of the box at three places—top (for the panel in the lid), bottom (for the box bottom), and along the lid's rabbet line. Join up the box, then after the glue has set, cut the box open to leave the rabbet in the lid. Finally, run the box part over the tablesaw to make the exterior rabbet that receives the lid. By varying the width and depth of the cuts, this method can be generalized up to blanket-chest size, where it ensures that box and lid are not only figure-matched but also the same size. Some people find it most efficient to saw the groove for the exterior rabbet in the box sides before glue-up, while the square-bottom grooving blade is on the arbor. This saves a blade change, and also leaves no doubt about where the lid begins and ends when you saw the box open. Allow for the box-opening kerf when you lay out the grooves. If you use the tablesaw to separate the two pieces, cut one side at a time, and shim each kerf open before cutting the next, to keep the box

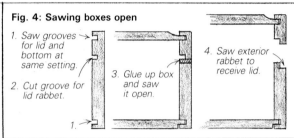

Fig. 4: Sawing boxes open

1. Saw grooves for lid and bottom at same setting.
2. Cut groove for lid rabbet.
3. Glue up box and saw it open.
4. Saw exterior rabbet to receive lid.

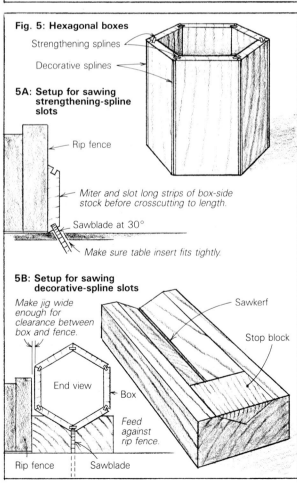

Fig. 5: Hexagonal boxes

Strengthening splines
Decorative splines

5A: Setup for sawing strengthening-spline slots

Rip fence

Miter and slot long strips of box-side stock before crosscutting to length.

Sawblade at 30°

Make sure table insert fits tightly.

5B: Setup for sawing decorative-spline slots

Make jig wide enough for clearance between box and fence.

Sawkerf

Stop block

End view

Box

Feed against rip fence.

Rip fence   Sawblade

from closing and pinching the sawblade. If you handsaw, first scribe a line all around the box with a sharp marking gauge.

Frame-and-panel lids don't have to be straight. The chestnut box shown on page 90 was cut open in a curve on the bandsaw. To form the lip that secures the lid, I inserted false sides in the box, then trimmed them to conform to the curve. Of course, false sides work just as well in a box that's been sawn open on a straight line.

In any frame-and-panel design, whether for a box lid or a piece of furniture, the way the edge of the panel is shaped affects, even determines, the look of the piece. Some of the options are considered on the facing page.

Hexagonal boxes—A dead hackberry tree yielded such strikingly spalted wood that I thought I'd try matching the corners all around a hexagonal box (page 90). The method works just like Bush's, except that you lay out the box to get three equal sides from each half of the resawn blank's length. In my box, because the pattern in the wood ran at an angle, each sawcut threw off the match a little bit. As I taped up the sides, I found that I could accommodate the loss by shifting each side upward in order to align the figure. This trick finally caught up with me at the last corner, which ended up being not a good match at all.

When the box's top and bottom edges had been trimmed straight on the bandsaw, I removed the tape at one corner, unrolled the box flat, and tablesawed a groove for the bottom. I had no hackberry left, so I made a glass bottom instead: I rolled up the box dry, traced its outline, laid a piece of glass on the tracing, and cut out a hexagon, allowing for the depth of the groove. The glass hasn't broken, even though this box does daily work holding pens and pencils. I've since added cross-splines to each miter joint, because spalted wood cut ¼ in. thick needs all the help it can get.

In another box, shown in figure 5 and on page 90, I planned to put lengthwise splines in the miter joints, both for strength and to make a pretty detail at the top rim. The box went together dry, but when I added glue, the splines swelled and forced open the joints at the outside corners. As I strained to get the joints tight, I became covered with slippery glue squeeze-out, masking tape and rubber bands, but I knew that if I tried to retreat, the mess would be even worse. I clamped up as well as I could and hoped for the best.

The corners dried open, but the splines were holding the box sturdy and tight. I rescued it by making another 2x4 jig (figure 5B), this one oriented to run a sawkerf the length of each corner. With the second round of splines in place, the box looks as if I'd planned it that way. For thin splines, such as in the little cherry box shown on page 90, you can kerf the corners on the bandsaw—no jig necessary.

A self-keying lid—While I was making the chestnut box with the false sides, I noticed that the top automatically aligned itself in one direction because of the crown in the bandsaw cut. I reasoned that if I could get the crown on both the long sides and the short sides (pine chicken-feather box, page 91), the top would align without my having to insert false sides. This meant that I would have to make the bandsaw cuts before the box was joined.

I resawed a piece of #2 common pine, about 3 in. wide and 14 in. long, then cut the sides to length, matching the grain the way Bush did. Then I ran a groove for the top and bottom. Next I bandsawed a curve on each side, taking care that adjoining cuts would meet at the box's corners.

The marks from the bandsaw blade were very obvious, but planing or sanding the edges would have altered the fit of the lid. Instead I ripped thin slivers of pine (half the thickness of the bandsaw kerf) to mask the rough edges on both the lid and the box. I glued the edge-banding in place before I mitered the corners, using tape for alignment and a vise for pressure. Because all four sides were the same height, I could glue up the first side, clamp it in the vise, then simply add the other sides to the stack as I got them ready.

While the stack was in the vise, I cut a mirror for the bottom and a piece of old picture glass for the top. The picture glass was so thin that it rattled, but, luckily, two pieces filled the kerf perfectly. To add some decoration, I stuck a few chicken feathers between the panes.

If I were making this box again, I'd do a couple of things differently. It is almost impossible to match the figure around the corners and match the bandsaw cuts as well. I'd forget about the figure, and concentrate on matching the bandsaw cuts—they're more important. Also, I'd seal the edges of the double glass with clear tape before I slid it in. When I sanded the resaw marks off the outside of the box, dust worked between the pieces of glass and muddied the clarity. I'd also take the time to catch a clean chicken, rather than just picking up any old feathers off the floor. □

Jim Cummins is an associate editor at Fine Woodworking.

Panels for lids

The simplest way to fit a panel into a frame is to make the groove the full thickness of the panel (**A**). In large-scale work, this has the drawback of requiring that the panel be very thin, or that the frame be weakened by a wide groove. So, usually, a panel is made thick enough to be stable, and then its edges are thinned down so that it fits a narrow groove in the frame. This process is called "raising" the panel, and it leaves a raised "field" in the center.

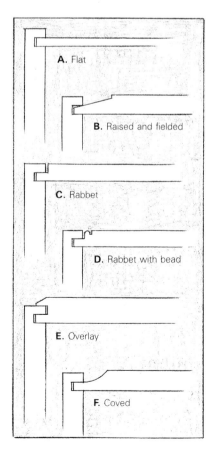

A. Flat

B. Raised and fielded

C. Rabbet

D. Rabbet with bead

E. Overlay

F. Coved

There are innumerable ways to raise panels, each with a different look.

For the little boxes in this article, treatment **A** succeeds because the pieces are so small that strength and stability aren't a factor. Also, the plain, flat panel doesn't interfere with your efforts to bookmatch the wood's figure.

In **B**, the edge has been tapered down and the center field defined by a little vertical shoulder, the traditional form of the frame-and-panel. In **C** it has been rabbeted, so seasonal wood movement will show up as variation in the width of the space between frame and field. The bead at **D** is an elegant touch that tends to conceal seasonal movement in the panel's width. It can be routed, but it may also be easily hand-worked with a homemade tool called a scratch beader. Any evidence of wood movement will be concealed by the overlay panel at **E**. You can run the cove at **F** against an angled fence, cautiously raising the tablesaw blade a little on each pass until you reach the depth you want.

Where you make the groove affects how much the panel is raised. The top groove, if near the edge, can raise the panel higher than its frame (**F**), which looks fine on the lid. But if the same spacing were used for the bottom, it would cause the panel to project too far—you want the box to rest on the edges of its sides, not on the panel's raised field. You can also shape the edges of the frame to complement the treatment on the panel itself. Such details can be delicate on the lid, but shouldn't be too fragile if on the bottom or they may break off.

All these variables are easy to work into the design if you plan ahead for them—many require just a single pass over the tablesaw. If you wait until the box is glued up, however, trying to add even a simple detail may very well tax your patience.   —*J.C.*

Starting and finishing— thoughts on design

by John Kelsey

A box is only a box. Still, there is an infinite variety of rectangular wooden boxes. What makes one simple box different from another? Three general considerations are the size and proportions of the overall form, the way the surfaces are decorated, and the detailing at corners and edges. These outline a rich universe of design possibilities.

The size and proportions of the boxy form often grow logically from function: what has to fit inside? Just as often, however, the box is being made simply to have a box, perhaps for a gift, and because *here's* a good-looking piece of wood. Some people have an eye for proportional harmony and somehow know when the components are long enough, wide enough, high enough. Other people prefer to devise some proportional scheme, instead of choosing dimensions at random or defaulting to the largest pieces possible within the given plank.

I like to think of proportion as the visual analog of rhythm in music. We see harmony in dimensions that interrelate. Perhaps we subliminally measure, by subconsciously comparing the time it takes the eye to traverse adjacent edges. As in music, simple proportional schemes are usually pleasant (figure 1, page 96). But the simplest, the cube, is dull as drumming until you embellish it. The double cube and the root-of-two cuboid are interesting; so is the 1:2:3 proportion. Whole volumes have been written on the intricacies of the golden

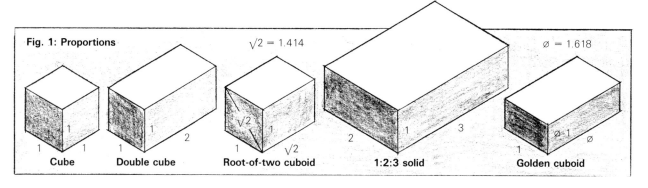

Fig. 1: Proportions

$\sqrt{2} = 1.414$ $\emptyset = 1.618$

Cube   Double cube   Root-of-two cuboid   1:2:3 solid   Golden cuboid

section: the division of a line into two parts such that the smaller part is to the larger as the larger is to the whole. It gives rise to the "golden cuboid." Many people think this looks just right, and its proportions are often rediscovered by artisans working entirely by eye.

"Surface decoration" usually means a design imposed on the form, worked out in paint, carving or inlay. But bookmatched wood figure is also surface decoration. The woodworker perceives and enhances what grew in the tree, instead of laying on what's seen in the mind's eye. A featureless corner joint, such as the splined miter, doesn't compete with the main attraction.

With woods that don't have flashy figure, we can play up corner joinery and tooled edges. Even people who shudder at glued-on gee-gaws can usually accept the decoration of careful joinery, because the joint isn't an afterthought, it holds the box together. The half-lap with square pegs shown in figure 2 requires only the ability to saw on a line. The pegs are split out square and whittled round for half their length, then driven with glue into round holes. Decorative nails would do instead. The cleanest edge treatment is probably a bold chamfer, straight off chisel and plane.

The dovetail isn't the most difficult joint, but non-woodworkers don't know that, so it can make a small box into a real show-off. Dovetailed boxes with

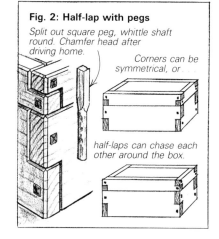

Fig. 2: Half-lap with pegs

Split out square peg, whittle shaft round. Chamfer head after driving home.

Corners can be symmetrical, or ..

half-laps can chase each other around the box.

paneled lids are customarily made closed and then sawn open, as shown in figure 3A. The grooves for lid and bottom usually exit through the sockets of the pins pieces, but they must be shaped in mid-tails, else a hole will show. Grooves are easy to stop when routed; if you tablesaw or hand-plane the groove, you can't make it stop, but you can whittle a peg to fill the hole. If your eye sticks on pegs and half-pins, chisel neat end-miters instead (figure 3B).

Antique dealers sometimes import veneered boxes from England. The best ones are dovetailed hardwood under the veneer, although most are made of pine joined by miters or rabbets, glued and nailed. Some boxes might even have se-

cret mitered dovetails, who can say?

When a box's reason for existence is its pretty wood, the quality of the finished surface is important. Varnish is too coarse and plasticky for little things. Bookmatched wood that's been planed smooth shows best under a glossy penetrating oil finish such as Minwax natural oil, a thin formula you have to build up and rub out hard. But it is an unforgiving finish, emphasizing flaws as much as beauty, and a waste of time if you've sanded your boxes, as grit and dust just muddy the oil's clarity. Watco Danish oil, McCloskey Tung-Seal and Minwax Antique oil complement sanded wood. They dry to a satin gloss when rubbed, and two coats are usually enough. Avoid linseed oil unless you want to smell it every time you lift the lid.

Oil finishes are no good for soft, absorbent wood or any wood that has spalted, because the oil soaks in, it takes forever to dry, and you have to apply so much to build up the finish that you'll bury the figure. One answer is a brushing lacquer such as Deft. Dense woods such as rosewood can take a high-gloss oil, but for best results you ought to fill the open grain. An alternative is a single coat of paste wax, buffed.

Finally, there's always no finish. Like a tool handle, small boxes acquire a nice patina from use. If what I'm calling "patina" looks like dirt to you, a light sanding will renew the wood.   □

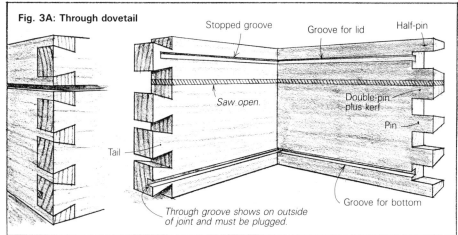

Fig. 3A: Through dovetail

Stopped groove   Groove for lid   Half-pin

Saw open.

Double-pin plus kerf

Pin

Tail

Through groove shows on outside of joint and must be plugged.

Groove for bottom

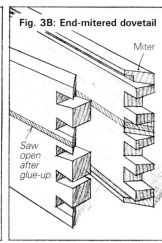

Fig. 3B: End-mitered dovetail

Miter

Saw open after glue-up.

French Fitting
Making the presentation case presentable

by John Lively

Though the term is most often applied to arms cases, a box, a drawer or a chest can be French-fitted to hold almost anything. Drafting, optical and photographic equipment, large pieces of jewelry, hand tools and musical instruments are but a few of the items that can benefit from being snuggled into a closely fitting, leather-lined recess. The method I will describe deals specifically with cases for handguns.

In the last quarter of the 18th century, a gentleman's purchase of a pair of new pistols was no casual matter. As much objects of art as instruments of defense, the custom-built pistols of Georgian times involved the cooperative efforts of many skilled artisans. Master gunsmiths, acting much like general contractors, retained the services of independent founders, barrelmakers, lockmakers, woodcarvers, goldsmiths, silversmiths and engravers. After designing the parts and farming out the various jobs, the gunsmith's work was done, except for collecting and assembling the finished pieces. Then the pistols were delivered to one more specialist—the casemaker. It is the work of these casemakers that has ensured the survival into our time of so many splendid examples of 18th-century gunsmithing. Thanks to them, it is not unusual for an auctioneer's bulletin to describe the condition of 200-year-old firearms as "excellent" or "original."

Though these cases served well enough for storage and display, they were designed for traveling by coach. They were usually shallow, rectangular boxes in sturdy oak or mahogany, dovetailed together, with their flush-fitting lids secured by hinges at the rear and an inlet, keyed lock at the front. On the outside, these cases were paradigms of unadorned simplicity, relying on the wood's figure and color for decoration.

Yet on the inside, things were not so simple. Muzzle-load-ing arms required a number of accessory tools that had also to be fitted into the case, and all the pieces had to be kept from coming into damaging and possibly dangerous contact with one another. Two distinct methods of casefitting arose to address this necessity—the English and the French. English casemakers found it expedient to divide the case into straight-sided, cloth-lined compartments, each conforming, more or less, to the shape of the piece it contained. The inside of the typical English case appears labyrinthine. The French casemakers chose instead to fashion compartments in the precise shape of the pieces. They created these negative spaces either by cutting the shapes into a solid panel of wood or by making molded impressions. In either event, they usually glued cloth inside the impressions as well as to the ground surface above, so it covered the entire inside of the case. Though elevations vary from case to case, the typical French-fitted box presents its contents in half relief, the metal of the pistols contrasting nicely with the cloth-covered ground.

The fitted pistol case remained an indispensable part of a gentleman's traveling gear until the advent of repeating arms and pocket pistols toward the middle of the 19th century. The wooden carrying case then gave way to the leather holster and the vest pocket. But as a presentation case for custom-made or special-issue arms, the fitted wooden case continued to be made, and even today the major arms manufacturers sell them as accessories. Their cases are inferior, however, and in recent years the interest of collectors in black-powder and reproduction firearms has created a new demand for custom-fitted presentation cases. The woodworker is in a good position to compete. Too, the marketplace is accessible via the well-attended gun shows held several times a year in most

Black walnut main case holds Colt dragoon revolver and powder flask, while cleaning and bullet-making tools fit into lidded inner box at right.

French-fitted presentation case, 21 in. by 18 in. by 5 in., is made of mahogany with padauk molding inside, and red leather lining. An inner lid (not shown) rests atop the molding inside the case.

Photos: John Barretto; Illustration: Ric Lopez

major cities. With samples to show, the casemaker is sure to generate considerable interest.

Before proceeding, I have to point out that my fitting method differs in several significant respects from the traditional treatment. First, I line the case with leather instead of cloth. I've found that fabric wears quickly where it contacts the pieces, and it eventually becomes grimy from gun oil and other residues. Also, it is almost impossible to line the cavities with fabric without unsightly wrinkles. Second, I don't make a molded impression of the pieces, but rather I cut the shapes into a solid panel of wood (called an inset panel), line their inner edges with leather, and secure the panel above a leather-covered cushion that fills the bottom of the case. Using wood rather than cloth as the visible ground not only allows me greater opportunity to create visual effects, but also makes for a more durable interior. And because it is small, the inset panel is the perfect place for using a nicely figured scrap from the stash under my bench.

Making the inset panel — French fitting begins where casework ordinarily leaves off, though it's good to have all the materials on hand before starting the case itself. If you want to use several different species of wood on the interior, you will need to coordinate these with the color of the lining material. Leather comes in lots of colors, but they may not all be available all of the time. At a leathercraft supply store, select upholstery leather that is finished on one side but left unfinished or sueded on the other. Buy enough to cover double the bottom surface area of the case.

Finished upholstery leather is many times more durable than cloth, its finished surface will not soak up oil and dirt, and it can be cleaned with a damp cloth. The leather's unfinished side has just the right texture for gluing to wood with contact adhesive, and its finished side will resist glue penetration. You can wipe off glue smears with your finger.

Once the case is made, cut four cleats ¾ in. square by its inner dimensions. Miter them to length and glue them to the bottom and inner sides of the case. Next, obtain a piece of medium-density upholstery foam exactly 1 in. thick, and cut it to fit snugly between the cleats. As you will see later, the ¼-in. difference between the thickness of the foam and the thickness of the cleats is important. Now cut a piece of leather to the inner dimensions of the case and tack it securely along

its edges to the top of the cleats, one tack every 1½ in. The leather should be taut, but not stretched across the cushion. When the leather is tacked down, there must be no wrinkles or bulges caused by uneven tension.

Start by making templates from the object that is to be fitted. Trace around the contours so that the completed outline is larger than the object piece by the thickness of the leather. Leather does not come uniformly off the cow, but if your outline is ¹⁄₁₆ in. larger than the piece you are fitting, your template will be close enough. First, clamp the object over a piece of poster board. I use a bench holdfast with a pad of foam and a small scrap of wood. To produce the outline, I used a scribing device that holds a pencil at a slight angle from the perpendicular with its point ¹⁄₁₆ in. behind the tracer. Because the scriber had to negotiate tight-radius curves and fit into little crannies, I made the base in the shape of a vee, with its nose under the tracer.

Once you have completed the template, dimension the stock you have chosen to the inside measurements of your case, and at least half as thick as the object you are fitting—¾ in. does well for pistols. Lay the template on the stock and move it around until you are satisfied; if more than one object must fit, try different arrangements until you find one that is both pleasing and practical. Trace the outline of the templates onto the bottom face of the panel. If you have a jigsaw, drill starter holes and cut out the shapes, being careful not to stray beyond the inside edge of the traced lines. Don't risk ruination by sawing too close to tight corners. These areas will be properly enlarged by filing later.

Rather than jigsawing, I prefer the band saw. But instead of attempting to weld a blade threaded through a pilot hole, I simply rip the panel in two so the saw kerf passes through all the proposed negative spaces at once. Joint the sawn edges, dry-clamp the two pieces together, and reposition the templates on the top surface to make new tracings corresponding to the ones on the bottom. This is necessary because the ripping destroys the original proportions. Then I unclamp, saw out the spaces, and glue the two parts back together. You will probably need to clamp from the inner edges of the sawn-out spaces, using several small handscrews, along with bar clamps at either end of the panel. Different panels will call for different strategies.

Before proceeding any further, saw a slot along each end-grain edge to receive a spline ¼ in. thick by at least ½ in. wide, the full width of the panel. Rip the two splines from solid material. They should seat tightly enough to require a few gentle taps with hammer and block. Do not omit this step or postpone it; without reinforcement, the short-grain portions of the panel won't stand up to subsequent handling, and it will crack the first time you give it a hard look. I usually take the additional precaution of boring through narrow short-grain walls and gluing in bits of ¼-in. dowel.

Now you should begin to clean up the bandsawn inner edges with bastard files—a half-round, a triangular and a small round. Assuming the entire width of your traced outline is still visible, as it should be, you will want to file the sawn-out spaces just to the other edge of the line. Do not obliterate the line, but leave a visible trace of it all around.

The next steps are quick and easy. Make sure the panel fits easily in the case, bearing in mind probable movement across the grain. With a marking gauge, scribe the panel's upper face ⅜ in. in from all four edges. Then mark equidistant

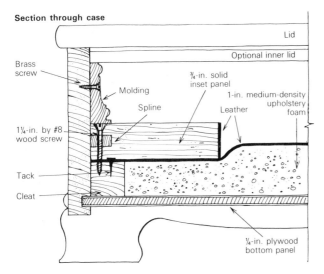

Section through case

Lid

Optional inner lid

Brass screw

Molding

Spline

¾-in. solid inset panel

1-in. medium-density upholstery foam

Leather

1¼-in. by #8 wood screw

Tack

Cleat

¼-in. plywood bottom panel

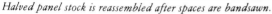

Halved panel stock is reassembled after spaces are bandsawn. *Leather is cemented into place. Note reinforcing spline in panel's edge.*

centers for pilot holes, three of them along the length and two on the width. Bore and counterbore on these centers for 1¼-in. by #8 wood screws. If you anticipate more than negligible movement, slot appropriate holes to allow for it. Transfer the centers to the leather-covered cleats on the bottom of the case, and bore pilot holes in them, too.

Lining the spaces — At last it is time for an initial fitting. Return the panel to the case and screw it down. Since the foam cushion is higher than the cleats, it will be compressed. Tighten the panel as you would tighten a drum-head—not all at once on any one side, but in even stages all around. When it is firmly seated, you will see that the covering has welled up into the cavities, forming a firm, neatly crowned pillow. Now you can nestle the items into their compartments. Cut several patches of leather and slip them between the edges of the cut-out and the object pieces at various places along their contours. Then study the unfilled spaces to determine whether a proper fit will be achieved once the entire inner edge is lined with leather. Remember that you want a smooth fit, but not one that is tight. Whatever you are fitting should settle into its compartment by its own weight. Once settled in, there should be an absolute minimum of slop. If you try to wiggle it around, it should not move more than 1/32 in. in any direction and preferably it should remain dead still. Shade the tight spots with a pencil, remove the panel from the case and file some more. Then test it again.

When the fit is correct, seal the surfaces of the panel so that they will resist the glue you will apply inside the cavities later. Take care to prevent the finish from dripping over the edges of the cut-outs, as this will interfere with gluing the leather.

When the faces of the panel are sealed, you are ready to line its inner contours with leather, which should be cut (straightedge and sharp knife) into long strips a uniform 1 in. wide. These strips must be long enough to run the entire distance—any attempt to splice will leave ugly gaps. Now lay the strips face down and apply three coats of contact cement to their unfinished sides, waiting for each coat to dry. Do the same to the inner edges of the panel. When the final coats have dried, clamp the panel in a vise and begin sticking the strips of leather to the contoured edges, allowing the strips to overhang about ⅛ in. to each side. Begin and end in the same

corner to make the junction as unobtrusive as possible.

Press the leather firmly into place with your fingers. For those tight little curves and culs-de-sac, use a round screwdriver shaft or the like to put pressure where it belongs. Don't rush this operation, and don't permit the leather to touch the tacky surfaces ahead of the spot you are working on. If it sticks to the wrong place and you try to pull it loose, half of the leather strip will remain stuck to the wood. Should this happen, pull all the leather loose and clean up the mess with lacquer thinner, which will probably also dissolve the finish on the panel's face. Be assured of a nasty tussle if you let the leather stick where it doesn't belong.

When the inner edges are lined, take a pair of manicure scissors and trim the leather flush with the top and bottom surfaces of the panel. Before going further, you need to work in a bead of yellow glue with your fingertip to stiffen the raw edges of the leather so that they will not roll over in use. When the glue has hardened, sand the face of the panel with 220-grit paper. A subsequent sanding with 400-grit paper will leave the panel ready for final finishing, which should be done before it is fastened to the cleats.

The final step is to design and make a molding to trim out the inside corners of the case. The only requirement of the design is that the base of the molding be thick enough to obscure the heads of the screws that fasten the inset panel. You might attach this molding with small brass screws, so you can remove the panel should the need for repair arise.

Having said little about the design of the case itself, I would like to close with a few prejudicial remarks. For a contemporary collector, a presentation case is seldom used as a traveling container. It's an article of household furniture with the specific function of preserving and displaying objects of significance and value. Though it may be carried about from time to time, there is no need to feel restricted by the design requirements of a traveling case. Apart from structural necessities, your design should be aimed at achieving harmony, balance and continuity between the case and its contents, so that the two can be perceived as one thing. □

John Lively, formerly an associate editor of Fine Woodworking *magazine, is now editor of* Fine Homebuilding *magazine.*

Bandsaw Boxes

The quick and easy way to make a complicated container

by John Alcock-White

The versatile band saw can be your primary tool for making small wooden containers. I have been experimenting with the band-saw technique and have found that with it I can produce attractive containers in comparable or even less time than by turning or conventional joinery. Since the container is made from a single (or laminated) block of wood and all the grain remains parallel, movement caused by humidity change is uniform—the bandsaw box is not adversely affected by changing moisture conditions. The method is so direct it has an inherent beauty.

Bandsaw boxes became popular and widely imitated after Arthur (Espenet) Carpenter developed his version back in the late 1960s (page 102). In addition to ingenious boxes, Carpenter made such things as pigeonholes and drawers inside roll-top desks. Carpenter, of Bolinas, Calif., is a quiet person who becomes shy when discussing his own work. When asked about bandsaw boxes, he replies that his technique is so simple it hardly needs explanation. Be that as it may, it has the elegant simplicity common to all important innovation.

I found this technique when I first began to use the band saw. The method is first to saw off the sides of a block of wood, to turn the block on its side and saw out the center, then to glue the sides back on. The procedure can be extended to make drawers (figure 1). After the sides of a block are sawn off, drawer pieces can be sawn out, resawn into smaller containers, and finally replaced in their original positions within the larger block. If the saw is set up correctly—top and bottom guides snug, blade sharp and tensioned as much as possible—the cut pieces can be glued directly back together with little or no smoothing. Because the kerf cut by the saw governs angles and clearances, very little fitting and measuring are required.

Although this technique had struck me as a marvelous way to make containers, I forgot about it for some years until a friend, who markets a line of bathroom accessories, was telling me how profitable it was to manufacture such items as oak toilet seats. However, to increase sales he had to offer a full line of accessories, most of them of good quality, simple design and easy construction. One exception was a box designed to cover a tissue package, constructed with an elaborate finger joint. He was getting $8 for it and it retailed for $15, and he admitted it was a money-loser but still an essential part of his line. Instead of sawing and gluing up the finger joints, I proposed he make the box from a solid or laminated block of wood. He'd then have only four operations: bandsawing, regluing, routing the opening, and sanding (figure 2). The waste wood would be used to make something else, and the $8 price might become more feasible.

This experience got me making bandsaw containers again, and I became convinced it is a viable technique with lots of potential. Mainly the method is fast, perhaps faster than anything else. It is economical if the sawn-out sections are used to make smaller containers or if they can be used in other phases of your operation. Expansion and contraction of the wood is not a serious consideration. Making these containers does not depend on a lot of equipment—apart from the band saw, a few clamps and some smoothing tools are all you need. Lastly, compared to traditional joinery, there is practically no measuring and fitting. You can build freehand and end up with some interesting shapes, without tooling contortions. Although purists may decide bandsawn containers are gimmicky, I find them an enjoyable relief from conventional, more exacting woodwork. They look complicated yet are easy to make, and best of all, people like them. I can sell for a profit what I make. I wish that were always the case. □

John Alcock-White makes furniture and bandsaw boxes in Nanaimo, on Vancouver Island, B.C.

Fig. 1: Bandsawing a container with drawers

Fig. 2: Bottomless finger-joined box compared to bandsaw box

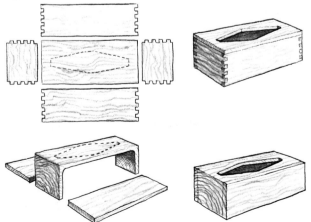

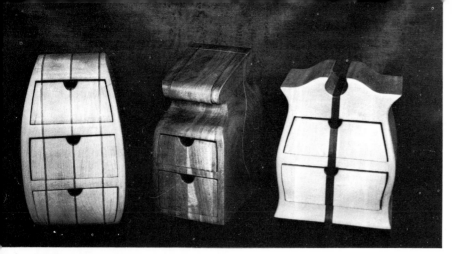

The boxes above, made by the author, have curved fronts and sides made by regluing along a curved kerf. The glueline is generally very clean; the major difficulty of holding the parts while sawing the interior is solved with improvised jigs and clamps.

A. To make a bandsaw box, start with a solid or laminated block of wood; shown are a small piece of myrtle taken from a bent section of the tree and a laminated block of Central American walnut with Honduras mahogany. Saw the block to contours you like, using a four-tooth, ¼-in. blade for heavy cuts and a six-tooth, ¼-in. blade for lighter cuts. Make simple containers with at least two flat sides before trying more complex shapes.

B. Set up a fence on the band saw and remove about 1 cm. (⅜ in.) from each side of the block. These pieces become the sides of the box, C, and since end grain does not glue well, saw them with the grain. The saw should leave surfaces smooth enough to reglue later, but for a perfect fit you can joint the cut-off sides and the central block.

D. Draw the interior of the container, and drill for the hinged lid. These boxes are fairly complicated, with a secret ledge above the drawer in the laminated block.

E. Saw along the lines, striving for smooth cuts. Resaw the blocks taken from the drawer openings. Rasp and sand any rough spots now, while they are still accessible.

F. Carefully glue the sides back on. Once the glue has set, insert dowels (or brass rods) through the hinges. Be sure the lid opens smoothly before driving the dowels home.

G. Trim off the dowels, cut a drawer pull, sand the outside of the box, and finish.

B

G

F

C

D

E

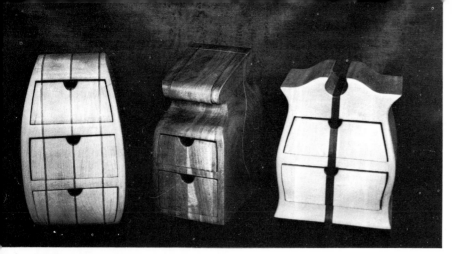

Boxes, Carcases and Drawers **101**

Photos: John Alcock-White

The Bandsaw Boxes of Arthur (Espenet) Carpenter

Arthur (Espenet) Carpenter began bandsawing boxes in the late 1960s. In the early three-drawer cabinet, below, only the front and the drawer openings are bandsawn; the carcase and drawers are conventionally joined. The kerf left by entering and leaving each drawer opening is glued up, thereby reducing the clearance around the drawer to the width of a single kerf. A five-drawer cabinet made in 1970, below center, shows how swiftly Carpenter made the transition to a fully laminated block. The entry kerf runs from the center bottom, up the right-hand side, around the perimeter and finally out the point of entry. In the process five drawer blocks—one of them within another—are isolated. They are then sawn to form the drawers. Later, the rear panel is glued to the back of the main block. Since the entry kerf runs across the grain, it is splined and glued with epoxy.

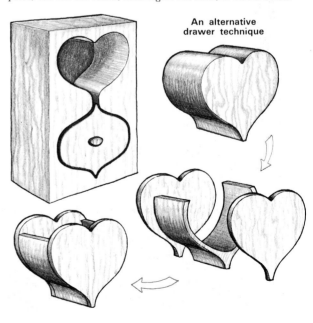

Carpenter also worked with solid blocks of wood, like this three-drawered piece made from a walnut branch. The first step in constructing a box of this type is to rip a flat on the back of the log. A kerf is then run up from the bottom, outlining three drawers. The entry kerf is reglued and the rear section replaced. Carpenter then makes two separate cuts to form each drawer, lining the pieces with felt to take up the slack. The protruding drawer fronts are smooth and epoxied a fiery red. Drawer bottoms made Carpenter's way might be weak, because of short grain. Instead of two scoop cuts, you can saw off the front and rear of the drawer piece, saw out the center, then reglue the ends, as shown below.

An alternative drawer technique

Carpenter doesn't make many bandsaw boxes these days, but he frequently uses the method in larger work such as roll-top desks, for shelving, drawers and pigeonholes.

Photos: Art Carpenter

Another Case of Box Fever

I was first impressed with the bandsaw-box technique when I saw a roll-top desk with bandsawn cubbyhole drawers by Art Carpenter at the California Design II show in 1971. I had had a shop for four years and was wondering where there might be other contemporary furniture makers. I was struck by that show; there was definitely a whole other world out there that I had not been aware of. I have had "box fever" ever since.

My earliest pieces (beginning the day following the design show) were called Hobbit Houses—tree limbs and burls that had small drawers free to open on either side. Turning Carpenter's technique on end led me to the lidded bandsaw box (below, left). First the top of the limb was sliced off, then the entry cut in the box bottom was made and the plug removed. Slices from the top and bottom of the plug were glued to the lid and to the box

bottom. Making boxes from dimensioned lumber revealed the possibility of opening up the entry cut and incorporating it as a part of the design (below, right) instead of gluing it back together. I continue to use this approach in my current designs. One of my latest pieces (bottom) has a solid back and a mechanism, integrated with the design, to open the drawers.

—*Michael Graham, Los Osos, Calif.*

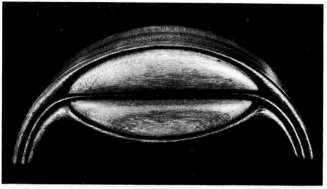

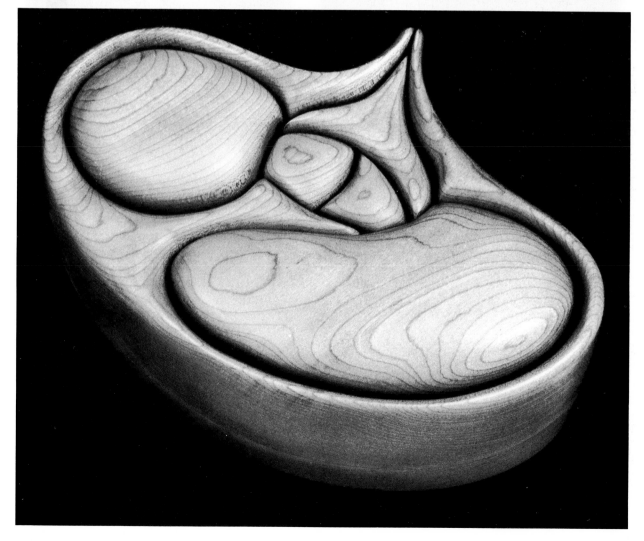

Photos: Michael Graham

Index

FINE WOODWORKING
Editorial Staff, 1975-1984:

Paul Bertorelli
Mary Blaylock
Dick Burrows
Jim Cummins
Katie de Koster
Ruth Dobsevage
Tage Frid
Roger Holmes
John Kelsey
Linda Kirk
John Lively
Rick Mastelli
Ann E. Michael
Nina Perry
Jim Richey
Paul Roman
David Sloan
Nancy Stabile
Laura Tringali
Linda D. Whipkey

FINE WOODWORKING
Art Staff, 1975-1984

Roger Barnes
Deborah Fillion
Lee Hov
Betsy Levine
Lisa Long
E. Marino III
Karen Pease
Roland Wolf

FINE WOODWORKING
Production Staff, 1975-1984

Claudia Applegate
Barbara Bahr
Pat Byers
Deborah Cooper
Michelle Fryman
Mary Galpin
Barbara Hannah
Annette Hilty
Nancy Knapp
Johnette Luxeder
Gary Mancini
Laura Martin
Mary Eileen McCarthy
JoAnn Muir
Cynthia Nyitray
Kathryn Olsen

FPCT

Fine WoodWorking

To subscribe

If you enjoyed this book, you'll enjoy *Fine Woodworking* magazine.
Use this card to subscribe.

1 year (6 issues) for just $16—$5 off the newsstand price.

Canadian subscriptions: $19/year; other foreign: $20/year. (U.S. funds, please)

Name _____

Address _____

City _____ State _____ Zip _____

☐ My payment is enclosed. ☐ Please bill me.

☐ Please send me more information about Taunton Press Books.

☐ Please send me information about *Fine Woodworking* videotapes.

FPCT

Fine WoodWorking

To subscribe

If you enjoyed this book, you'll enjoy *Fine Woodworking* magazine.
Use this card to subscribe.

1 year (6 issues) for just $16—$5 off the newsstand price.

Canadian subscriptions: $19/year; other foreign: $20/year. (U.S. funds, please)

Name _____

Address _____

City _____ State _____ Zip _____

☐ My payment is enclosed. ☐ Please bill me.

☐ Please send me more information about Taunton Press Books.

☐ Please send me information about *Fine Woodworking* videotapes.

NO POSTAGE
NECESSARY
IF MAILED
IN THE
UNITED STATES

BUSINESS REPLY CARD
FIRST CLASS PERMIT No. 19 NEWTOWN, CT

POSTAGE WILL BE PAID BY ADDRESSEE

The Taunton Press
52 Church Hill Road
Box 355
Newtown, CT 06470

NO POSTAGE
NECESSARY
IF MAILED
IN THE
UNITED STATES

BUSINESS REPLY CARD
FIRST CLASS PERMIT No. 19 NEWTOWN, CT

POSTAGE WILL BE PAID BY ADDRESSEE

The Taunton Press
52 Church Hill Road
Box 355
Newtown, CT 06470